Feminist Criticism

Feminist Criticism

Women as Contemporary Critics

Maggie Humm

Co-ordinator of Women's Studies
North East London Polytechnic

THE HARVESTER PRESS

First published in Great Britain in 1986 by
THE HARVESTER PRESS LIMITED
Publisher: John Spiers
16 Ship Street, Brighton, Sussex

© Maggie Humm, 1986

British Library Cataloguing in Publication Data

Humm, Maggie
    Feminist Criticism.
    1.   Feminist literary criticism—History
    I. Title
    809   PN98.W64

    ISBN 0-7108-1048-2
    ISBN 0-7108-1124-1 Pbk

Typeset in Plantin 11/12pt by Graham Burn Typesetters,
Leighton Buzzard, Beds.

Printed in Great Britain by
Biddles Ltd, Guildford and King's Lynn

THE HARVESTER PRESS PUBLISHING GROUP
The Harvester Group comprises Harvester Press Ltd (chiefly
publishing literature, fiction, philosophy, psychology, and science
and trade books); Harvester Press Microform Publications Ltd
(publishing in microform previously unpublished archives, scarce
printed sources, and indexes to these collections) and Wheatsheaf
Books Ltd (chiefly publishing in economics, international politics,
sociology, women's studies and related social sciences).

For Dan, the future

CONTENTS

PREFACE

This book grew out of courses that I teach at North-East London Polytechnic. For some time, my women students have been reading and writing about feminist literary criticism. They feel that critics are making a distinctive contribution to feminism. They cannot understand why publishers are not publishing more feminist criticism nor why there are few useful accounts of this body of writing. This book is for them and also for general readers concerned with issues of gender and writing.

It is an introduction to, and analysis of, the feminist literary criticism which has been written in England, America and France from 1970 to today. The reason for the dates is that in 1985 we are at an important moment in the history of feminism as well as the history of literary criticism. The period from the 1970s has been propitious for the establishment of women's centres, women's publishing and women's studies. Over the last fifteen years both feminists and literary critics have created a number of significant practices. Now, in 1985, Black and lesbian critics in particular are contributing methods which must be described as revolutionary. Drawing on women's politics, it is time for feminist literary criticism to claim a firm position in the territory of literary theory.

This book is an account of women critics and their methods rather than women writers. But of course criticism cannot be read in separation from women's writing. I therefore assume some knowledge of women writers and the main kinds of women's literature. My account is horizontal rather than historical because I have chosen texts which reproduce the spectrum of contemporary feminist criticism and arranged them loosely in order of their ideas. The second part is a look backwards at Virginia Woolf and Rebecca West, as the writers most cited by contemporary feminists, and an account of Adrienne Rich, who is my personal guide to a feminist future.

I want to move away from past descriptions of feminist literary criticism, which tend to be narrative rather than theoretical, because I find that the terrain is spreading too quickly to be encompassed without the help of theory. There have been well-formulated definitions of feminism. The most useful perhaps is supplied by Linda Gordon: 'an analysis of women's subordination for the purpose of figuring out how to change it' (1979). But the term feminist literary criticism raises problems. It is not always the same in different countries or even within one country. Of course, the activity of literary criticism itself is no longer simple. My own feeling is that feminist literary critics must enjoy being women and being with other women. They must enjoy reading the work of women writers and helping other women to enjoy reading women's literature. They must be women choosing to read women as women. I want to demonstrate that in the body of writing that is feminist literary criticism there is now such a range of techniques and ideas that feminist literary criticism can function as a forum of feminism and perhaps may well be the *only* literary criticism needed by women students.

This book owes as much to people as to criticism. After my students, I want to thank women here in Britain and in the United States, Amsterdam, Australia, Berlin, Brussels and Canada who have taken time to send me bibliographies, contacts, advice and sponsorship. There are too many to select just a few. The British Annual Women's Writing and Theory Conferences and the group Network have been an important source of ideas and friends. Giving papers there, at the British Association for American Studies, or at women's studies conferences, has helped me rethink my work.

For their support and interest I want to thank Peter and Daniel Humm and my other close friends. I particularly want to thank, for their very useful comments on earlier drafts of this book or on my other writing, Helen Carr, Renate Duelli-Klein,

Elizabeth Garrels, Moira Monteith, Sandra Runzo, Johanna Stuckey and Shelagh Wilkinson, my anonymous Harvester Reader and also Sue Roe for showing that women in publishing can be feminist. Finally this book depended most of all on the meticulous typing skills of Joan Smith.

PART I

1

FEMINIST CRITICISM

Once upon a time, and a very sad time it was, though it wasn't in my time, nor in your time, nor in any real time, there was a man who told secrets to other men. And the man was a Critic King and the other men were his vassals. And no woman ever heard the secrets. And no woman ever read the books which the secrets were about. But the king had a daughter. And, one day, the daughter read the books and heard the secrets. And the daughter saw that the secrets were not real secrets and the books were not real books. And she was very angry. So she talked to other daughters. Through nights and days and dreams and waking the daughters talked together. And the king and his vassals grew old and died. The daughters looked at each other's golden faces and heard each other's golden voices. And they lived long together in the land, whole again, which they called Feminist Criticism.

In the process of hearing the golden voices of feminist critics I learned a good deal about myself as a teacher and writer. But I also learned a good deal about the exclusion of women and the ideological use of the subject 'literature', and literary institutions, by men. Nonetheless, developing and writing about a woman-centred perspective in literary criticism may not seem the most revolutionary of feminist acts. Why concentrate on the generation of ideas and theories in literary form when we should be addressing the more immediate social forms that sexual discrimination takes? Why not concentrate on the expression of male power in medicine, legal relations or sexuality rather than literature?

A quick answer to this would describe the contribution criticism has made to the evolution of feminist thought, and hence to feminist action. It is not surprising that in that pioneering text of contemporary feminism *Sexual Politics,* Kate Millett chose to attack patriarchy through literary criticism. To question the representation of a raped woman in literature is to demystify the secret of patriarchy and hence subvert the social role played by rape, and the fear of rape, in the power that men have over women. The growth of the feminist movement itself is inseparable from feminist criticism. Women become feminists by becoming conscious of, and criticising, the power of symbols and the ideology of culture.

A more long-term trajectory would trace the exaggerated role that literature and, hence, literary criticism have in national cultures. Criticism, as Bourdieu shows, has always been part of the public expression of cultural power, whether in education or in periodicals.[1] In England the teaching of criticism in the nineteenth century was a viable alternative to the decline of theology. The opportunities of professional writing were greatly increased by the expansion of Victorian periodicals in the mid nineteenth century. Yet that very expansion, by securing for periodicals the role of interpreting contemporary thought and making it accessible, forced academic criticism into becoming a specialism.[2] Critical essays satisfied the ideological need of Victorian capitalism. Their imagery provided the decorative outlines of patriarchal ideology. Matthew Arnold gave criticism an institutional base by advocating its incorporation into the curriculae of universities and schools. The teaching of reading in eighteenth-century charity schools, through nineteenth-century elementary schools, or private boarding schools, to twentieth-century training colleges for women, may have used different texts, but the role of English was central and crucially homogeneous.[3]

Reading English in a nineteenth- or twentieth-century curriculum meant, in effect, the learning, by rote, of patriarchal culture:

> Amongst girls . . . there are great mistakes made by their longing to 'better themselves', as they say . . . Service, like other trades, is one that must be learnt young . . . But the girl who gets angry if told her needlework is so bad that she must be taught how to hold her needle properly, or the boy who

declines learning the multiplication table perfectly . . . will probably go backwards [*Fifth Standard,* School Managers' Series of Reading Books, ed. Rev. A.R. Grant, 1871]

The official government view has been endorsed by the universities with the publication of myopic texts like *The Cambridge History of English Literature,* which surveyed a restricted range of 'literary' texts, and by a methodological specialisation of English 'subjects'. The reconstruction of English in higher education and in government reports became, in the twentieth century, a form of professional certification, with state schools using English as the compulsory hoop through which students had to jump. Criticism, or 'English', did not deviate, in other words, from the original Greek meaning of *krino*, 'to judge'. The Victorian practice of Matthew Arnold continued through the writings of T.S. Eliot, Cleanth Brooks and Northrop Frye, keeping intact the concept of criticism as judicial. With deconstruction, criticism becomes not only a judicial theory of literature but a form of theology. Of course, only males can be ordained as priests.

English, as a compulsory subject, will always be about power, and criticism, its weapon, will always be about the power to name, what to choose and who to exclude. Since what has been excluded, along with dissenters, is any concept of woman as an independent professional, then clearly feminists, in order to appropriate the land and the weapons, will have to make literary criticism an integral part of feminist struggle.

The institutional argument for feminist criticism is now more secure with women's studies having some place in education, and thus women's writing receiving critical attention and re-evaluation. But the argument for a specifically feminist criticism is not only to give more adequate attention to women writers but, by giving a space to the woman critic, to give space to the idea of women theorists. When I started to compile a bibliography of feminist criticism I was not surprised to find that women, in the public sphere of publishing, are conspicuously underrepresented in those subjects, in particular philosophy, psychology and criticism, which formally require skills of abstraction, logic and evaluation, more than in the humanities and arts. Patriarchy, as represented in publishing or in education, might tolerate the idea of creative woman but resists the woman academic. The restricted classification of *The Cambridge History of English Literature* is duplicated in contemporary anthologies. Berenice Carroll has revealed the explicit denegration of women in a standard American bibliography, James et al., *Notable American Women* (1971) which describes criticism written by women as 'superficial'.[4] In an overview of twenty-four widely used student anthologies of literary criticism two feminist researchers discovered that out of a total of 653 essays only 16 (2.4 per cent) represent the work of women.[5] Yet if I mention only a few names of women who each wrote substantial and significant literary criticism, we can see that exclusion is a political rather than aesthetic judgement. George Eliot, Madame de Staël, Simone de Beauvoir, Winifred Holtby, Olive Schreiner, Kate Millett, Adrienne Rich, Virginia Woolf, Rebecca West, Mary Wollstonecraft, George Sand.

Yet an impatience with patriarchal uses of criticism will not re-address the devaluation of women critics by men. Feminist criticism must redefine literary theory as the programmatic understanding of women's experience in literary form to violate the taboo on participation in theoretical exposition that is set up for women from adolescence. An even more important task for feminist criticism, then—more important than re-evaluating women's writing, or re-evaluating the misrepresentation of women's intellect—is to re-evaluate the whole terrain of criticism itself as mapped out and colonised by men; that is, to change the language of literary criticism from one of power and possession to one of emotion and caring. So what is, or could be, feminist criticism?

Rebecca West pretended not to know. 'I myself have never been able to find out precisely what feminism is: I only know that other people call me a feminist whenever I express sentiments that differentiate me from a doormat or a prostitute' (Marcus, 1982, p. 219).

Adrienne Rich chooses to define feminism more directly. 'Feminism is the place where in the most natural, organic way subjectivity and politics have to come together' (Gelpi and Gelpi, 1975, p. 114).

All critics writing what they call 'feminist criticism' seem to share three basic assumptions. The first is that literature and criticism is ideological since writing manipulates gender for symbolic purposes. The experience of gender in writing and reading is symbolised in style, and style, therefore, must represent the articulation of ideology by any particular writer or critic reader. For this reason feminist criticism needs to include general interpretations of the cultural theory or ideology of each individual writer. But the definition of ideology, tautologically, contains the notion of contradiction. This is because ideology is what we construct to explain our experience, and the experience of others, to ourselves. Ideology is our way of coping with the contradictions of experience. Inevitably the ideology of women critics is likely to encompass more contradictions than the ideology of men since women are provided with many more confusing images of themselves than are men. But when one turns to feminist psychoanalysis one learns that the instability of the feminine which Freud reveals as his great fear in *Female Sexuality* can be a source of woman's power.[6] By exposing how critics cope with contradictions we can see what are the fundamental contradictions for all women in everyday life, through feminist criticism.

The second major assumption is that there are sex-related writing strategies. Virginia Woolf's now famous comment on the technique of Dorothy Richardson tells us what to look for. Richardson had invented or developed 'a sentence which we might call the psychological sentence of the feminine gender'.[7] Of course, how women wrote is how they were allowed to write. In the nineteenth century the socialisation and subordination of middle-class women limited their access to, and means of, expression, as much as did the exclusion of working-class women from shipbuilding or public utilities to means of employment. But in linguistics, from the work of Robin Lakoff onwards, researchers have pointed out that, given a dependence on social process, men and women do *use* language in different ways, they have different vocabularies and put their vocabularies in different kinds of sentences. Women speak in a sexually distinctive way from men.[8] These linguistic studies have influenced feminist criticism which by using phrases like 'a woman's style' assumes that, metaphorically at least, women writers use imagery and vocabulary around themes which create a different literary iconography from that of male writers.

To celebrate the multiplicity of women's writing rather than simply its difference (thereby avoiding the dangers of 'oddness') is to prove the extent, and normality, of women's experience.

The evidence of specifically female forms in literature can be easily catalogued. It would contain patterns of disjunction, animal and plant imagery, uses of the supernatural, science fiction or otherworldliness, dress iconography, anxiety motifs and so on. Traditional criticism has not adequately attended to this enlarged idea of literary creation. Women critics, on the other hand, who do pursue the question of difference, can contribute a special knowledge from their gendered experience. A criticism which describes language habits unacknowledged by the male literary tradition; which describes writing like diaries that cannot be accommodated in existing male genres; which appreciates the vocabulary of menstruation, reproduction or craft work—this is feminist criticism.

The last assumption in feminist criticism is that even if some male critics acknowledge the first two postulates of feminist criticism (and I am very dubious that they can in full), the continuing tradition of literary culture, like the economic and social traditions of which it is a part, uses male norms to exclude or undervalue female writing and scholarship. Virginia Woolf in 1929 found when she went to the British Museum that professors and sociologists, journalists and novelists, 'men who had no qualification save that they were not women' had written hundreds of books describing women.

The page was headed quite simply, WOMEN AND POVERTY, in block letters; but what followed was something like this:
> Condition in Middle Ages of,
> Habits in the Fiji Islands of,
> Worshipped as goddesses by,
> Weaker in moral sense than,

Woolf, [1929, p. 25]

Contemporary criticism also betrays an exclusively male frame of reference, which, by restricting women's writing and criticism, creates categories which are as inaccurate and distorted as those that Woolf discovered. Feminist critics question the appropriateness of traditional generic classifications based on texts about men being applied to women's modes; terms like 'intuitive' applied to devalue women's forms; and aesthetic criteria which overvalue the 'alienation', say, or the 'existentialism', of the bourgeois artist and therefore give preference to the male view of world literature.

As a sixth-former I was trained to scan 'unseen' passages for clues to ownership. My passport to higher education, the 'A' level certificate, depended on me acquiring this skill. Yet the whole concept of origin, of establishing the 'blood' father of a text is, as Foucault has established, not simply a bourgeois notion but has a much longer history in patriarchy.[9] Numerous aspects of criticism, like the idea of normative values (of sorting out legitimate from illegitimate readings of a text) are part of the promotion of the paternal. To question ownership is feminist criticism.

This is not to say that male critical concepts are totally wrong but simply that they must be situated within a larger textual system. At the moment they are all we are allowed to use. Virginia Woolf had the same difficulty with the concepts of her contemporaries. Describing the writings of Swinburne, Professor Saintsbury and Sir Walter Raleigh she said:

> It would appear, then, that there are at least three schools of criticism: the refluent sea-music school; the line-irregularity school, and the school that bids one not criticise but cry. This is confusing; if we follow them all we shall only come to grief [1979, p. 166]

Good advice, but clearly too, in the process of reading and rereading about contemporary male criticism, present-day feminists have learned a good deal about literary meaning and what alternatives to tradition can be proposed. Post-war American critics like Wayne C. Booth and Walter Gibson write within the confines of a formalist position: one which assumes the value of uniqueness of the literary work of art. Semiotic and structuralist approaches in the work of the French critics Barthes, Genette and Riffaterre developed the idea of the reader *in* the text and took the literary activity, not to be about assigning meaning as such, but about codes that make the text *readable*. Their analysis remains, however, firmly committed to the assumption of textual objectivity. The more phenomenological approach of Wolfgang Iser paid attention to the reader

9

actively producing textual meaning. As with Norman Holland's Delphi seminars, male critics *have* begun to relate people's reading experiences to their life experiences.

Yet, although continental theories have been of use to both male and feminist American critics, in 'The Interpreter's Self' Walter Michaels makes a revealing suggestion. American males, Michaels argues, from the American pragmatist C.S. Pierce on, are frightened by the notion of an anarchist self. Feminists, on the other hand, as Hélène Cixous claims in 'The Laugh of the Medusa', *are* anarchic. Feminine texts pulsate with a rhetoric of rebellion and rupture.

Clearly it would be wrong to ignore the influences on feminist criticism of particular critics such as Riçoeur, particular texts such as Barthes' *S/Z*, and particular stances, such as Geoffrey Hartman's definition of reading as a 'dialogic' and creative act. But there is a way in which the reader who emerges from those male critics has (for Booth and Gibson) no privileged status. He (and it is a 'he') takes a very abstract approach to reading (for Iser and Riçoeur). And, for psychoanalytic critics such as Holland, he is the totally unified self dear to American ego psychology.

Again recent theories of reading by critics, like David Bleich or Stanley Fish, seem close to feminist criticism with their attractive descriptions of communities of interpreters engaged in a conscious process of negotiation. They say, in other words, that one's criticism or reading is a direct result of the interpretative strategies we possess, not something necessarily in the text itself. This is attractive because it gets us away from a fixed hierarchy of texts—James Joyce 'good'/Georgette Heyer 'bad'—but becomes more paternal than the old-fashioned idea of a hierarchy of texts by replacing this with a hierarchy of readers.

Most reader-response criticism carries with it the implicit assumption of a 'free' reader apart from external realities engaged in an old morality of self-development. Clearly this is a reader without children or Sainsbury's shopping. In *Is There a Text in This Class?* Stanley Fish is horrifically paternal in the way he deliberately plays with, and puns on, the insecurity of a young female student. Fish prefers the kind of literature which deliberately renders readers insecure. Students in Fish's classes have to discount what is idiosyncratic in their own response because, as a male critic, at the heart of his criticism is the wish to deny that his activities have any consequences. Fish is at an opposite pole from feminism.

If academic male critics are mishandling literature as much as they mishandle their students, surely left-wing male critics will be more tolerant when they address feminism. Before he died Herbert Marcuse wrote an essay about the relation of feminism to marxism.[10] The eradication of what Marcuse describes as the social conditioning of the female comes, he claims, with 'feminist socialism'. Yet Marcuse's ultimate solution is still firmly within a patriarchal frame since feminism, for him, is only a short-term stage on the road to a future society.

In Britain Terry Eagleton claims to be able to write feminist criticism. It is 'the second' of his three critical approaches in *The Rape of Clarissa*. In a sense Eagleton might be pardoned for his attempt. His critique is about discourse in that larger mould which sees that the problem of writing *is* the problem of women. The writing of *Clarissa*, Eagleton says, is about sexual politics since its epistolary form encodes the sexual relation between Lovelace and Clarissa. But Eagleton can never *centralise* gender. He cannot explore the full extent of the victimisation of women because he is male. *Clarissa*, the novel, it seems to me, is not only about a woman raped and excluded from speech but about a woman who, like many women, excludes *herself* from speech. Eagleton manages to write a whole book about *Clarissa* while ignoring features like the way Clarissa is mutilating her own discourse and her own body in an anorexic refusal to eat. These are features which would probably be crucial for a feminist critique. Richardson is a man not a feminist writer. *Clarissa* has no vision of an alternative sexual standard and contains the heroine within a prevailing definition of Christianity. What Eagleton finds most interesting in Richardson is his own self mirrored. He describes the way Richardson enjoyed soliciting the views of the women to whom he read his works aloud, in a kind of teasing erotic play. They were 'a group of perceptive, well-educated, critically astute women; and Richardson's compact with them is best seen as a crucial act of solidarity' (Eagleton, 1982, p. 11). This is, rather, Eagleton with his adoring coterie of Oxford women. In male Marxism, texts resolve their own ideological problems while their male or female authors slip away. Other male critics, like K.K. Ruthven, do not wish to 'possess' feminists as dramatically as does Eagleton. In *Feminist Literary Studies* Ruthven takes feminism seriously as a critical practice. Yet, as ever, there is an implicit agenda of male supremacy. By refusing separatism Ruthven aims to recuperate feminism. He ignores Black and lesbian writing and hence depoliticizes feminist criticism turning it simply into another pedagogic skill. *The* major departure from this tradition is feminist criticism, in the way that feminist criticism works *first* as archaeology (discovering the past of women) *then* as theory rather than the other way round.

Why describe this long catalogue of the failures of 'friendly' or unfriendly male critics? If we accept my earlier argument that we need to establish a feminist position in literary criticism very quickly because criticism is central to the hegonomic power of education, why not just get on and write a feminist criticism? I think I have established, if only in a roundabout detour through the patriarchal terrain, that it is actually very hard to write feminist criticism without being aware that every critical handle, like 'author', is itself tainted and suspect. Every critic, male or female, is trained in the techniques of paternal criticism. We need to reverse the situation where male critics talk about the syntactical defences and distortions of women writers, and identify instead the way male readings are themselves full of specific defences and distortions before we can provide correctives. But above all, what the catalogue does is to demolish the whole argument of male criticism in which the perspective of a non-aligned male critic is assumed to be sexually neutral while a feminist is seen as a case of special pleading. Feminist criticism must be more than simply an addition to 'structuralism', 'Marxism' or whatever. It is male criticism, not feminism, which has the ideological blinkers. How can we replace sophistry with Sappho? Of course, the previous few pages contain one, as yet unexamined, problematic. My critique describes the limitations of male critical interpretations in terms that male critics might be prepared to accept. We need to move on. We need to take the same stance to ourselves as women readers and critics that Ros Coward took to women writers when she said that a woman's book is not necessarily a feminist book because it is written by a woman (Coward, 1980, p. 53). Reading as a woman is not necessarily what occurs when a woman reads: women can read and do read as men. We have to think through just what it implies to ask a woman to read as a woman—which is what I take as feminist criticism.

Jonathan Culler, in *On Deconstruction*, asks himself the same question: What does reading as a woman mean? He concludes that reading as a woman is to 'play a role', that critics, male or female, can set up the hypothesis of a woman reader. But this will not do. A male reading as a feminist, is not a feminist critic because he carries with him the possibility of escape—into masculinity and into patriarchy.

To be women readers and therefore feminist critics we have to understand that a gendered reading must foreground several perceptions simultaneously. Taking 'concept' in its original sense of a class of objects or comparisons, the concept of gendered reading, then, involves three gender comparisons or transactions. We simultaneously read with the experiences of our biological sex (whether from menstruation or re-production). We read with a gender identity—with our self-created condition of femaleness (from mother-identity or childhood). And we read with a gender role—with a consciousness of the social construction of femininity. In other words, we are different readers, and therefore different critics, from men because our gendered reading is both essentially different *and* one produced by our agreeing to read 'difference' as a crucial paradigm of cultural construction. The *extent* of difference is therefore infinite. It is in a syntax of subordination and subversion. It is in the whole difficulty for women of engaging with the materials of language itself as a signifying practice.

So we are back on earth, safely returned from the tech-nological 'star' wars in the space of male criticism. We debrief ourselves and step out of the contaminated space suits woven by established patriarchal aesthetics. But how do we ad*dress* as women readers in a freshly gynocentric world? If a womanly aesthetics is not a series of normative judgements about the evolution of art but about the way art may help women to evolve, criticism will automatically have a new focus. It will help us more easily to see what women actually write and find out why they write it. One obvious challenge will be to the aesthetic norm where 'good' is to be avant-garde. For women, 'good' writing may not need to be stylistically innovatory if a woman writer finds that the 'reactionary' form of romance, for example, provides her with a useful epistomology.

Pluralism can replace normalism. Because feminism ends in 'ism' its pluralistic nature is often overlooked. Feminist critics may share one single assumption that literary history is a constructed male fiction, but feminist criticism is not one unified technique. Because feminist criticism confronts the centrality of 'literature' in literary history and examines the implications of centralising literature itself, it involves historical explanation, reconstruction and a recognition that reading is always rereading. Because feminist criticism centralises 'woman', it is sociolinguistic in nature, describing women's writing with a practical attention to the physical use of words.

Stephen Heath defines a masculine discourse as one 'which fails to take account of the problem of sexual difference in its enunciation and address' (1978). And at best difference is usually defined in its epistemological aspects—women think in circles rather than lines, we tend to be holistic rather than partial; we prefer open to closed systems; we employ associational rather than sequential logic; we are obsessed with detail and with pattern; that we write sentences to quote Virginia Woolf 'of a more elastic fibre than the old'; that we are subjective and naturally attracted to interior spaces, children and animals.

This is to deal with difference without constituting an opposition. What feminist criticism addresses and opposes are three problems in literary criticism. First the problem of a gendered literary history is addressed by re-examining male texts, noting their assumptions and showing the way women in them are frequently moulded within tight cultural and social constraints. This criticism is thematic—focusing on women's oppression as a theme in literature and assuming a woman reader as a consumer of male-produced works. It can then replace this oppression with a new literary history which gives full weight to texts of neglected women, and women's oral culture, previously regarded as extra-literary.

Second, feminist criticism confronts the problem of creating a gendered reader by offering her new methods and a fresh critical practice. Such practice focuses on those techniques of signification—as the mirroring of mothers and daughters, or role playing and transvestism, whose language can become 'literary'. Third, feminist criticism has to make us *act* as women readers by creating new communities of writers and readers supported by a language spoken for and by women. This practice treats criticism as a contractual genre where women readers collectively can become a counter-tradition in academia providing new ideas about the interaction of author, character and reader. Feminist criticism is not simply training sensibility in an updated political guise. Yet, although feminist critics tend to use models from the social sciences and techniques from psychoanalysis, writing an account of models of feminist criticism is as difficult for literary critics as writing feminist history is for historians. Women writers are excluded from the centre of 'literature' by men, and some radical French feminists like Cixous are refusing to be called feminist at all. We are in difficult times.

Part of the problem comes from the way in which feminist criticism developed in the 1970s. This is best summed up through considering the writings of four critics—Ellen Moers, Patricia Meyer Spacks, Elaine Showalter and Florence Howe. In their work they began to develop a female annexe to male literature. This led them to redefinitions of the topic of criticism because recognition of a new group of works turns out to be more than a simple process of addition and at some point feminists needed new critical tools. The new grouping, or configuration, tended to alter our definitions and hierarchies and our understanding of how those definitions and hierarchies came into being. But the approach is problematic. It creates a crude utility model using criticism to sustain feminist consciousness, as Marxists manipulate class representation for symbolic purposes. It also depends on a too-generalised conception of women.

The writings and reception of Elaine Showalter illustrate the issue very clearly. In 'Towards a Feminist Poetics' Showalter divides criticism into two distinct varieties. For Showalter the first type is concerned with woman as reader, as the consumer of male-produced literature, and with the way in which the hypothesis of a female reader changes our view of a text. The second type of feminist critic is concerned with woman as writer, with woman as the producer of textual meaning, with the history, themes, genres and structures of literature by women. Here she theorises the more empirical revisionism of her earlier book *A Literature of Their Own* (1978). Showalter went on to develop her ideas in *'Feminist Criticism in the Wilderness'* and subsequent writings (1982). This categorises what might be called working techniques of criticism in her discussion of biological, linguistic and psychological models of 'different' discourse.

But the reactions to, and attacks on, Showalter's writings by other feminists reveal the difficulty of locating feminist criticism in this way. Showalter's failure to adequately address issues of race and sexuality, to these later feminists, is symptomatic of the inadequacies of white, heterosexual women's studies in American universities. Carolyn J. Allen set out a role for criticism as a political act in her response to Showalter's essay (Allen, 1982). Elly Bulkin, more than others, has attacked the homophobia and racism of Showalter and those critics most influenced by her like Annette Kolodny (Kolodny, 1980). Feminist shifts seem often breathtakingly speedy to outsiders, but the most significant lesson from this debate is the recognition that literature and criticism must be related to gender *and* class and race and sexual preference.

I have chosen, therefore, to describe and analyse the directions of feminist criticism and then use those directions to study, in depth, the writings of Virginia Woolf, Rebecca West and Adrienne Rich. Chapter 2 'Pioneers' sets out the questions and provides some historical context to the answers that later feminists provide. A starting point in post-war feminist criticism is the assumption that culture is emblematic of patriarchal social attitudes. Reading the work of Kate Millett, Simone de Beauvoir and the populists Betty Friedan and Germaine Greer is to be interrogated by their encompassing questions of literature and culture. All four are addressing the sex caste system as represented in literature and culture, and their criticism balances narrative with moral debates. They are fundamentalists because they try to find basic, universal explanations: they ask what features of culture represent the subordination of women and what literary techniques perpetuate this pattern? The agenda of Millett, de Beauvoir, Friedan and Greer set out a major new direction for post-war feminist criticism. It was the first time that the interrelation of sexual ideology and culture was addressed as a fundamental condition of critical form.

While the legacy of Millett or Friedan has given feminist criticism its attractive pragmatic amalgamation of techniques from the social sciences and the arts, such fundamentalism has lost much of its appeal in recent critical theory. Their approach depends on a static conception of patriarchy and, paradoxically, none of the four really tackled the institutional nature of literature itself. Perhaps because Millett and de Beauvoir, in particular, see education and the humanities as *the* vehicle of social change, they left to later feminists the work of making an adequate account of 'experience' and the subconscious.

Language and Psychoanalysis

The writings of Julia Kristeva, Hélène Cixous, Mary Daly and Monique Wittig read the feminine as rooted in language and subjectivity. They describe the emotional power of feminism and challenge the unity of the subject and hence the traditional relations of art. Other psychoanalytic feminist critics like Sandra Gilbert and Susan Gubar began with the psychodynamics of female characters, but the more fundamental deconstruction of the realist approach comes with French ideas of an alternative women's time, the semiotic, or an alternative women's place—androgyny or absence. While providing a fresh semantics in their attack on the possession of language by men, the French feminists can lose sight of the *reconstruction* in criticism of linguistics *with* social motifs.

17

Marxist-Feminism

The representation of women's social experience in literary form is the topic of critics like Lillian Robinson, Michèle Barrett, Gayatri Spivak and the feminists within the Birmingham Centre for Cultural Studies. It is the conjunction of the subject *and* her history as part of discourse which is their concern. It should be understood that there is a blurring between critical standpoints and political positions. Those who I term 'Marxist-feminists' are not necessarily committed to orthodox Marxism. I use the division mainly to indicate that the themes and kinds of collective, or ethnographic techniques, they use in feminist criticism are derived in some way from their political theories, which are maybe anywhere on the continuum from socialism to Marxism. Like the pioneer critics, Marxist-feminists are renegotiating the creation of literary values from a gendered point of view. It is in their practice—whether of group writing or mixed-media analysis—that Marxist-feminists have contributed most to feminist criticism.

Black and Lesbian Criticism

More than most feminists, Black and lesbian critics show that the personal is political in their examination of self-definition in literary form. For Barbara Smith, Audre Lorde or Adrienne Rich new forms of critical experience depend on rejecting the idea of a coherent classical academic tradition. One of their most powerful contributions to feminism is their understanding that every act of criticism is political in its shaping of personal as political experience. The coming out of silence makes both Black and lesbian critics intensely interested in language, but to some extent they are still having to construct a Black or lesbian reading as much as a Black and lesbian theory of criticism.

Myth Criticism

A new area in feminist criticism is the ecology of myth. The construction of cultural archetypes of power useful to women is, for Mary Daly, Annis Pratt and others, a psychological tool to avoid tradition while remaining within criticism. Their writings are both deconstructive *and* futuristic in their reformulation of Motherhood and vivid re-creation of early female images and symbols. Setting the radical otherness of women against the patriarchal disorder of the present, however, may lead to a false universality when such criticism avoids race or class.

A number of problems arise when we try to sketch out feminist criticism in this way. First, as one might expect, it is very difficult to contain a writer like Mary Daly within one kind of criticism. Second, by taking different critical positions and projecting them as differences *between* critical methods, the approach appears to assume an artificial homogeneity within critical schools. It might be more realistic to note down our own reading experiences, which can range from Marxism to myth, occurring not as *levels* but more as moments in a single reading.

Clearly this notion that criticism might originate as the critic/reader's experience and that the function of criticism is to re-create or relive this experience makes literary criticism very reductive. It both assumes that a writer is speaking in the same time as the moment of reading and that the function of criticism is basically therapeutic. The project of feminist critics is precisely to relate reading to other kinds of social activity. The strength of feminist criticism is in its refusal to accept the dislocation of literature from other social practices, and this has far-reaching institutional implications. The very difficulty of reconciling feminism's 'isms' suggests that feminist criticism *has* undercut traditional assumptions about literature and criticism. Whether or not it displays any single or major critical style, feminist criticism's impact on the reading and teaching of literature is due to its centralising of women's experience. Feminist criticism rests on the notion of the relation of women's reading to writing experience. Virginia Woolf called her collection of literary criticism *The Common Reader* because it was written with an ordinary woman in mind who was reading for pleasure. If we women readers explore in our own language our own needs in our own study groups, we can glimpse what a non-patriarchal criticism might look like. Virginia Woolf first described it in *Three Guineas:*

> Obviously, then, it must be an experimental college, an adventurous college. Let it be built on lines of its own . . . The poor college must teach only the arts that can be taught cheaply and practised by poor people . . . The aim of the new college, the cheap college, should be not to segregate and specialise, but to combine. It should explore the ways in which mind and body can be made to co-operate; discover what new combinations make good wholes in human life. [1938, p. 40]

Contemporary feminist criticism has solved in its very style the major problem confronting all cultural theory; that is, in its symbiotic relation to the Women's Movement, feminist criticism can address and help support a viable counter-culture. Throughout the 1970s and 1980s feminists have built a series of feminist institutions. They have equipped feminism with its own bookshops, libraries, theatre groups, book clubs, magazines and newspapers, arts centres, community centres, local authority women's committees, women's transport and social facilities, nightclubs and women's film and video in a whole range of cultural spaces. This audience, supported by consciousness raising and education groups, enables feminist criticism to be part of a broader movement. Potentially, feminist criticism can be engaged in one of the most important jobs in any intellectual activity—that of the critical in-terrogation of ideology for a readership who can seize on images and ideas for feminist action. Within the space of feminist criticism, feminists can explore a huge variety of cultural symbols and motifs in articulating their personal reading experiences. Feminist criticism can be nothing less than the political appropriation of culture. It could be a land of golden voices.

2

PIONEERS

It is no accident that in our post-war period, literary criticism has a central place in feminist theory. The pioneering texts—Simone de Beauvoir's *The Second Sex* and Kate Millett's *Sexual Politics*—appropriated literature for feminism. Feminism and cultural criticism unite in the work of Betty Friedan's *The Feminine Mystique* and Germaine Greer's *The Female Eunuch*. These writers provide by far the most systematic feminist criticism because they ask major and encompassing questions of literature and culture. De Beauvoir asked, 'What is woman and why is she misrepresented in male texts?'; Millett asked, 'What are sexual politics and how are they represented in literature?'; Friedan and Greer, although writing in a cruder style, were asking, 'Why are particular stereotypes potent and why do women accept them?' In some ways all four are only tentatively or partially feminists because it provided models of how these questions could be *approached*, most importantly through an analysis of cultural forms. All four writers set out to address the key need of feminist criticism: how to describe and subvert the cultural repression of women in contemporary society.

All four choose to answer their questions by examining the sexual caste system as it was represented in contradictory images in literature and culture. Yet their feminist criticism was written in isolation from the traditional practices of literary criticism. De Beauvoir's training was in philosophy, Millett's debt was to the social and sexual historian Steven Marcus, and Friedan and Greer were journalists. Although Millett used her research for a doctorate and Greer was teaching at the University of Warwick, their criticism was a novel alternative to traditional academic criticism. It was revolutionary in scope for it amalgamated critiques from the social sciences and the arts. But what is most revolutionary was the importance this criticism attached to the language of sexuality. It is for these reasons that the feminist criticism of de Beauvoir, Millett, Friedan and Greer represents an enormous breakthrough in describing women's oppression in literary form.

Each of the texts is very much part of their own cultural 'moment'. Because issues of women's oppression do not figure in the French Left critiques of the 1940s, de Beauvoir was more consistent about male constraints and much vaguer about women's alternatives. From 1971, when she organised the Right to Abortion Campaign and joined the MLF (Mouvement de la Libération des Femmes), de Beauvoir has consistently supported radical feminists (Schwarzer, 1984). Millett thought the key male writers were Mailer and Miller because their notions of 'Hipster rape' were popular in the macho libertarian sexual climate of the 1960s. It was the startling conservatism in replies to questionnaires which Friedan gave, in 1957, to Smith College graduates that made her start writing. Greer claimed that her book depended on the forcing house of the New Left. If the oppressive mechanics of post-war culture forced each writer into print, the historical contexts which inspired each writer also limited their notions of women's possibilities. Yet, having said that, there is an attractive way in which all four writers refuse the radical chic of their times—most evident in Kate Millett's brave attack on Eldridge Cleaver (the symbol of American Leftists) for his hostility to women.

The distinguishing feature of post-war feminist criticism as established by these writers, was its hybrid mixture of cultural and literary criticism. All four compare images of women and the conditions of femininity, as defined by males, with the reality of everyday women. They present a cultural analysis centring on the female self as cultural fabrication in the myths of male authors. Culture is treated as emblematic of male social attitudes and literature is seen as representative of male emotions and fears. In other words, literature is analysed to 'confirm' each writer's general account of myths of the feminine.

Literature (or, in the case of Friedan and Greer, popular

culture) emerges in their writings as having a formal homology
with the working of patriarchy. Texts, literary or cultural, are
read as models of patriarchal power. All four writers engaged in
a psychosocial critique intent on unveiling the ideological
nature of 'beliefs' and 'values'.

If their use of a hybrid form links these geographically distant
writers, the titles of all four books are similarly revealing. Each
is about sex. Indeed, each analysis is pervasively animated by
the sense that women's status is gender determined. For
example, de Beauvoir understands that Claudel's misrepresentation of character is not the result of bad writing but of
Claudel's sexual politics. Millett's *Sexual Politics* is a handbook
of male sexual techniques. She judges texts in relation to the
sexual nature of their authors; Swinburne's poetry, for example,
reveals his impotence or algolagnia. Sexual politics, for Millett,
even determines a writer's choice of genre. For example,
Tennyson's use of fantastic forms, Millett claims, stems from
Tennyson's sexual ambivalence. Friedan and Greer take
popular culture's major ideological service to men to be the
restriction of women's sexuality to stereotypes of marriage and
children. The justification for claiming this criticism for
feminism is in the thoroughness of each account of sexual
politics, even if (as in the case of Friedan and Greer) some
explanations seem superficial.

Why was literature so particularly important to these writers,
and what implications does that interest have for subsequent
techniques of feminist criticism? By taking literature and
popular culture to be totally illustrative of all social issues—totally
incorporative—each critic was able to describe literary or
cultural forms as instruments of socialisation. Novels are then
collections of social and psychic attitudes. De Beauvoir and
Millett focus more on male than female characters since, they
say, the characteristics of women in texts written by men are
there only for what attributes of male authors they might
correspond to. They find the representation of women to be
very similar in otherwise disparate authors.

Millett is primarily interested in the 'autobiographical'
representation of male authors in their male characters. She
therefore examines narrator viewpoint and terminology in
relation to authorial moral or ethical norms. Since the only way

to social change for these critics is a rather Reichean[1] belief in personality change, then the investigation of the representation of personality and identity in literature must be very crucial.

Friedan and Greer, too, analyse images of women in women's magazines as if they are documentary evidence of a male psychic need for childlike women. Imagery here, whether in literature or popular culture, is reflective. If the role of literature and culture is to be reflectionist, then the implication for feminist criticism is that its techniques will be primarily illustrative rather than constructive. But, clearly, what and how criticism illustrates is rather different for each critic. The ideological legacy of post-war feminist criticism indeed comes from the two different orientations set by these writers. On the one hand, there was the pragmatic, anti-theoretical, writing of Friedan and Greer; on the other, there was the theoretical, literary version of sexual politics developed by de Beauvoir and Millett. Where de Beauvoir and Millett take patriarchy itself as the source of sexual repression, Friedan and Greer take women's response *to* patriarchy as the issue. The two divergent paths of feminist criticism ended in different solutions. Friedan and Greer, by advocating consciousness rousing, promote education as the agency of change; while de Beauvoir and Millett, although ultimately reformist, speak of radical coalitions between feminism and negritude or lesbianism.

Simone de Beauvoir

The architect of post-war feminist criticism is Simone de Beauvoir. *The Second Sex*, published in 1949, is her now classic study of women's repression and the construction of 'femininity' by men. It pioneered ideas and techniques acknowledged by feminists from across the range of academic disciplines. Betty Friedan 'Americanised' *The Second Sex*, Shulamith Firestone dedicated *The Dialectic of Sex* to de Beauvoir and Juliet Mitchell called *The Second Sex* the 'most important of the "totalising" studies on the oppression of women' (Mitchell, 1975, p. 300). Although 'The Myth of Women in Five Authors' (that part of *The Second Sex* which is specifically literary criticism) is short, it exemplifies the ideology of the rest of the text. It is there, as de

Beauvoir says, 'to confirm this analysis of the feminine myth as it appears in a general view' (de Beauvoir, 1972, p. 299). Just as in her fiction and autobiographies, de Beauvoir uses long book-lists and comparisons with literary heroines like Jo March to establish character identity, so in *The Second Sex* it is literature which vividly illustrates de Beauvoir's philosophical frame-work.

The theoretical issues raised over thirty years ago in *The Second Sex* continue to be central. How is woman constructed differently from, and by, men? What explanations from psychoanalysis or Marxism can help women understand this construction? What particular perspective does literature offer? And from this can we distinguish between women and femininity in a useful way?

Although *The Second Sex* occupies a crucial place in contemporary feminism, critics have been less than fair to de Beauvoir's achievement. Early reviewers were hostile. François Mauriac attacked *The Second Sex* in *Le Figaro Littéraire* and Elizabeth Hardwick, four years later, when the heavily edited English translation appeared in America, said '*The Second Sex* is so briskly Utopian it fills one with a kind of shame and sadness' (Hardwick, 1953, p. 321). Contemporary feminists are more worried that de Beauvoir's existentialism and commitment to notions of transcendence prevents her from understanding the deeper contradictions of desire or eroticism (Walters, 1976; Evans, 1980). But it was precisely de Beauvoir's training in philosophy that enables her to ask her more abstract question 'What is a woman?' and hence write such a thorough reply.

The Second Sex begins with facts and myths drawn from psychology, history and biology as well as from literature. These are man-made myths where women are passive objects from prehistory to the coming of suffrage. Book II describes the life of contemporary Western women, using autobiographies as well as psychosocial studies to focus on how women themselves live experience. Woman is constructed 'differently', then, by men. For de Beauvoir, physical distinctions between women and men have meaning only from social arrangements, so that biological characteristics can only explain, but never determine, differences between women and men. It is because women have been denied social liberty that they become narcissists, since the essence of 'femininity' is dependence. What strengthens de Beauvoir's critique is her use of theoretical approaches drawn from psychoanalysis and Marxism. The Freudian model de Beauvoir finds too deterministic, and its concepts, as with penis envy, are part of men's symbolic power. Similarly de Beauvoir considers Engel's analysis of capitalism and the oppression of women to be an inadequate explanation for the interaction between the economic and the symbolic oppression of women by men. Just as in her fiction and autobiographies de Beauvoir describes alternative object models for woman, so in *The Second Sex* she tries to disentangle woman from the symbolism of femininity. In order to do this she synthesises images of women in myth and literature, with the intellectual scheme established in the early part of her text. Asked by Alice Schwarzer how she would prefer to be remembered—as a philosopher or a writer—she replied 'I set my store by literature' (Schwarzer, 1984, p. 23). Literature and myth are important since it is there that the sense of woman as Other is given a stronger elaboration by men. When reading the work of Claudel, Lawrence or Breton, de Beauvoir shows how each writer reflects collective myths—of woman as Flesh, as Nature, as Muse. The privileged Other in literature is de Beauvoir's version of Virginia Woolf's 'The Angel in the House'. In literature women are 'compensation myths' for men. De Beauvoir suggests that feminist criticism should be interrogative and establish in the name of *what* women are to be condemned. De Beauvoir shows how, because Motherlant wanted to be God, for example, he made horrifying mother images. Breton devalues women as the incarnation of Nature. Even Stendhal, who allows a more human woman to develop in his fiction, is still condemning his women to dependence.

The construction of difference in de Beauvoir's literary criticism is more sophisticated than her rigid distinctions between men and women in her philosophy. She gives a more accurate account of Lawrence, for example, than Kate Millett later was able to do. De Beauvoir claims that Lawrence's idea of sexuality does not simply demand the subjectivity of women but the transcendence of subjectivity by most women *and* male characters. In Lawrence men and women use each other instrumentally, with men arousing symmetrical demands in women. For example, de Beauvoir interprets Gudrun's 'masochism' in *Women in Love* to be only caused by Gerald. Only the male character who functions as the autobiographical representation of Lawrence himself has subjectivity. The ideal of the 'true woman' which Lawrence offers us, de Beauvoir concludes, is a woman 'who unreservedly accepts being defined as the Other' (1972, p. 254).

Yet, although her account may be adequate as a feminist phenomenology of literary features, it is inadequate as a form of literary criticism. Characters in de Beauvoir's criticism are static entities. Certainly de Beauvoir shows that her literary authors, like any other males, have a rigid hierarchical view of society that depends on women's social submission. But the title of de Beauvoir's literary critique 'The Myth of Women in Five Authors' is very revealing. De Beauvoir paraphrases literature into philosophy. Looking at literature, as she does, as a continuous line running from the agnostics suggests an external fixity of male aggression. De Beauvoir trivialises the whole issue of why some myths of women *are* fictionalised at all. By setting out a panoply of male myths and checking them for 'ambivalences' and 'contradictions', as a well-trained philosopher should, de Beauvoir is in effect checking *internal* consistency in a very atemporal way.

This is not an adequate totalisation of the female I in literature since de Beauvoir does not counter male myths with an any more significant or contingent female individuality. The erotic is always mediated by male desire. It is not there as an autonomous state because that would involve de Beauvoir in describing the subjective and the unconscious as a part of the feminine. Yet literary criticism depends on an imagery of the unconscious as another mechanism for explaining fantasy or desire. But the parallel de Beauvoir draws between representation *and* construction—that men need to *represent* (in myth or literature) before they can construct women's dependence—makes literature, and therefore criticism, important to feminism. What de Beauvoir was able to establish in *The Second Sex* is that male writers share a deep conservatism about women, and therefore to use *only* traditional terminology to describe writing modes is clearly inadequate. Literature is an important site because in it each male writer reveals, in his descriptions of women, the gap between his general ethics and his fantasies. In other words, de Beauvoir claims, male writers only write about women to learn more fully what they are themselves.

The problem with de Beauvoir's agenda for feminist critics is not that her interpretations depart from the context of understood critical vocabulary. It is that, like Millett's, they sometimes depart from the actual world of the novels themselves. Women are too often extrapolated from the specific context of specific novels, and as feminist critics, we need to look at women existing *within* the worlds of novels as well as within a 'real' world. Perhaps de Beauvoir's best legacy to feminist criticism and what links her with Millett and Friedan is her implicit assumption that women can *never* be adequately portrayed by male authors, determined as *they* are by their own male myths.

Betty Friedan

Betty Friedan's reworking of *The Second Sex* in *The Feminine Mystique* was a pragmatic version of the same arena—women's passive acceptance of the cultural stereotypes of femininity as constructed by patriarchy. Although an overtly populist text, *The Feminine Mystique* set out for feminist criticism a useful mode of cultural analysis which has been more problematically developed in the writings of Angela McRobbie, Lillian Robinson and Judith Williamson. Friedan's discussion focuses on the cultural isolation of American suburban women of the late 1960s. Like Catherine Beecher Stowe before her, who questioned 200 friends in 1846 about the origin of their psychosomatic illness, Friedan questioned 200 Smith College graduates about their dissatisfaction with suburban culture. *The Feminine Mystique* is a very period text, tied to a moment in Cold War history and the post-war boom, and presents a demographic account of a particular generation. But, although a far less radical writer than de Beauvoir, Friedan was trying to answer a similar question: Why did women (albeit affluent college graduates of the late 1950s) narrow the boundaries of their lives to marriage and children?

The Feminine Mystique is written by an American journalist whose previous articles had appeared in *Good Housekeeping,* and it catered to an American fascination for statistics, anecdotes and autobiography. Contemporary feminists have attacked Friedan for shrinking de Beauvoir's concepts and endorsing the American dream of individual ambition and competition (Dijkstra, 1980; Eisenstein, 1981). But, although the political appeal of *The Feminine Mystique* was to the liberal individualist consciousness of affluent America, in observing the process by which Friedan selects and transforms de Beauvoir's philosophical ideas into a popular language we can witness, problematised, a central dilemma for all feminist criticism: how to be both rigorously feminist and yet readable.

The appeal of *The Feminine Mystique* comes, obviously, because it offers an easy introduction to snippets of women's history, a simplified Freud, and familiar aspects of social and educational discrimination. Friedan says that she has no theory and implicitly suggests that the 'mystique' of suburban woman stands for women's problems in general. But Friedan is useful to feminist criticism both in the way she analyses culture and because she offers cultural solutions to the social needs of her audience. We need to know, not so much why Friedan is addressing such a narrow class group in her obsession with the nuclear family, but how *such* a cultural analysis clearly satisfied and might still respond to feminist concerns.

Friedan describes the media and consumerism by comparing the more active personae of women's magazines of the 1930s with those contemporary to her. Her explanations are ideological rather than institutional. She describes the way women's magazines were serving the political exigencies of post-war America. Magazines, or culture itself, are not a cause of women's oppression but rather the means. They service patriarchal ideology. *The Feminine Mystique* includes well documented interviews and statistics about cultural products, and Friedan starts with these as an anthropologist might start with the observed rituals of a social group. Friedan moves from observed point to observed point within a narrow trajectory of documentation. Some of her critical motifs are based on interesting evidence. Friedan found that American magazines were not creating a simple idealised stereotype of women's passivity but continually moving between 'genres', creating 'documentary' evidence of feminine stereotypes for their female audiences. For example, the same magazine *Ladies Home Journal* combined picture essays of split-level homes with a social series like 'Political Pilgrim's Progress' of women working to improve playgrounds. Friedan notices the match between form and ideology. Thus, the type size of women's magazines was enlarged and simplified to meet the cruder and simpler image of women being presented. The unconscious of women is a most potent threat to patriarchy (although Friedan would never use these terms) since fiction, where women's dreams are located in magazines, Friedan found to be more stereotyped and less honest.

If Friedan reads like a product of undergraduate workshops in creative journalism—'I was on the trail of the problem that has no name'—her understanding of how culture actually functions in American society remains relevant to feminist criticism. It is an ideological rather than intrinsic criticism. A more problematic analysis would reveal women's pervasive psychological need for repeated cultural motifs by an account of how motifs are put together. For example, Friedan quotes the story of 'The Sandwich Maker'—a woman, saved by pregnancy, from having to earn money with home cooking—without analysing characterisation or domestic imagery. Friedan ignores the quality of images and that they in *themselves* are unrepresentative of the hard and uncongenial (not only tedious) daily suburban housework. A fully feminist reading needs to combine an intrinsic with an ideological reading. Friedan does try to identify the institutional source of myths because she interviews magazine editors, but she is not able to estimate their influence.

It is when writing about sexuality that Friedan is most revealing. As a good sociologist she has at least to mention Kinsey, but Friedan is locked into a nineteenth-century feminism of sexual abstinence. Like de Beauvoir, Friedan wants to separate sexuality from women's lives. Friedan's fear of sexuality is evident in her use of extreme vocabulary—love and desire are a 'parasitical softening' (Friedan, 1982, p. 244). Sexuality is always heterosexuality. Friedan's attacks on homosexuals are particularly crude. Males are 'no less than the female sex-seekers, Peter Pans, forever childlike' (1982, p. 239). Not only does Friedan lack a theory of sexual politics, her solution to the problem with no name is asexuality, 'to postpone present pleasure for future long-term goals' (1982, p. 214). The vocabulary is telling. Any reshaping of women's culture, to Friedan, will be by individual not collective effort. Friedan is attracted to the strong pioneer woman and creates a 'New Life Plan' of hard paid work. 'She must learn to compete, then, not as a woman, but as a human being' (1982, p. 328). After consciousness raising, Friedan feels, there will be no constraints preventing women from questioning their own self-images. But changing the concept of oneself as a woman is of course part of a larger social and class reality, and feminist criticism needs to deconstruct patriarchal ideology as it is represented in different and *always changing* cultural forms. Finally, the ideal woman model Friedan offers is herself with her 'lifelong commitment to an art' (1982, p. 302).

The Feminine Mystique does represent an important cultural 'moment' in feminist criticism. We must not only acknowledge Friedan's popularity (and therefore women's need for populist texts) but examine what kind of cultural agenda it delimited. The humanities are crucial to Friedan. Her educational 'shock treatment' comes through 'an intensive concentrated re-immersion in, quite simply, the humanities' (Friedan, 1982, p. 324). At the organising conference of NOW (the National Organisation of Women Friedan set up in 1966) she chose seven task-forces to investigate discrimination against women. These were in the fields of education, employment, religion, poor women, women's image in the mass media, women's political rights and the family. The list, like Friedan, rests in the realm of ideas, with education as first vehicle of social change. Friedan's is a superficial solution specifically antagonistic to separatism. She does not ask women to look at alternatives *outside* patriarchal culture but remains reformist, accepting the canon and simply altering its scope. Feminist criticism would need to move beyond Friedan's horizons.

Germaine Greer

The British progeny of *The Feminine Mystique* is Germaine Greer's *The Female Eunuch*, published in 1971. By spending a moment examining Greer's text we can see the problems with Friedan's limited conceptualisation evident in Greer's more diminished form. Greer documents images of women as they appear in popular culture and literature. She makes a direct use of literature as evidence for social roles in her assumption, for example, that Shakespeare is representing in a one-for-one relation the social parameters of romance and marriage. *The Female Eunuch* is an early British example of popular culture criticism when it comes to Greer's analysis of the stylistic features and themes of popular romance. But, although Greer is making an ideological analysis of aspects of misogyny in culture, her text is superficial. The style—of simple paraphrase into a contemporary everyday vocabulary—was dictated by her commissioning editor. Yet it is not the accessibility of *The Female Eunuch* which creates a problem for feminist criticism but rather Greer's deradicalised refusal to make value judgements. Why, then, mention *The Female Eunuch* in a chapter on pioneers? Because, like Friedan, Greer was widely read and had a clear impact on feminist thinking. Prophets of women's emancipation will always be untheoretical, easy to read and pragmatic. But by examining the process by which they translate more comprehensive critiques we can praise the more readable journalese while being very careful to refuse the ideological pattern.

Both Friedan and Greer refuse to distinguish between different representations but lump them together in an unclassified approach to male misogyny. They give no materialist analysis. Women only know who they are supposed to be according to the cultural definition of feminity. The solution to the problem for Friedan or Greer, therefore, is to free women from the destructive *mental* dependence that patriarchal culture breeds. The agenda for cultural criticism set out by Friedan and Greer cannot be easily dismissed. It recurs in much subsequent feminist criticism in patterns of plurality and a refusal to set value criteria. As where a text can claim to be feminist because it claims 'all' Black, lesbian, working-class women's lives are there. Historically, Friedan and Greer played an important role in encouraging consciousness raising, but feminist criticism needs a more problematic and comprehensive methodology.

Kate Millett

The radical core of de Beauvoir's analysis is the dynamic of *Sexual Politics* by Kate Millett. But Millett made a critique of ideology central, whereas de Beauvoir does not. Feminist criticism is centralised in *Sexual Politics* since Millett uses literary analysis to examine gender difference in the way subsequent sociology or historiography would examine other contemporary discourses. Millett confronted literature as the record of the collective consciousness of patriarchy. The book was a revelation of sexism in the work of Lawrence, Mailer and Miller and revolutionised the way women and men were reading, or misreading, contemporary literature. Millett took her writers to be archetypes of particular social values within capitalism—the values of violence, sexuality and the cash nexus. She takes issue with the way these writers have generalised male values (as with Mailer's endorsement of violence against women) and made male values seem *the* human condition. Millett argues that sexuality is *the* site in which male power is expressed, and that literature reveals that sexual mastery of men over women as the central symbol of patterns of dominance and subordination in culture; in other words, that forms of thought *and* means of expression are made and controlled by men.

There are three kinds of charges in *Sexual Politics:* first, that male writers distort male and female characters; second, that they misrepresent sexuality by associating deviance with 'femininity'; and third that the narrative structure of fiction is a representation of masculine culture. The first half of *Sexual Politics* provides the social and political background to these literary charges. Here Millett argues that the political power men have over women amounts to a more fundamental political division in society than class. She provides a range of evidence from biology, sociology, education, anthropology and psychology which shows patriarchy as archetype. This section is less precise in its use of the language of caste and class than the criticism section, and Millett, by playing down feminism as a subversive alternative, presents, as a result, a somewhat static notion of patriarchy.

As Norman Mailer gleefully pointed out, Kate Millett *is* an annoying critic—and not just to Mailer. 'A hard-hat has more curves in his head' (Mailer, 1971, p. 119). She paraphrases at length, confuses author with character and generalises to make all-inclusive points. Rereading Kate Millett is a little like watching black and white television after years of colour. But her faults come, I think, from not knowing her audience. Millett lacked what is now a feminist constituency, and she was trying to create one. Hence she spends time with lesser fiction where sexist themes and techniques are more explicit.

But Millett goes further than simply exposing sexism in one work after another, because she provides interpretative strategies for reading writing rather than merely denouncing men. The writers are chosen because they wrote about particular institutions and can therefore reveal a range of institutional ideology, whether it is the American army in Mailer or colonialisation in Genet. The critical technique is first one of paraphrase. Millett treats criticism as an act of translation in order to change the way we apprehend male texts. The key indices to Millett are then vocabulary and point of view, and her own vocabulary is full of extremes, of 'exalts' or 'dazzling', to successfully emphasise the power of words. Millett says male characters are authorial surrogates. Rojack in Mailer is emblematic to Millett 'like one of Faulkner's ancient retainers of a lost cause' (Millett, 1977, p. 16).

Although as a method of literary analysis *Sexual Politics* has limitations (clearest in the way key literary episodes are not analysed, and often relegated to footnotes), by judging everything in terms of identity creation Millett does produce interesting critical criteria. Particularly intriguing is her notion that genres can be distinguished by the way they reveal different aspects of personality. Criticism, she says, is like ego construction. Novels are the id and poetry represents the unconscious (Millett, 1977, p. 148). *Sexual Politics* is a psychoanalytic critique of literature as much as an ideological one.

The radicalism of *Sexual Politics* can be highlighted by situating it within American psychoanalytic criticism of the time and the context, at its time of writing, of American feminist developments in psychoanalysis (such as they were). It is tempting, when writing about the psychoanalytic milieu of the 1960s, to speak of a split into right and left wing. From Erik Erikson's famous description of women's 'inner spaces', through the behaviour therapy of E.G. Skinner and cybernetics of Norbert Weiner, all forms of conservative psychiatry translate individual dynamics into those which can function in the practical terms set by American post-war society. A good example is Erich Fromm's *The Fear of Freedom.* Fromm explains that he analyses the psychological processes operating within individuals only to understand the dynamics of the *social* process. Psychological forces are 'historically conditioned responses to economic change' (Fromm, 1960, p. 252). Fromm and his contemporaries were reviving an idealistic ethics for a period of American white male affluence.

The power of the therapeutic was the answer of the Left to this technology of the instincts. Wilhelm Reich, Norman Brown and Herbert Marcuse emerged as major theorists among the disaffected student generation of the 1960s. They offered the young concepts appropriate to a youthful desire for a sexually liberated society. Reich emphasised the extent to which sexual repression is enforced by capitalism, Marcuse proposed the idea of a libidinal morality; there were the hallucinogenic promises of Timothy Leary and Allen Ginsberg. This psychology of alienation has its Baedeker in Theodore Roszak's *The Making of a Counter Culture.* Roszak plans eventually to substitute for Western militarism a 'shamanistic world view', which he draws from a psychotherapy very much concerned with the symbolic vocabulary of dreams. Both right- and left-wing solutions ignore the historical *and* gendered dynamics of social psychology.

There was not, as yet, a feminist alternative. Definitions of 'femininity' were set out in Helene Deutsch's definitive two-volume *The Psychology of Women* (1944). Although Deutsch does not trace *all* women's problems to penis envy, she does claim to have found that successful career women suffer a 'masculinity complex'. She did not revise the psychoanalytic descriptions of sex roles. What Kate Millett transforms is the language *and* dynamics of psychoanalysis. By distinguishing between sex and gender, Millett could assess how literature contains and creates an ideology of sex roles. Using literary criticism to deconstruct the attributes of 'femininity' and 'masculinity' in male writing, Millett was able to reveal the misogyny of literary constructions.

That is not to say that Millett ignores materialism. She is able to situate Henry Miller's descriptions of sexual relations in a social world by analysing the bourgeois commercialism of his vocabulary. In any case, Miller has, Millett shows, a distorted psyche since he is unable to describe real sexual behaviour. What Millett particularly resents in Miller is his objectification of the feminine into the prostitute. Servicing, to Miller, is both bourgeois and sexual. It was, in 1970, a radical interpretation of Miller's apparent libertarianism. Her training in comparative literature enables Millett to address the social construction of gender in her account of Jean Genet. By aping 'masculine' and 'feminine' social roles, Genet—Millett feels—reveals the essence of what heterosexuals take to be masculinity or femininity. Millett is interested in authorial characters who can challenge gender identity like Genet's drag queens. But her strength is that Millett can draw comparisons between female stereotypes in literature and women in the real world, as with her comparison between the artificial representation of *The Woman that Rode Away* and African women lobbyists at the United Nations.

Millett moves easily between genres, comparing *The Woman that Rode Away* with *The Story of O* not because she herself confuses good and bad writing but precisely to situate literary form by association with, and contrast with, the unfamiliar. Cora Kaplan, among others, has attacked Millett for wanting literature to contain intent and motivation (Kaplan, 1979). But Millett's polemic *is* based on careful reading. For example, she shows how Hardy uses different modes for different characters on the basis of gender. She is unhappy with Hardy's biological essentialism, since she attacks him for using hereditary traits in character. Gender, to Millett, is about the representation of environment and conditioning in personalities in fiction.[2] Millett describes the gender structure of character as if it is the gender stucture of society.

There are occasional severe misreadings. Millett takes Ursula in *The Rainbow* as an example of Lawrence's notion of unfulfilled femininity because he apparently distrusts Ursula's educational values. Since Ursula's educational sympathies, even her educational techniques, were similar to those of Lawrence, as far as we can establish from biographical evidence, then Millett is clearly oversimplifying Lawrence. If he *is* locating a notion of 'femininity' in these episodes, we would have to understand that characters have a more problematic relation to authors than male authors simply being 'in' male characters.

But literary criticism is clearly important to Millett. Book II of *Sexual Politics* contains a long account of the history of English criticism. She describes the work of John Stuart Mill and Ruskin as a projection of the unconscious fantasies of Victorian sensibility. The question we want answered is 'What *was* the role and function of criticism?', and Millett evades the issue by only describing ideas and themes in Mill and Ruskin. But the section is an unusual ingredient in an American text.

Millett is a very moral critic and is a very moral writer. All her writing is an autobiographical and critical quest for an alternative feminist heroic, as are her writings on Angela Davis (Millett, 1972, p. 54). We can read *Sita* or *Sexual Politics* as a balance between narrative and interrogative moral debates. Both in her fiction and in her criticism Millett helps us to a 'lived-through' experience. In *Sita* life and art are interdependent. The narrator's relationship with Sita has to end so that the journal can. The hatred of the 'real' evident in the *text* of *Sita*—its unstable narrator and her use of imagistic repetitive monologues—are joined by hatred of realism in its content, in both characters' preference for photographs, scrapbooks and personal notes rather than actual encounters. In *Sita* Millett gives us the all-American feminist, 'all the woman I never was', just as in her criticism she demolished the all-American male.

It is difficult to impose categorical readings on Millett since she refuses imposed structural patterns. The fluidity of sexual desire expressed in *Sita* in reflections on bisexuality is ideologically enlarged in the juxtaposed columns of 'Prostitution:

A Quartet for Female Voices'. Millett's exploration of the lives and self-perception of prostitutes is an attack on the sexual codification of patriarchy, just as her literary criticism attacks the sexual codes of a patriarchal literature. Millett dislikes the artificial rhetoric of writings on prostitution—whether in sociology or in romance. She replaces this rhetoric with an innovative choice of critical form. She interweaves the speaking voices of academic and prostitute, shifting accounts from column to column on the page to point up the impossibility of using social compartments (Millett, 1971).

Millett is engagingly self-conscious about the act of writing, trying to bring the private into the public by a critical perspective of immersion not distance. Millett presumably moved into autobiographical fiction in order to relate more closely the private and public worlds of women since the diary is the classic form of private writing. And hence Millett prefigures that later concern of feminist criticism to use creatively the power of autobiography to alter and thus to release experience. 'Prostitution' is a deliberate attempt to evade critical categories. The form prohibits the reader from finding a single organising principle. By experiencing the feelings of loss and disjunction recounted by prostitutes, we abandon the illusion that critical experience can be discreet. The attitude of ambivalence, of uncertainty, about her role as critic is appealing. Millett's critical texts are really about what criticism demands of women. Her training in both European and American literature allows her to question the usefulness of a coherent line of literary criticism. But it is in her portrayal of the *arbitrary* sexual designations of patriarchal culture that she is most effective.

Millett's own bisexuality became a *cause célèbre* in 1970, when *Time* magazine publicised it to discredit the American feminist movement. The sales of *Sexual Politics* may have dropped that year but feminist women publicly supported Millett's honesty. In her criticism, as in her life, Millett's major contribution is the dramatisation of the political contexts of sexuality. In the end Millett's restricted methods of literary criticism may have denied feminist criticism the contradictions it needed to set up (Kaplan, 1979, p. 14). Her aim is reformist, even evolutionary, since she thinks feminism is to be 'accomplished by human growth and true re-education' (Millett, 1977, p. 363). But both for her radical coalition with Blacks and gays, and for her autobiographical dramatisation of sexuality in critical form, Millett is *the* post-war pioneer of feminist criticism.

How then do these four critics see their criticism enabling the end of patriarchal culture? All agree that critical analysis can help women to break out of their objectification and act as authentic subjects in society. De Beauvoir adds the more radical context of democratic socialism. What does their criticism establish? First, it establishes that male writers are deeply conservative and women can never be represented adequately in male texts since men writing about women are more alike than unlike. Of course, the logical correlative might be that men can never be adequately represented in *women's* texts. Second, it establishes that the critical mode for feminism is one of mixed disciplines. All four represent the first thorough attempts to write feminist criticism by mixing arguments from biology, psychology and historical materialism as well as from writing traditionally designated as literature. One of the great strengths of feminist criticism has been to challenge where the boundaries of 'literature' are located. If Friedan and Greer remained superficial, Simone de Beauvoir and Kate Millett were able to enlarge their criticism by clearly articulated philosophical and moral themes.

The texts *are* pioneering but not without problems for a feminist future. All four critics present a somewhat static notion of patriarchy. Looking forward to *Sex and Destiny*, Greer's writing still *reflects* social trends rather than subverts them. Her arguments are not new. Her slogan for the 1980s is 'Improve fertility management'. This does not move us on from Rebecca West's linking of sexuality and male power in the 1920s. Here, as in *The Female Eunuch*, Greer never questions Western sexual values. Although de Beauvoir in particular tried to break the link between women and femininity by describing femininity as each male author's Other of woman, there is, in her work, too absolute a barrier between the sexes. For example, in *The Woman Destroyed*, women and men are psychological opposites—supported by an imagery of black and white contrasts. De Beauvoir structures her fiction around scenes of psychodrama where women and men reveal their differences. In *Memoirs of a Dutiful Daughter* de Beauvoir ignores the value of 'feminine' moments in order to train herself to think like a man, to move into a man's world. Her fiction describes a social world where women can only make impossible choices—to be artists *or* mothers and, in any case, are always vulnerable to the sexual politics of men. Male aggression has too eternal a fixity. Just as women's 'moments' (whether of childbirth or eroticism) are not central moments in de Beauvoir's autobiographies, so she, and the other critics, give little space to women's alternatives. Their criticism is pessimistic not progressive. In their critiques women respond *to* men rather than act. Lately de Beauvoir, in her interviews with Alice Schwarzer, does regret not having written more about eroticism. 'I would like to tell women about my life in terms of my own sexuality because it is not just a personal matter but a political one too' (Schwarzer, 1984, p. 84). Yet the very fact that eroticism is suppressed in *The Second Sex* is a very obvious example of the ideological constraints of post-war French culture as to what can/cannot be written/published. It takes later critics like Firestone or Daly to enlarge these categories of masculinity and femininity. The real absence in any of these critics is a serious attempt to deal with the unconscious. Literature, and hence criticism, is deprived of a whole area of experience. Later critics like Coward and Spivak had to redress this imbalance just as the work of Susan Griffin on the juncture of feminism and ecology has enlarged the relation of woman to nature in another direction.

If the social ideas of these critics were loaded with undeclared class assumptions, so too their version of literary criticism is often imprecise. Literature is central to Millett, for example, in that she thinks literature presages social reform. But, because Millett, like Friedan, also believes that creative energy is *only* located in high art, she remains locked into a modernist notion of the avant-garde. The institutional nature of literature is not adequately addressed. But, although these critics see women as potentially 'free' once patriarchal ideology is lifted, and although masculinity and femininity are unproblematically represented in different modes of writing, many later feminist concerns *are* prefigured. De Beauvoir's analysis of the image of women in myth foreshadowed similar analysis by more contemporary critics as Ortner, Chodorow and Griffin. Adrienne Rich develops her conceptualisation of lesbianism from both de Beauvoir and Kate Millett. The cultural analysis provided by Friedan and Greer prefigures subsequent media studies. Juliet Mitchell, and many other critics, have praised the welding of disciplinary modes.

These critics *did* change literary values and the forms with which we apprehend those values by expanding the content of criticism to reveal things that had not previously found their way into criticism. It is this expansion of the field of criticism on which later feminist criticism is dependent. The pioneering critiques of de Beauvoir and Millett (even Friedan or Greer), by altering the images through which we think of culture, altered the very experience of reading. To defamiliarise literary experience and to incorporate the previously unacknowledged reality of women was to open feminist criticism to a new perception.

3

LANGUAGE AND PSYCHOANALYSIS

Language

The pioneers of feminist literary criticism established that one of the features of patriarchal literature was its ability to use language to 'naturalise' stereotypes of women as an inevitable part of literary production. Only by making literary criticism be a flexible mixture of cultural themes *and* linguistic techniques, they held, could feminist criticism mount an adequate attack on the patriarchal institution of 'literature'.

Since May 1968 the barriers between disciplines like psychoanalysis, philosophy, literature and linguistics have come down in feminist criticism. The most dramatic reworking of the map comes in the texts of Julia Kristeva, Monique Wittig, Hélène Cixous, Luce Irigaray and, in America, Mary Daly. All these writers share a desire to destroy not only the male tradition of criticism but also the very language in which it is transmitted. In *Les Guérillères* Monique Wittig even claims to 'screen every word'. But have these writers created a women's phoenix from the burnt embers of male stylistics? Is it possible, in other words, to destroy, and re-create without some debts, without some 'unconscious' influence?

The dialogue between literature and psychoanalysis is invaluable for two reasons. Psychoanalysis has traced the psychic relation of mothers and daughters as represented in features of speech. And in discussion of a specifically feminine writing, emphasis is often put on the voice. Second, the whole idea of the powers of authors, the ownership and possession of texts by writers or readers is thrown in doubt by the rethinking of power in psychoanalysis. This twofold contribution has enabled critics to address the special problem of language in relation to literature since literary uses of language are crucially different from other uses.

The problem is that literature, as defined by the critical tradition, is an institution ruled by the regulations of genres and histories. Writing (*écriture*) is defined by its practice, not its past, as an activity. What then can be the role of women's language in literature in enabling women to deconstruct the historical values of that institution? Cixous or Daly would see language as a *dynamic* system, not as a stable body whose elements need classifying and organising. They study the interaction of signifiers and signified, of texts and people in order to *explode* the unity of the sign. For example, Cixous suggests that all women writers of force give birth to words flowing in accord with the contractual rhythms of labour (Andermatt, 1979). The *tempo* of women's writing, in other words, will be in cadence with lacunary moments and 'jets of letters'. There are many other possibilities. Using memories of our bodies rather than the 'free' generalising of men, we do, in any case, read texts in a different way. We ask questions which implicitly carry with them gendered values. What is the relation between sex and politics as represented in the relations between authorial voice and heroine? Is a woman writer envisaging on the level of language the questions she poses theoretically? The markers are a writer's intimacy with her heroine or her doubts about the ability of language to tell.

It is not surprising that a search for a woman's language should begin in France. In French traditions of philosophy like existentialism language was always more than a cultural concern. Simone de Beauvoir, in *The Second Sex*, describes the importance of philosophical assumptions and their implications in language to writers choosing political positions. The new trends in feminist criticism are much indebted to her ideas, whether or not they diverge from them. The creation of a woman's language by French feminists must be seen in this intellectual context where the transformational powers of language are always part of political practice. The intellectual debates and plethora of publications in recent years in French have all centred on the problems with, and possibilities of, a woman's language. The French language itself could not represent a better example of the suppression of the feminine with its 'mute *e*'. The French writers Monique Wittig, Julia Kristeva, Hélène Cixous and Luce Irigaray all oppose phallocentric language, but they envisage different forms of resistance and different ways of moving ahead. What they do agree on, however, is that language has been the central mechanism by which men have appropriated the world. The linguistic means by which men colonise women is that they devalue sensuality in favour of symbolism.

How then is the symbolic discourse of men and its signifying practices to be resisted? Julia Kristeva uses psychoanalysis to help her clarify her concept of the semiotic discourse, a phase of language occuring between mothers and children before the symbolic language which society imposes. Irigaray and Cixous, more radically, use psychoanalysis to formulate a discourse which, by *only* expressing women's sexuality explicitly, denies male egress. If female physiology is, for Irigaray or Cixous, a source of critical metaphors, they do not, however, describe language in any idealist sense. As their educational background suggests, they reflect on women's discourse in order to change both the phallocentric order of language *and* of culture.

If the defining characteristic of the French feminist project is its attentiveness to the libidinal rather than the sociocultural, in Britain Marxist-feminism, as we shall see, has used French theory more to rethink Marx's theories of ideology and reproduction in terms of women's representation (which of course includes language). The one area useful to *écriture feminine* is the considerable work of feminist linguists which has not received the attention it deserves. Some American critics, like their British sisters, may deny the concept of a separate woman's language but, in the epistemology of Mary Daly, feminist practice is both a detailed and a thoroughgoing 'difference' from male academic concerns.

This divide between a recuperable and hence more accessible language and the alternative of a feminised libidinal linguistics is one common to other movements like modernism. The debate between sociorealists and the surrealists in the 1930s also centred on concepts of idealism and the unconscious and what *can*, or should, be represented in a literary text. As an activity the debate was more politically significant for writers than reader/critics. As far as feminist criticism is concerned, the worry is less about a writer's formal allegiances to, or traces of, 'the avant-garde' or 'humanism'; it is about what women are saying and how they manage to say it. Not only is the notion of a special language related to the general debates of modernism but it also relates to the more contemporary debates about humanism. Louis Althusser's attack on the humanism of Jean-Paul Sartre has echoes of the modernist debates in his similar setting up of choices between the realistic 'givers' of people's lives and the more radical deconstruction of the subject.

It helps to see that, in a certain way, the debates within feminism have some of the same characteristics. There are similar problems in defining feminist criticism. Is it to document women's social oppression and, therefore, methodologically, slip towards the social sciences (in literary terms: realism); or should it train women linguistically for a transformation of language? This does not imply that any continuation of the debates of modernism or contemporary philosophy into feminist criticism necessarily diminishes feminism. Given that any criticism carries some debt to earlier debates, what then are the defining features of feminist criticism about language?

Julia Kristeva has it both ways. She proposes to juxtapose the poetic with the analytic in attempting to uncover the repressed signification of sexuality. Methodologically, as her outline in *Tel Ouel* on 'recherches féminines' shows, this will demand a mixture of Marxist, Lacanian, and structuralist and post-structuralist approaches. Kristeva appears closer to critical patterns established outside feminism particularly in her analysis of the milieu of George Bataille. Hélène Cixous is also aware of her debts. She cites Derrida in her key essay 'The Laugh of the Medusa', using deconstruction to avoid describing women only as the negative of men. To change the stock of the Imaginary is an important part of her work. Cixous is a more personal critic than Kristeva. Her own technique is to mix autobiography with sentence fragments and portmanteau words and publishes fiction in order to speak freely in a 'feminine' voice, as in *Angst*, of female body rhythms.

Luce Irigaray's attempt to write a language of the body is methodologically similar to that of Kristeva and Cixous, but she adds other elements to their approaches. In 'Ce sexe qui n'en est pas un' Irigaray enacts linguistically Alice's adventures through the looking glass. 'Le Miroir, de l'autre côté' of woman's language is not *one* style but a mixture of intellectual discourse, simple body descriptions and occasional silences. Although the commitment to a separate linguistic identity for women is very clear to these writers, *what* it might involve is less certain. Perhaps only in France would writers reply so fully to the questionnaire 'Does writing have a sex?', sent out by *La Quinzaine Littéraire* in 1974. The answers reveal explicitly this methodological problem in feminist criticism. The periodical asked whether writers *when writing* are conscious of gender and whether that influences the text. Some writers, like Marguerite Yourcenar, largely evade the issue by suggesting that the *content* of a piece would determine the role gender might play. For example, if a writer was describing her experiences as a mother autobiographically, then clearly gender would be a factor, but not necessarily otherwise. Nathalie Sarraute thinks that writers would choose to emphasise masculine or feminine qualities if they wanted to possess them. However, the notion that there *are* gendered qualities stays intact in the replies *(La Quinzaine Littéraire,* 192 August 1974).

Perhaps I am exaggerating the divide in feminism between what might be termed accessibility versus narcissism, between realism and libido. Clearly language in any strict sense must be essentially discursive. It is not so much whether writers choose the symbolic in some logocentric gesture or opt for the world of their bodies that is the issue. It is the *mode* of handling experience, rather than *what* is written, that characterises this group of writers. A movement is characterised more by the *formulation* of its problems than by its *solutions* of them. Rather than grading writers in terms of their debt to male discourse, it might be better to see feminist criticism on language more as a series of positions related to the linguistic dilemma: How *do* women writers work with a language produced by men, and what technically can they accomplish?

Two different approaches emerge. The first describes specifically female experience. In fiction this tradition includes Colette, Gertrude Stein and Virginia Woolf, and in criticism appears in the critiques of Ellen Moers or Patricia Meyer Spacks. Such fiction and criticism register the detail of day-today experience, emphasising women's relationships, their domestic environments and above all their modes of oppression. As critics, Moers and Spacks seem not to doubt the viability of language to express the world of women. But putting together lists of women's experiences in order to determine how one writes like a 'woman' can incur the danger of biological determinism.

The second approach, in Cixous or Irigaray, questions this decision to accept language. They understand that feminist criticism must read texts in order to support writers and readers who are developing a specifically female discourse very different from language as we know it, a language that allows the eruption of the semiotic into the symbolic in a rich new form. The difference is between criticism that seeks to explain the persistence of representations of woman in terms of a general structure of the subject 'woman' and criticism which is freer to look more flexibly at writing practice. The centrality of the heroine in the first kind of feminist criticism is like the centrality of the subject in theories of ideology. The concept might obstruct consideration of all the possible writing forms of women because it relies on a homogeneous representation of women's oppression. All that needs to be postulated, say the second group of critics, is that there must be a difference between men's libidinal expression (as valorised by our culture) and the libidinal expressions of women (as repressed in our culture) which incurs a necessary difference in language.

Simone de Beauvoir's description of woman as Other, in *The Second Sex*, is obviously the beginning point for this feminist criticism of a gendered language. De Beauvoir was the first to philosophically demonstrate the mechanisms by which men use symbolic language to exclude and objectify women. But the first wave of post-war feminism, in America, although attacking this male misrepresentation of women, aimed to *reduce* women's difference from men. The American collection *Women in a Sexist Society*, edited by V.G. Gornick and B.K. Moran, is a good example of this kind of criticism. It attacks the construction of women's difference by men in American culture. In essays by Elaine Showalter and Cynthia Ozick, among others, there is a long catalogue of sexism and censorship in advertising, fiction and pornography. The challenge for these critics is to invalidate idealist notions of femininity which result in literary and social stereotypes. Ozick calls the whole idea of a gendered language 'The Testicular Theory of Literature' and prefers to gain the territory of men rather than construct a new language for women (Gornick and Moran, 1971). The female aesthetic here is simply a version of the aesthetic practice of any non-hegemonic group. The first book in America to promote a language for women is *Of Woman Born* by Adrienne Rich. This shifts feminist criticism to a woman-centred perspective by substituting maternal imagery for masculine culture. Rich's voice of American feminism parallels Kristeva in a rethinking of maternal iconography as a basis for a gendered and different feminist aesthetic. The American critic closest to Cixous is Mary Daly, who in taking the male Logos back to its roots has articulated a feminist language in all its linguistic manifestations.

The impossibility of an 'absolutely' new language underlies Daly's approach. Her books are lessons in how to find *in* patriarchal language images and signs of matriarchal sources which patriarchy disguises. For example, she describes how patriarchal archetypes like the Virgin Mary are distorted versions of what she calls living moving 'Archimages'—which rhymes with 'rages'—(Daly, 1984).

Of course, there are problems in this shift from first- to second-wave feminism. Any insistence that woman has an essentially feminine style can perpetuate long-held stereotypes about women as natural, and hence anti-intellectual, objects. A single *écriture féminine* can flatten out the linguistic differences *among* women which respond to racial, class or national groups. However, women's physiology *does* have important meanings for women in all cultures, and it is essential for feminist criticism to express those meanings rather than submit to masculine language.

The most sustained rejection of male discourse is in the astonishing *Gyn/Ecology* and *Pure Lust*. What Mary Daly does is to move outside male-centred, binary logic altogether into a new female syntax. *Gyn/Ecology* and *Pure Lust* are the most notable example of *écriture féminine* that we have to date, and the most exciting. Daly changes syntax, the whole *process* of language, not just male vocabulary. We must, Daly claims, connect our language and our bodies to 're-member the dismembered body of our heritage' (1978, p. 23). Daly takes on the political implications of vocabulary change in a quest, like Rich, for a common language for women. Her technique is to fragment standard discourse into its parts, 'de-partments which depart from departments' and replace it with the female continuity of the solidus (1978, p. xiv). It may seem paradoxical to want a holistic woman's world yet take a path to it by word-splitting and fragmentation. But Daly has politicised etymology. She expands the elements of a word both in form *and* sense. *Gyn/Ecology* itself, Daly claims, is a 'gynocentric manifestation of the Intransitive Verb' (Daly, 1978, p. 23). Changing nouns to verbs is more than a linguistic game. It emphasises the importance of action. Prefixes particularly interest Daly. She employs alternative meanings for prefixes as *'re-cover* actually says "cover again" ' (1978, p. 24). One characteristic of prefixes is, of course, that they act to intensify nouns. So by separating out prefixes from what Daly understands to be patriarchal nouns, male discourse begins to lose its power.

Dictionaries (by males) always divide vocabulary into racial groups—those words native to the speaker and those from foreign intruders. Mary Daly uses dictionaries as semantic resources but proposes an alternative classification of language for women. This is one of connotative value where literary vocabulary can take its place in the ordinary words of women's speech. *Gyn/Ecology*, for example, ends not only with a customary general index but adds to it an 'index of new words'. Language is Daly's theme from beginning to end. The outstanding feature of her approach is her recognition of the ideal value of many vowels normally obscure since unstressed. In a woman's syntax these vowels return to their full quality as in 'a-mazing'. Again, hyphens enable Daly to create new double forms, like 'Crone-logical', with differences of meaning since the hyphen can add clearness to, or emphasise, the function of the prefix.

Gyn/Ecology is nothing less than a fresh semantics. Daly is not a detective simply collecting evidence of male linguistic crimes but conducting a full enquiry into male language by analysing as far as she can some of the issues that were there inside the vocabulary. In her enquiry Daly therefore chooses words which relate to the central experiences of women, which involve our ideas and values, in order to attack the 'shared' meaning of words in general used by men. Hers is an attack on the *possession* of meaning by men, which is bound up with a certain way of seeing gender. Vocabulary is *the* element in sexism and therefore, to Daly, a form indicative of male power.

Critics who take an empirical approach to semantic change and linguistic history would object that Daly does not describe specific *sites* for her revolution. They could claim that Daly is at odds with the way feminist discourses still have to circulate through the gate-keeping academic world of men. But this approach, by seeing the issue simply as one of pedagogy, is basically accommodative. Daly would retort quite rightly that the aim of feminist criticism is to replace male pedagogy, not to make compromises with it.

Despite Daly's unique verbal richness, however, her books are primarily philological and etymological, with the effect that Daly is much better dealing with variations than with making connections. But she is making a specialised analysis of what is involved in meaning. To pick out a word's own internal structure is a necessary start to understanding the larger system of language itself. Especially if you believe, as Daly does, that significance comes from the male construction of language. The importance of naming patriarchy to Daly is that 'they—in effect—drop dead' in what she calls a criticism of 'Positive Spooking'. In other words, Daly is trying to make linguistic judgements be judgements about sexual politics. 'Exorcism requires naming this environment of spirit/mind rape, refusing to be receptacles for semantic semen' (Daly, 1978, p. 324). This is language as a sexual battleground. One of Daly's key strengths, it seems to me, is her refusal to be silenced, her refusal of absences, of slippages. Daly shows how a language of the body can communicate, can serve women's interests. To use a sexualised semantics is not a 'surrender' to an essentialist mode of discourse but a genuine act of creativity. Daly's is a mature style in which the extension of vocabulary and the resources of language are necessary to her intensity and precision about women's bodies.

Monique Wittig is a French writer, now living in America, who is also, like Daly, in this wave of feminist critics constructing a new language. Wittig's writing career, however, spans over twenty years, from her first novel *L'Opoponax*, published in 1964. She is probably best known for her novel *Les Guérillères*, written during the political revolt of May 1968, which describes the possibility of a new language for women. But it is in *Lesbian People's Material for a Dictionary* that Wittig makes women the namers of a new feminist lexicon. To create a new erotic discourse Wittig takes language away from patriarchy. She does not document in an unpoliticised way the details of women's bodies but encourages her reader to rethink the relation between language and identity. One of her tricks is to experiment with pronouns and nouns. In the *Dictionary* she goes so far as to reject the name 'woman' altogether since it means 'one who belongs to another'.

It is this feature of Wittig's writing—that she is in her employment of language simultaneously a critic of language—which links her with the manifesto of *écriture féminine*—'Le Rire de la Méduse', written by Hélène Cixous in 1975. Like Daly and Wittig, Cixous attacks patriarchy by attacking patriarchal language. The only alternative to male domination, Cixous says, is to construct a woman's language which is both separate from male discourse and can exemplify sexual difference. In 'Le Rire de la Méduse' Cixous asks women to take up writing in order that they can break apart the dominant mode and replace it with a feminine one. If the vague aim of *écriture féminine* is for women to write with their bodies, Cixous manages to make this aim more precise. In 'Castration or Decapitation' she begins by telling stories—the story of Hera, of Chinese Wives and of Sleeping Beauty. There are stories about the relation between women's names and their sexuality. Little Red Riding Hood is the little clitoris—the female sex with her little jar of honey caught in a chain of male metaphors. Cixous attacks the classic dualist oppositions of activity/passivity or superior/inferior in systems of symbols as a kind of male war. She finds a critical focus here, therefore, for the relation in language between knowledge and power.

What women have to do, Cixous says, is bring about a shift in the metalanguage. First, they should attack the institution-alisation of language in universities and disciplines where 'doing classes' is like military service—a way to keep women in the service of men. Next, women should learn how to read for themselves women-centred texts. How can we do this? By creating, Cixous claims, a site of language, a feminine Imaginary shaped by the libido and spoken about in savage tongues. The main feature of this feminine textuality will be its endlessness. There is no beginning and no conclusion to a female text. Clearly Cixous is interested as much in the *féminine* as in *écriture*. By publishing only with feminist presses, Cixous, more than other critics, commits herself in her practice and in her theory to linking language and woman's libidinal difference.

Exploring the geography of female pleasure is never simple for these feminist writers. Perhaps this is why both Cixous and Irigaray tell stories. They create sexual fables about signification because none of these feminists believe that language should make definitive statements. But although Irigaray and others are not giving us 'content', they are, at best, giving us a critical *procedure*. The geography of female sexuality becomes the very shape of these critics' texts. Their writings might be better described as prose accounts of female love told in the form of fable. If the French texts signify a new rhetorical structure for women's language, they are no more than poetic versions of Mary Daly's American mapping. Both French and American linguistic feminists are calling for a complicity between woman readers and writers not unlike therapy. For, although we may not be able to *apply* their methods directly in a one-to-one relation with literary texts, there is a way in which we are changed by them in our reading practice. Our reading, like our writing, can now have a sex.

Contemporary feminist activists are also preoccupied with language, and these writers have helped feminism by raising fundamental issues in the area of psychoanalysis and language. They take language seriously. They describe the ways in which verbal minutiae are used by patriarchy to create and maintain cultural values. Above all, they answer the question of difference by insisting on a fundamental difference in women's language—a language which is no longer constructed by negativity, with women the complement of men, but one which is radically non-unitary, grounded in female anatomy. These critics are all concerned with the condition of existence of a new order of discourse and how language can change women's lives. Their work represents the way feminist criticism can connect language to social life. Although from different countries and different disciplines, Daly and Cixous, Kristeva and Mitchell, shed light on one another and reading them together gives us a richer picture of language in women's lives. Since fairy tales are the expression of desire and imaginary fulfilment, it is perhaps not surprising that Cixous, Irigaray, Wittig and Daly chose a form which gets at an emotive content much deeper than objective experience. Fairy tales are always being told. As Cixous maintains, 'It is impossible to *define* a feminine practice of writing . . . It will be conceived of by subjects who are breakers of automatisms' (1976, p. 883).

Psychoanalysis

It is psychoanalysis which puts the 'feminine' into '*écriture féminine*'. Contemporary theories of a women's language depend on the relation between the female libido, woman's unconscious, and their representation in female discourse. Not all feminist criticism is immersed in debates on the status of psychoanalysis in the interpretation of women's reading and writing. Literary criticism, within feminism, is still producing biographies of women writers, histories of literature and thematic studies which are not concerned with theory. But psychoanalysis shapes the more exciting and energetic feminist criticism of recent years by offering women somewhere to go (a woman's place) and something (a woman's language) in which we can make our journey.

The texts of Kristeva, Cixous, Wittig or Daly could not have been written twenty years ago. It is only very recently that psychoanalysis has shown criticism how 'the feminine' is consciously produced and organised in language. What Kristeva, Cixous and Irigaray do in common is to oppose the phallic symbols which have structured Western thought and writing with women's body experiences as decoded by psychoanalysis. They read psychoanalysis (or, in Mary Daly's case, philosophy) in order to answer the basic question: Can a woman's body be a source of her language?

Juliet Mitchell's *Psychoanalysis and Feminism* is the first feminist text to fully explore the theories of Freud, Lacan, Laing and feminism as explanations of women's experience. From psychoanalysis feminists understand that women have a gendered difference from men which is constructed in and through their bodies, culture and language. The problem with a psychoanalytic construction of femininity *per se,* is that it overlooks important contemporary changes in women's sexuality and culture. In other words, language as a system of signs must be read as both a consequence of the social construction of sexuality and a mechanism for re-evaluation and change.

The concept of *écriture féminine* derives from psychoanalysis. Since so many feminist critics deal with the possibility of an analogy—and a very attractive one at that—between the female psyche and an *écriture féminine,* it is important to examine their writings in detail to see how well they can answer the question: Is there a woman's language which speaks of psychic experiences ignored or devalued by the dominant discourse? 'Psychoanalysis' locates the starting points and defines the intellectual ambience of this new linguistic trajectory. Psychoanalytic criticism articulates a problem that is inherent in all feminist criticism: that of linking the place of the social with what are private, perhaps even totally individual, feelings.

Yet psychoanalytic criticism is one of the most valuable and fruitful additions to the literary theory and methods of feminism. If we make a list of major feminist critics, we find that Kristeva, Cixous and Irigaray from France, and Daly, Heilbrun, Gilbert and Gubar, Spivak from America, and Coward and Mitchell from England are all indebted to psychoanalysis, albeit in very different ways. In spite of those determinedly seeking their base in experientialism, uses of psychoanalysis have made more theoretical much of the feminist nervousness about validating the 'feminine' and defining the relation of gender to language.

What psychoanalysis does is to offer a reading of the feminine rooted not *entirely* in the social construction of femininity (which nevertheless organises the feminine), nor *entirely* in biology, but through language and subjectivity. Indeed, even in 'purely' medical psychoanalysis case studies of the private lives of women, their fantasies and early experience are initially read as language before being read as medical symptoms. Even those preverbal experiences of the unconscious or the semiotic are constituted linguistically, as it were, by psychoanalysis.

What is so often difficult about psychoanalytic criticism is not its insistence on relating the literary text to early childhood; it is, rather, its avoidance of the *process* whereby the private fantasies of individual women can become public and collective for all women. Yet, paradoxically, psychoanalysis offers descriptions of subjectivity and desire which can give the social face of feminism an emotional power and place.

Psychoanalytic cases as well as literary criticism have a tendency to be written as *texts*. Both openly reveal their status as fiction without, of course, abandoning their search for a single 'true' meaning in the discourse they examine. Psychoanalysis tries to read the 'text' of each subject in terms of her dreams and style of speech. To do this, it focuses in particular on 'literary' forms—on absences, distortions and slippages—which may provide useful access to hidden parts of a subject's personality. Literary criticism does something very similar. By examining metaphors, similes *and* absences in the literary text, or subject, it tries to reveal the hidden subtext of an author.[1]

But, although, clearly, psychoanalysis and literary criticism are methodologically akin and psychoanalysis offers feminism a useful hermeneutics or mode of interpretation, the theoretical ground plan of psychoanalytic feminist literary criticism lacks many explorers. There is a very simple explanation. The feminists who contribute most to articulating a theory of psychoanalysis are not primarily concerned to do this in literary criticism (Irigaray, Coward, Daly); conversely, those who have linked psychoanalysis with literature are literary critics first before they are feminist (Moers, Felman). This leaves those of us who are trying to read literary texts both psychoanalytically *and* with a feminist perspective running between the camp of the theorists and the camp of the technicians. But by describing—even if in a sketchy fashion—a full range of feminist psychoanalytic insights within the *ambit* of literature, I can, perhaps, describe concerns which make up, if implicitly, that larger hermeneutics.

There are challenges which psychoanalysis and feminism together offer to traditional literary criticism. The greatest challenge both make is to the unity of the subject. Psycho-analytic critiques, like feminist criticism posit the writing of many rich and random multiple realities. Another, and crucial, challenge is to the traditional relations of art, politics and society. There need no longer be a hierarchy of relations with one or other having a more privileged status in explaining an individual psyche or text.[2] The popular text (like women's magazines) may be as useful as a modern novel in offering explanations of women's desire. Feminism itself, both as a political movement and as a literary practice, offers an analogy with psychoanalysis. Both use a model of repression. Feminists think that women's sexual experience is too often unconscious or repressed. Consciousness raising in feminist groups is like the bringing 'up' of the repressed into consciousness in therapy or the raising of the sub-text in literature—all ways of learning about the previously unexpressed effects of patriarchy.

What are the main modes of feminist psychoanalytic criticism? There are several different forms which include Freudian theory, Lacan and object-relations analysis. The French feminists Kristeva and Cixous focus attention on the semiotic/preverbal and define the symbolic as patriarchy. The semiotic is the organisation of instincts by rhythm and intonation which proceeds the imposition of the symbolic, a system of meaning created in language.[3] The American feminist Ellen Moers uses the term 'symbolic' in a more conventionally Freudian sense to supplant patriarchy's symbolisation, or stereotyping, of femininity with her own more appropriate feminine metaphors. Juliet Mitchell, influenced both by R.D. Laing and by Winnicott, describes a phenomenology of childhood and its relation to female identity. All combine in identifying feminism with a subversive female discourse.

The feminist work being done in psychoanalytic criticism is thus very rich and multiple. It includes study of the psycho-dynamics of women characters (Moers, Hardwick), a psycho-analysis of textual metaphor (Spivak, Mitchell) and study of the psychodynamics of readers reading (in Britain the cultural studies approach to popular romances, or in America Shoshana Felman). Although writing about gender difference is central to all feminist psychoanalytic theory, the examination of gender *strategies* is also a great strength of some male psychoanalytic and left-wing criticism. It would be wrong to treat feminist criticism in isolation from this male background. Holland, Marcuse and Bloom also address cultural assumptions and psychological attitudes as ideologies within the discourses of power. But although both male and feminist critics use psychoanalysis to link individual issues to the larger ideological structures in which they operate, there is a difference in focus and method which marks out the feminist critique.

The literary criticism of orthodox male Freudians has tended to remain locked within the notion of an individual author's, or individual reader's, single experience. At its best, in his *The Dynamics of Response*, the American critic Norman N. Holland thinks literature can open up the reader to his unconscious fantasies. But of course Holland has none of the *equality* of response stimulated by shared feminist readings. Indeed, Holland claims his criticism is a scientific quest for a *single* distinctive identity theme in literary texts. Similarly, to the critic Simon Lesser in *Fiction and the Unconscious*, literature serves mainly to reassure and hence stabilise a unitary reader. The multiplicity of women's experience has no space here. In contrast, the synthesis of Marx and Freud projected by Marcuse and the Frankfurt School *does* examine the individual consciousness as part of shared, capitalist, relations but hence tends to leave little space for the unique case histories of particular subjects as women do in their autobiographies. Harold Bloom *has* influenced American feminists with his uses of Freud in *The Anxiety of Influence*. If other male identity theorists assume that constancy is a desirable goal for writing development, Bloom, in effect, rewrites literary history in terms of the Oedipus complex to read all poems as poets' deliberate misinterpretations of a precursor poem or poet. Yet Bloom's theory, too, is inadequate for feminism. Not only are Bloom's poets always male, he seizes on a quantitative notion of sublimation. That is to say, Bloom assumes the *value* of a poem to come from the amount of sublimation a poet exposes in his poem.[4]

This male tradition suggests a need for models which are not locked, either into an opposition between the individual and the collective nor into a quantitative piling up of literary experience, but are rather able to think about discontinuities in a radically different way. In 'Women's Time' Julia Kristeva suggests that feminist psychoanalysis is about the arrangement of new spaces in a new time. Kristeva's is an arresting and useful metaphor. Like Kristeva we can ask feminist psychoanalytic critics: From what place and in what way do you speak/write differently from men about literature?

Ellen Moers or Sandra Gilbert and Susan Gubar would answer that they speak from the place of female bonding in the images and symbols of nineteenth-century literature. Kristeva would answer that she speaks from the place of the mother and the semiotic. While agreeing with Kristeva that the mother is a central focus in much of women's literature, Juliet Mitchell aims to speak from the space of the hysteric. Carolyn Heilbrun finds a very 'different' space in the form of the androgynous heroine. Mary Daly and Gayatri Spivak speak from the place of absence about a new language, and Felman and Irigaray read literature as a whole morphology of female sexuality. Feminist critics of popular culture enlarge the space to bring in the psychodynamics of a body of readers.

On this view, feminist psychoanalytic criticism must signify a major force in literary theory. It might be asked what can Freud or Lacan now be saying of any use to these innovative critics? There *are* still crucial connections however between feminism and Freud and Lacan which must be spelt out. Rather than briefly recapitulating the theories of Freud and Lacan and hence oversimplifying their ideas, it might be better to consider what is so influential about their work. Freud, for the first time, made the very status of femininity the centre of Western theoretical discourse. In analysing the individual histories of female patients, psychoanalysis begins by trying to understand how psychological femininity (and masculinity) came about. Freud, in systematising manifestations, offers objective knowledge about how femininity is lived in each woman's mind. It was Freud who changed the interpretive strategy of medical psychology from a use of *sight* (the main technique of Charcot in the 1880s) to a use of the *ear* and hence to language. By separating psychoanalysis from biology, Freud shifts analysis from physiology to the spoken and subsequently the written word.[5]

Similarly, for Lacan, the unconscious is structured like a

language. Lacan, like Freud, reads subjects as texts. We grow as children, Lacan says, by making imaginary identifications, but these are always difficult and will often be fictive. The first stage of our ego identity comes from the sight of ourselves in a mirror—an image which in itself blurs subjectivity and objectivity. The unconscious also, Lacan claims, is 'a sliding' of what he calls signifieds and signifiers; that is, a mixture of fixed meanings and metaphors. 'Femininity' is now a construct of metaphors, in some senses a language.

It seems abundantly clear that feminism's focus on language is in debt to the transformation of imagery begun by Freud and continued by Lacan. Any literary debate about femininity must start with their particular links between femininity and the unconscious. For Lacan the unconscious reveals the fictional nature of sexual categories. Lacan develops his account of subjectivity in reference to the idea of a fiction. It is this relation of language and fantasy that attracts feminist critics to Lacanian analysis. Language, to Lacan, is what identifies us as gendered subjects. The acquisition of identity and hence subjectivity occur only as we enter into speech. But Lacan gives feminist literary critics an even more useful elaboration of this idea of subjectivity. Not only is a girl identified through her language, rather than by innate biology, but Lacan suggests that the idea of a coherent subject is itself a fiction. Sexual identity is always unstable, it is susceptible to disruption by the unconscious and disruption manifests itself in the discontinuities and contradictions in everyday language. The meaning of the feminine can only be gleaned from language—from the ways words are signifiers.[6] Additionally, the idea of femininity will always be open to redefinition.

The way Freud and Lacan treat psychoanalysis as a linguistic exercise enables feminist psychoanalytic criticism to emerge. Freud's idea of interpretation had another immense advantage for feminists. It is halfway between a pure interpretive method—providing a single meaning through the connection of stable terms—and the questioning of the interpreter herself. In other words, both the author and the critic in the act of literary interpretation are, like the analysed and the analyst, inter-pretable objects.

Yet the influence of Freud, and more specifically Lacan,

clearly poses a problem for feminism. It is the Oedipus complex in Freudian and Lacanian theory which forces us into a symbolic order. Language (and hence literary criticism), in simple terms, is now controlled by the law of the father and would be the interpretation of a linguistic chain of symbols. Female metaphors are in a realm *outside* the symbolic—in romance, fantasy or transcendental imagery. For example, Irigaray's descriptions of women's semi-confidences, exclamations and 'babble' would be outside the symbolic which is based on proper names and meanings. So feminist literary critics cannot, therefore, simply celebrate maternal symbols in language and literature because this implies a celebration of patriarchy. As we shall see, Julia Kristeva and to some extent Luce Irigaray evade the issue by creating their imaginary 'literary' world in *pre*-symbolic, pre-Oedipal patterns which Kristeva calls the 'semiotic'. Although this does establish a source of 'difference' in something other than a castration complex, a further problem in (male) psychoanalysis still remains. For Lacan there *is* no prediscursive reality, and therefore for feminists to privilege that world is to assign femininity to an archaic form of expressivity.

In the current attempt at a radical questioning and a general 'deconstruction' of the range of psychoanalytic practices, feminism encounters *the* major challenge of contemporary thought. The problem, in fact, is common both to psychoanalysis and to feminism: How can one speak from the place of the Other? Where and what are the places and spaces of the Other? How can women in literature, or for that matter men, be thought about outside the existing Masculine/Feminine framework. According to Derrida, Western metaphysics depends on a system of opposites (Presence/Absence, Identity/Difference) with the 'positive', or masculine, term being of greater value. In other words, how can women break away from the logic of oppositions? How can women break out of this (psychoanalytic) imposition of the place of suppression without having to enter the masculine space of the symbolic?

The first place chosen by feminist psychoanalytic literary critics was the novel. Ellen Moers and Sandra Gilbert and Susan Gubar take novels to be narratives about the location of gender identity. To them, novels or narrative poems allow women's desire for affirmation to manifest itself. These critics seek in women's writing for a certain knowledge about the repressed and unconscious features of women's identity. The novel, they think, is a space of fantasy and subversive imagery outside of the frustrating order of social signs. Their method is basically to trace the psychodynamics of character represent-ation in fiction. They build on the earlier writings of the American psychoanalyst Karen Horney. In 'The Dread of Women' Horney had described anxiety images in the poetry of Heine and Schiller which, she claims, reveal men's secret fear of women and caused men to write about 'a feminine type which is infantile, non-maternal and hysterical' (1932, p. 360). Con-temporary critics, using the same techniques, could now oppose these alienating models of women, with mothering and female bonding as a potentially positive source of identity for women. Redefining Sartre's dialectics of Otherness and Lacan's use of mirroring, feminist critics were able to show how mothers and daughters and friends mirror each other in the imagery of women's writing. In their textual analysis of these psycho-analytic images, feminists showed how 'the reproduction of mothering', in Nancy Chodorow's terms, is also mirrored in the production of the daughter's text.

Ellen Moer's *Literary Women* (1977) is a classic example of the psychodynamic approach. *Literary Women* translates aspects of female culture into the problematic relation between female consciousness and forms in female writing. Moers claims that there are specific female modes (the Gothic), specific female myths (birth imagery in *Frankenstein*) and specific female symbols (like Anne Frank's bird). Women's social resistance becomes, for Moers, a matter of style—the no-saying of Jane Eyre is an attack by Charlotte Brontë on the cultural conditioning of young girls. *Literary Women* does open up a new way of thinking about the literary inheritance of women writers. Ellen Moers describes the warmth and regard of women writers for each other like George Eliot and Harriet Beecher Stowe, or Emily Dickinson's debt to Elizabeth Barrett Browning.

But Moers sees literary form in very functional ways and mainly for its function in the characterisation of white heterosexual heroines. The drawback to Moers' project is her very unproblematic assumption of a writer's intention. Critics also attack Moers as homophobic since she centralises Western, white heterosexual writing (Gardiner, 1982).

Sandra M. Gilbert and Susan Gubar's *The Madwoman in the Attic* (1979) shows the utility of Moers' model. They describe the works of Jane Austen, Mary Shelley, the Brontës, George Eliot, among others, and claim that it is in images (of enclosures, of doubles, of disease and landscape) that women writers strategically redefine themselves, art and society.

The Madwoman in the Attic is one of the most cited texts in current feminist criticism. This must be because not only does it firmly 'save' writers like Emily Dickinson from patriarchal critics but it attempts a feminist poetic. The book throws out a number of interesting ideas—that women writers are closest to characters they detest, that their images are anxieties about their own creativity. But the form of *The Madwoman in the Attic* is revealing. Its 718 pages show how much Gilbert and Gubar depend on narrative, on paraphrase rather than precise analysis. They go from writer to writer with no concluding chapter. They cannot conclude because they have constructed no argument. It is a curiously static text which gives little sense of why we *should* read one writer more than another.

The book's narrative rather than analytic form is partly due, as Gilbert and Gubar themselves admit, to its derivation from a course they taught at Indiana University. Similarly, Patricia Meyer Spacks' *The Female Imagination* (1977), which is also a thematic study, is organised around teachable titles which can encompass a variety of otherwise disparate works. Her titles of 'power' and 'passivity' resemble Gilbert and Gubar's 'angel' and clearly enabled them, as teachers, to swap around texts from year to year.

These American feminist critics, then, have used psycho-analysis in the main to deconstruct the imagery of femininity in literature. Certainly female stereotypes in women's literature are its most accessible feature, but these motifs are equally accessible themes in much else of Western literature. Not only are they vague handles for literary critics but they lock in the disparate qualities of any text to crude polarities. Charting the psychodynamics of characterisation uncontextualised does not explain why one stereotype is more useful than any other. More important are the metaphysical implications of the 'female heroine' approach of these American critics. By conceptualising the female heroine as an integral subject coincident with her own consciousness, such critics suggest a unitary subject—the female. The implication is that women could be free agents. But what does 'speaking *for* women' imply? What is 'to speak in the name of woman'? Does this repeat existing patriarchal oppression where women are inherently *spoken for* by men? For critics to 'speak in the name of' women heroines and women writers is to appropriate and control textual discourse.

To a certain degree this feminist problem about the status of women in narrative is not new. It is itself a reflection of the same attempts in modernism to eliminate subjects from literature. In a more general way, the dilemma shows that feminists need to develop more sophisticated conceptual instruments about subjects than simply to use symbols of character identity. This important theoretical question about women's representation has been addressed more adequately in a different psycho-analytic direction by Hélène Cixous.

In 'The Character of "Character" ' (1974) Hélène Cixous claims that it is only with the removal of 'character' altogether that the question of the nature of fiction can come to the fore. Characterisation, Cixous suggests, is the mechanism by which literary criticism 'markets' literature to a reader. Character-isation is, by necessity, a kind of social coding or connotes conformity, even censorship. Feminist psychoanalytic critics should refuse this ideology of a *whole* knowable subject. It is, in any case, an impossible notion to use in analysis. To support her argument Cixous cites the example of Virginia Woolf creating multiple individualities in a single discourse in *The Waves*. Feminists have to destroy logocentrism and choose to read the subject as 'an effort of the unconscious . . . which is unanalysable, uncharacterisable' (Cixous, 1974, p. 387).

If Cixous is unable, or unwilling, to develop a specifically literary criticism, Julia Kristeva has brought the methods of psychoanalysis to literature. In 'Women's Time' Kristeva describes how feminists in France sought, after May 1968, to give language to the intrasubjective and corporeal experiences left mute by culture in the past. Either as artists or critics these women explored a whole dynamic of signs. Later, in *La Révolution du Langage Poétique* Kristeva describes how her own theory of language derives from Lacan's distinction between the imaginary and the symbolic order.

To Lacan, Kristeva states, what constitutes the subject during his or her insertion into the order of language is his penis or her lack of one. Kristeva opposes Lacan's trajectory with *her* subject who is constituted *before* 'the castration phase', in the semiotic—a space of privileged contact with the mother. In French 'la sémiotique' is 'semiotics', the science of signs, and Kristeva starts by using *'le* sémiotique' to refer to the organisation of instinctual drives as they affect language. If castration marks out the symbolic contract, Kristeva asks, what can woman's place be in such a sacrificial order of language? The answer is for women to reject the symbolic and its social code and paternal function. We must, she claims, find a discourse closer to the body and emotions, to the unnameable repressed by the social contract. But if the semiotic is basically a pre-symbolic oral life we could, in turn, ask Kristeva: What connection can there be between a semiotic process and literary form?

Kristeva's answer is that if the semiotic occurs in a previous time chronologically to the symbolic, it is also simultaneously present as the sub-text of symbolic discourse. The semiotic occurs, in literature, as a pressure on symbolic language: as absences, contradictions and moments in a literary text. In 'Psychoanalysis and the Polis' Kristeva analyses the novels of Louis Ferdinand Céline. Her literary criticism has two foci: the segmentation of sentences and recuperable syntactical ellipses. This is where the locus of emotion, or the semiotic, will appear. Not only does Kristeva provide us with specific critical techniques, she is also concerned to provide specific aesthetic criteria. Great writers, she says, are those who, thematically, can immerse their readers in the unnameable semiotic of disruption. The task of critics is to help writers and readers (whether male or female) affirm this crisis in the symbolic function of literature itself.

What Kristeva elaborates, then, is not a critique about the female imagination as represented in symbols in women's writing but a theoretical and technical alternative to the 'neutrality' of (male) literary criticism. She proclaims the indelible association of women's bodies with language, whether in texts written by women or men. The concept of 'woman' or 'the feminine' is both a metaphor of reading and part of the topography of writing which Kristeva poses as a deliberate alternative to paternal metaphors or symbols. The most fruitful example, to Kristeva, of 'the feminine' is the representation of motherhood in Western culture (Kristeva, 1980). The subject's special relationship to the mother manifests itself in art or literature through a heightened tension *between* the semiotic and the symbolic. Like other feminists writing on the myths of motherhood, Kristeva is consciously aware of difficulties inherent in any definition of 'the feminine' which depends on 'motherhood'. Kristeva suggests however that the man-subject is as much a product of the interrelation of motherhood, the semiotic and discourse as is the woman's subject. Some male writers, like James Joyce, can also be seen as marginal to the symbolic order. Our problem might be not with Kristeva's essentialism but rather with her displacement of social and political concerns. She seems, at points, to be arguing that a linguistic disruption by the semiotic is as great a revolutionary gesture as a radical political practice.

At the same time, Kristeva *has* forcefully drawn attention to those moments in literature where women can deny patriarchy even if this best occurs only in 'the eruption of the semiotic', or across the border into 'Freudian' hysteria (Kristeva, 1980, p. 125). Kristeva's recognition of hysteria brings her close to the theories of another feminist psychoanalytic critic, Juliet Mitchell. But where Kristeva allides hysteria with bourgeois features of narrative, Juliet Mitchell believes that the literary power of the novel is in its portraits of hysteria. In contrast to *The Madwoman in the Attic,* Mitchell does not seek to endow madness with romantic glamour. Hysteria cannot be a *social* alternative, *it is* simply that the place of hysteria in literary texts is another place from which the psychoanalytic critic must speak.

Juliet Mitchell builds on the documentation compiled by Phyllis Chesler in *Women and Madness.* Chesler mixes statistical data about mental health with subjective accounts by individual women and sets them in the context of literary excerpts from the novels and autobiographies of women writers. Chesler aims to let women speak for themselves rather than be spoken for. But

Chesler collects evidence in a very American, pragmatic fashion and Mitchell's is the more theoretical contribution. The problem with Kristeva's semiotic, to Mitchell, is that it has its own ludic space set up by patriarchy. For Mitchell it is precisely *in* the symbolic but in a *new* symbolism that women must establish feminist criticism. In order to be published, Mitchell claims, women writers use a masculine language to talk about female experience. Inevitably their symbolic 'order' will always be 'hysterical'.

Mitchell has two kinds of psychoanalytic insights in her literary criticism. The more important because more theoretically thought out is her discussion about the 'imprisonment' of woman's style in male discourse. The focus is here on syntactics. But right from the beginning of her criticism Mitchell uses another psychoanalytic technique which is the more conventional, but no less useful, translation of narrative into psychoanalytic life history. She describes *Wuthering Heights,* for example, as a series of stages, of composite crises as represented metaphorically in Catherine's adult life. Again, when reading George Meredith, Mitchell constructs an existential phenomenology of Meredith's treatment of childhood (Mitchell, 1984). The focus here is on structure. The assumption behind these techniques is that narrative form *as well as* character representation must simultaneously define femininity. Mitchell is using both a psychodynamics of character *and* a psychoanalysis of the text. The effect of Mitchell's psychoanalytic critique is to make us look for relationships, for metaphors of Lacanian games or Winnicott's mirror imagery, and Mitchell is able to use psychoanalysis to pose a question central to feminism. Where is 'difference' constructed in a literary text? Mitchell's answer is the place of the hysteric who is articulating both the acceptance of *and* refusal of sexuality in contemporary culture.

While Mitchell's approach has the advantage of making it impossible to read literature outside of the construction of gender, other critics, trying to free sexuality from gender restrictions, *were* stepping outside into androgyny. In *The Second Sex* Simone de Beauvoir pioneered a serious consideration of the sexually androgynous. But, to de Beauvoir, androgyny implies masculinity (her word is 'brotherhood'). Carolyn

Heilbrun in *Toward a Recognition of Androgyny* uses the concept of androgyny to invalidate existing concepts of masculine and feminine within traditional literary criticism. In a line from Virginia Woolf's *A Room of One's Own* Heilbrun claims that androgyny is useful to feminism because it moves away from Freud's notion of bisexuality, which reinforces gender difference as binomial. Heilbrun claims that androgyny circumvents literary patterns of dominance and submission associated with rigid paradigms of gender.

Heilbrun looks at the psychology of sex differences as they are represented in literary descriptions of transexualism and cross dressing. Androgyny in literature, Heilbrun says, does not reflect authorial *confusion* about gender. The problems of female identity presented in women's poetry and prose are rarely difficulties in knowing one's gender; more frequently they are difficulties in learning what being a female means culturally. Androgyny shows that sex roles are societal constructs which can be abandoned. There is, of course, a significant nineteenth-century tradition of writing about androgyny and transvestism, but the difference, for Heilbrun, is that androgyny now could name not what is sadly *fixed* but what could be fluid. Many female modernists, including Woolf, Stein, Barnes and McCullars, create fictional universes questioning traditional assumptions about gender ascription and identity. In that work, and in the more contemporary writing of Ursula Le Guin, the androgynous future is, to Heilburn, a hopeful Utopia.

But another place where feminist criticism *could* speak about what has not and cannot be written in male discourse, is from the place of absence. Using textual slippages, feminism could speak out from the gaps in texts to subvert traditional ways of reading. For example, Jean Rhys deliberately disrupts her novels with ellipses to reveal the disrupted psyches of her heroines. In the work of Mary Daly and Gayatri Spivak, criticism looks to the abnormal not as the hysteria of character but as the 'hysteria' of the text—to what has slipped from the norm. They read texts not so much for what happens but for what is *not* happening—in the background of language and the original meanings of vocabulary. The text becomes what can only be 'got at' sideways in the margins. For example, Virginia Woolf constructs monologues where the speaker slips in and out of character to remind us of their absent pasts and the impossibility of speaking one truth in single names. Psycho-analytic criticism can emphasise women's exile from language as well as from society. Paradoxically it can invert patriarchy's refusal to represent woman as other than a lack, as a minus of man.

Mary Daly unites the psychological with the physical in her concept of a 'Hagocentric psychic space' (1978, p. 341). Criticism for Daly is a means to reach this space by helping us break out of our mental set through focusing on forms of meaning different from simply the cognitive. Glances, touch, the not-said in narrative and the semiotic space can reveal women's psyche and other kinds of identity. Mary Daly suggests that a useful critical technique is to build absences by 'paring away the layers of false selves from the self' (1978, p. 381). Eventually she chooses the absent *in the place of* patriarchy, by opting for an entirely separate women's culture in the 'Otherworld' journey of *Pure Lust.*

The best example of this method of psychoanalytic criticism is in the writing of Gayatri Spivak. In 'The Letter as Cutting Edge' Spivak suggests that any critic who has attended to the main texts of the new psychoanalysis has learned that the act of language is made up as much by its absences as by the substance by which the absences are framed. The task of the critic, Spivak claims, is to discover rhetorical slips and dodges in texts. The follower of Lacan will interpret these textual gestures as the eruption of the Other onto the text of the subject. To Spivak, the job of a feminist psychoanalytic critic is to look at imagery and signifiers of desire in a tropological cross-hatching of the text. Sometimes Spivak is very diagrammatic about these symbol-ogical lexicons, but she does allow psychoanalysis to help her question 'overt' meaning in a text. Spivak says, psychoanalytic criticism is caught in a double bind. Psychoanalysis frequently has to break with apparent sense to dig deeper into the psyche, yet literary criticism must operate as if the critic is making a sensible interpretation. What can criticism do? Spivak's solution is to name *frontiers,* borders and boundaries where the text becomes a sub-text. In addition, she suggests, feminist criticism should use psychoanalytic vocabulary to try for a frontier *style*—breaking the boundaries of formal criticism.

It is tempting not to ask the obvious questions. If 'the woman' is absent in male discourse, how can she speak in books? Who is speaking, and who is asserting the Otherness of woman? If woman's silence and absence constitutes her feminism, how can she ever speak in the name of women? This problematic—the enunciation of 'the feminine' in discourse—is the main concern of Luce Irigaray. In *Speculum de l'autre femme* she examines the polarity of masculine/feminine as it is represented in analogies, repetitions and oppositions in discourse. Through endless word-play Irigaray aims to create a place in writing where opposites might more creatively exist. 'Don't fret about the "right" word. There is none. No truth between our lips' (Irigaray, 1980, p. 76). She offers women a syntactically startling language as an alternative to what she regards as Lacan's exclusion of female expression. Western discourse, Irigaray claims, has far too long used its solidity to beat out the fluidity of feminine discourse.

Yet Irigaray does not ignore the relation of criticism to other forms of political practice. Although concerning herself with the subjectivity of sexuality, Irigaray is trying to think the feminist question through to some logical end. That is, she perceives that women's oppression exists both materially and in the very foundation of the language through which material meaning is acknowledged. Irigaray's specific contribution to literary criticism is the way she forces us to see 'femininity' as much more of a rhetorical category than a 'natural' one. Irigaray's criticism is a fundamental deconstruction of the realist approach. The critic can no longer be simple-minded about literary names or identities when identity is fluid. Like other feminist work on mother–daughter relationships (Kristeva and Rich) Irigaray opposes the 'hopelessness' of realism with the hope of defining a self in relation to m(other). As a result, the female identities we look for in literature will be double or even multiple.

Irigaray, like Spivak or Felman, is setting up a double question. Literary criticism has both to ask: What is sexual difference and (simultaneously) how is sexual difference intervening in the act of reading? It has to define difference while trying to find it out. The way ahead is to threaten the authority of the patriarchal code as such, to find signifiers of 'masculine' or of 'feminine' in texts which no longer fit into the social or institutional codes of their period. For example, Shoshana Felman describes how, in Balzac's *Adieu*, the text itself questions a masculine need for the authority of proper names. Balzac, Felman (1975) says, is staging theatrically Stéphanie's 'recognition' of her lover Philippe in order to tell us, unconsciously, that patriarchal naming is illusory. Only by showing how the cultural process of name-giving is no longer working in an individual text can feminists disrupt the male authority of naming.

A key place for psychoanalytic criticism is the romance. Romance is founded on absence—on frustration, of what will happen next. Tania Modleski, in *Loving with a Vengeance*, (1982) uses psychoanalysis to show how films and mass-produced narratives contain elements of resistance. A psychoanalytic framework has proved very useful to feminist critics of the romance whether in Kristeva's account of desire or Beauman's more anecdotal account of popular fiction. Other psycho-analytic critics like Ros Coward have investigated the imaginative dimensions of romance discourse and female complicity in the creation of a culture of romance. Just as psychoanalysis understands dreams to be fantasies of repressed pleasure, so romance fiction is a fantasy of women's repressed narcissism. Both kinds of 'rhetoric' aim to express the amorous state of women—psychoanalysis by specifying psychic rules for amorous discourse, romance by allowing the psychic play of women's amorous imagination. Romance is a major category of the feminine imaginary. By centring the question of pleasure, psychoanalysis helps us understand why the vicarious satis-faction of psychic needs (created in women by a patriarchal culture unable to fulfil them) are often satisfied by romance fiction.

The critical debate about romance fiction is between Marxist critics like Ann Snitow (1984), who feels (however sympathetic-ally) that romance keeps women in their socially and sexually subordinate place, and critics like Janice Radway (1983) who refuse this restricted notion of female false consciousness. I instance this final example of psychoanalytic criticism not so much to investigate its topography but because it summarises the main issue of a psychoanalytic debate. Snitow argues that romance fiction is a mirror image of pornography since women's price for emotional intimacy is passivity. Women read romances, to Snitow, by accepting a delimited invitation to artificial warmth. Radway, on the other hand, thinks women *resist* any artificial regulation of female sexuality in the Harlequin texts she considers, because they read ironically, and hence are exposing the inherent instability of gender.

The scene of this critical debate is thus itself a repetition of the possibilities dramatised by the romance text. The stylistic echoes of the text re-emerge in the very style of the polemic. Snitow asks what in the text invites and Radway what in the text resists the place and role of sexual identity. Romance can create sexual identity only through a precise sequence of cliff-hanging moments. Psychoanalysis narrates the topography of the unconscious in a set chain of signifiers. Romance critiques pose questions: What is a reading? What does the text have to say about its own reading? Both centre on the ownership of interpretation. Romance critics ask: Is the reader 'owned' by romance or does she own her own reading? In psychoanalysis the subject is both invited to interpret herself and be interpreted.

Psychoanalytic criticism gives feminism elbow room. It offers places in which we can ask questions. Using psychoanalysis to investigate desire, gender identity and linguistic construction feminists can deconstruct the gender hierarchies of literature and the gender hierarchies of society. Juliet Mitchell even claims psychoanalysis is an exemplary instance of Gramsci's 'optimism of the will' since its practice is to change will. At a simple level psychoanalysis emphasises a multiplicity of female expression and of possible interpretations. But by doing so it pinpoints the difficulty of the feminist critic in today's critical discourse. The challenge facing feminist criticism today is nothing less than to 'reinvent' language, to relearn how to speak. What psychoanalysis best offers feminism are modes of speaking which are outside phallocentric structures.

4

MARXIST-FEMINIST CRITICISM

To speak of literature and life as two separate phenomena is, for Marxist-feminists, a meaningless distinction. Literature, to them, *is* life since it incorporates both ideology and experience. 'Marxist-feminism' is not a precise term. Critics who might be considered as Marxist-feminist include writers like Michèle Barrett, who have an explicit allegiance to the ground *outside* of literature, others who move between Marxism and socialism, and those, like Mary Poovey, who examine social concepts only as they are encoded in literary form.

If we look at the development of Marxist-feminist criticism over the past ten years in order to assess its contribution, to point to certain weaknesses and to evaluate its future, the problem at issue is the state of Marxist criticism itself as much as the uneasy marriage between Marxism and feminism. Where all Marxist-feminists agree, however, seems to be that Marxism has something to teach literary criticism about the material conditions of women's cultural products and practices. This assumption enables feminists to interrogate the representation of women's experience in literature in terms of social determination.

Neither Marxism nor feminism can totally incorporate each other. What Marxism argues is that women are defined by the work they do or do not do. Work is the means by which people construct and change their material and imaginative worlds. Feminism argues that women are defined by the sexuality which they express or are repressed by. Sexuality is the means by which people create and mould their social and imaginative experiences.

Yet Marxism and feminism are both theories about the power of the 'real' world and its impact on literary imagination. They both give accounts of how culture relates to class and political change. But the key question for Marxist-feminist literary critics is whether Marxism itself provides an intact correct paradigm for comprehending women's literature or instead if a new, or modified, mode of analysis is needed. What, if anything, can Marxism, as read by feminist critics, teach us about literary form, and what is the utility of the Marxist method of literary criticism?

What Marxism can give feminism is a way of analysing literature in terms of the historical contexts which produce it and which it helps to produce. Psychoanalytic criticism, as we have seen, is responding in a different way to the same dilemma. But rather than setting up a 'woman language' as an *alternative* to social problems, as Wittig possibly does, Marxists foreground the problem of literature by rooting it in the real historical conditions of its production. The function of Marxist criticism is to prove that art derives from social-historical processes. Not only this, but Marxists understand that, from time to time, literature may be the *only* available source of historical ideas, feelings and values. The very forms of literature—its imagery, syntax and style—thus have a direct relationship to the ideological world which it inhabits. For feminist critics seeking to understand the representation of women, Marxism offers both a way of finding historical evidence of women's oppression and can describe how writers consciously, or unconsciously, transpose that evidence into their texts.

Finally, why Marxism is so attractive to feminists is that it understands that literature cannot exist as a distinct bounded object of discourse since culture, as a collection of signifying practices, transforms the notion of 'good' writing. The repression or misrepresentation of women can be methodically exposed and analysed when you believe, as Marxism does, that discourse is a form of power.

These are very exciting possibilities for feminist criticism. In addition, Marxism, by providing a revolutionary ontology for women's daily experience, gives historical significance to the everyday and hence redeems the notion of 'lived experience' for cultural activity. The terrain of literature is massively enlarged for feminism since Marxism shows that all culture is vitally bound up with personal identity. Rather than cultivating sensibility in a tiny minority, therefore, criticism is given a much broader project. Women will need to know much more about the role that art plays in their social consciousness and, in order to break their silencing, need criticism to actively encourage a feminist voice. By challenging the institution of literature and existing literary relations between writers and audiences, Marxism helps feminism to interrogate and re-negotiate the creation of literary value.

But in most versions of Marxist criticism written by men *language* is not assigned a central or even a distinctive role. Language as itself is never at their centre. Although Marxist literary criticism is not a school like structuralism, if we sample the strategies developed by male Marxist critics we can see a specific mode of explanation developing which devalues the one feature of social experience, language, most crucial to women.

Marxist literary theorists, in this century, read literature as a document of social change and the growth of a correct social consciousness. What Lukács, Gramsci and the cultural theorists of the Frankfurt School (Adorno, Marcuse, Benjamin), Goldmann and Brecht have in common is a concern with the social function of literature over its 'literary' character. They want to *utilise* aesthetics rather than be wary, as feminists must, of any concept, such as the social determination of ideas, which is created by the male bourgeoisie.

Echoes of this utilitarian approach to the study of literature can be found in England in the work of the English Marxist Christopher Cauldwell and writers connected with the magazine *Left Review.* The main argument of English literary Marxists was that the function of art is to assist a return to community. Because these critics wanted to relate social class and ideology *directly* to literature, they avoided actual textual analysis in favour of finding themes and examples appropriate to the class struggle.

A more subtle account of the relationship between ideology and literature is provided by Althusser and Macherey. The transformation of ideology within literature is their focus, and Macherey adds the suggestive idea that the literary work is continually distancing itself from the ideology contained within it.[1]

Yet when one surveys the many male approaches to the Marxist study of literature one conclusion is surely inescapable. None of these theories have much to do with language. They tend to deal with language only as a function or vehicle of some higher principle of social form. Adorno at least emphasises the formal laws of literature by putting a premium on 'difficult' texts because they could less easily be 'negated' by the culture industry. Yet through the 'culturalism' of Raymond Williams and the structuralism of Althusser and Eagleton what male Marxist critics are seeking is to link indissolubly the historical situation with the structure of a literary text. In other words, although some Marxist critics concentrate on the class-bound elements of literature and others on the revolutionary iconography of literature, literature itself must always be the symbolic precipitate of the materialist world. In Bakhtin language is even the material embodiment of social interaction.

To take one example of how feminism has to extend Marxist theory, in the work of Julia Kristeva the materialist life develops into a psychoanalytically based theory of experience able to deal with all language, marginal or otherwise. Kristeva attempts to show, by linking Freud and Lacan with Marxism, that what determines the power of language cannot simply be understood in terms of class struggle but must take account of how woman as subject is constituted in language. Since Kristeva was considered above in detail in Chapter 3, 'Language and Psychoanalysis', suffice it to say that feminism has enabled Kristeva to emphasise the revolutionary nature of literary language. She is able to argue that all social activity should be treated as signifying systems—as a series of texts.

In Marxist-feminism the Marxist indictment of capitalist repression is changed into a revolutionary account of women's existence. From the beginning, feminists, like Christine Delphy, were distinguishing very carefully between Marxist concepts (appropriate) and Marxist criticism by men (which is inappropriate). Delphy suggests that each woman has within her a dialectic between feelings and existence which she can manifest as social language or as literary imagination. Over and above this, Marxism, for feminists, must now insist not only on the unity of writer and her background but on a unity between a literary work and its audience. Literature must embody a specific set of relations between woman writer and woman reader. The question of literary value is bound up to some extent to Marxist-feminists with the problem of how works of literature relate to the real world. For example, a woman writer can have value for her documentation of social technology not just for her manipulation of the technology of art.

Marxism itself, as Kristeva and Delphy show, cannot be incorporated directly into feminism. There are problems with its categories and the way it constitutes subjects. To take the question of language first, if Macherey's work is useful to feminists since he argues that texts are never complete but are written around silences, there is a way in which women themselves are silent here too. The problem with Macherey, just to instance one male Marxist critic, is that, to him, the literary text is always de-centred. Marxist criticism is sex-blind. The Marxist text has no central essence whereas the feminist text must centre on women. Marxists tend to theorise the role of language and the subject descriptively in relation to class rather than moving *from* ideology to question the whole foundation of symbolic language itself. Hence Marxist critics' continual preference for the realist text in their obsession with nineteenth-century novels (Eagleton, 1976).

But rather than point up the inherent weaknesses in Marxist literary criticism as written by men, if male practice is where Marxist-feminism came from, its energy has a new direction. To the extent that Marxist theory and criticism has a more developed history than that of Marxist-feminism, the sketch can suffice as a grid of points within which feminists construct their own dimension of Marxist criticism. So the feminist critics I shall now describe may not necessarily *themselves* outline these theoretical priorities but are critics attempting to formulate a Marxist feminist critical method when reading literature and culture.

The opening argument came from Juliet Mitchell in an article 'Women: The Longest Revolution' published in *New Left Review* in 1966. Mitchell's crucial contribution was to recognise the ultimate centrality of the economic level yet describe the equal significance of other aspects of women's experience. Mitchell's work, at that stage, is theoretical rather than literary critical, but describing the relations that *could* exist between culture and the world of social action is the objective of Lillian Robinson. In *Sex, Class and Culture* Robinson believes that it is futile to author a feminist critical theory unless it proves adequate to women's history. So, first, she redefines the mode of criticism in order to replace traditional academic operations. Second, she uses this mode to examine 'low' and 'high' art by mixing pieces on What's My Line? with those of Virginia Woolf. Her essays continually move back and forth between literary and historical events by describing how that relation operates in her own political and literary activity. Robinson defines literature as being about the social roles of women. She asks questions like 'What are the social effects of literary conventions?' and sees a text as a reflection of social pressures rather than in terms of how women might read it.

'Criticism: Who needs It?' is a good example of her approach. The essay is about her home Buffalo, and she describes ethnic and class groups before describing any cultural features. Robinson places her own autobiography ethnographically, to show up the gap that she feels exists between current critical concerns and the everyday life of women in a typical American town. It is clear from where Robinson expects feminist critics to start. First, we should describe the social needs of an area and *then* ask what we can find in literature that is of use or might interest people who live there. The technique is basically one of juxtaposition, but Robinson offers a very positive future for literary criticism as a practice (not as an institution) since it can respond to the unformulated everyday political needs of women.

While providing very 'readable' accounts of historical romance and soap operas, Robinson seems to stop at the edge of the TV screen by limiting herself only to what is being represented and why. Although she sensibly starts with a specific use of Marxist theory—for example, using Marx's analysis of commodity fetishism on works of art—her criticism suffers from the reflectionist fallacy of vulgar Marxism. It is a very reactive criticism. If 'social experience is not only different from private experience but, that, acknowledged or not, it is the dominant force in the making of art or criticism', most of what Robinson writes could apply equally well to men (Robinson,

1978, p. 60). Particularly since Robinson is, in any case, antagonistic to a common feminist approach (1978, p. 87).

Lillian Robinson's version of Marxist-feminist criticism is finally extra-literary in the sense that she reads primarily to collect concepts and definitions, not to analyse literary experience. She understands literature to be a social agent not a symbolic representation of psychic need. If Robinson disparages formal aesthetics, she makes unconscious value judgements. While calling for literature, as an institution, to widen its brief to media studies, Robinson herself accepts the literary canon when she says that her essays on 'low' culture stem from her more private interests. If Marxist-feminist literary criticism does not give us notions of aesthetic *form*, then it remains just an epistemology. It needed to develop a vocabulary and conceptual tools to deal with the differential symbolic power of women and men in *literature* as much as in life.

What methodology could feminist critics use that would link the making of literature as an institutional practice with the making of literature as a creative act? Michèle Barrett finds her answer in literary history. In *Women's Oppression Today* Barrett sets out theoretical arguments which underpin her critical practice in 'Feminism and the Definition of Cultural Politics' and other writings. Barrett argues for a historical approach over what she calls the biologistic arguments of writers like Shulamith Firestone. In challenging the apparently universal and transhistorical categories of Firestone, Barrett is calling for a more precise construction of definitions and distinctions. These must, she feels, have an explanatory rather than descriptive character if 'realist analysis' is to move ahead. Literature cannot provide a *single* site for that analysis since, although we may learn a great deal while reading about the ways in which meaning is constructed in a particular historical period, 'our knowledge will not add up to a general knowledge of that social formation' (Barrett, 1980, p. 98). Obviously, for Barrett, it is the *context*, not the mode, of literature which is the basis for analysis.

There are obvious problems for literary criticism in Barrett's construction of Marxist building-bricks. If literature can only provide one (of many) 'sites for the construction of ideological processes' we could ask: Why bother with literature at all?

(Barrett, 1980, p. 97). Barrett would answer that although cultural practice is not a privileged site, it is at least essential to understanding the *bounds* within which particular means are constructed.

Barrett is firmly based in Marxist-feminism. Her scenario is one where literature expands if it engages in a living dialogue with many different cultural products. Criticism tries patiently to locate literature in the history of any period. But the critic must not tolerate the idea that some works are more valid than others. We have solved one group of problems—of the isolation of literature from determinations surrounding literary practice—but are immediately into another group. We are no nearer the *material* reality of literature itself. How do we set about reading fantasy, symbols and metaphors—the textual surface of literature—and yet remain polemically Marxist if need be? Marxism, in Barrett's world, seems very functional, concentrating only on the steps towards cultural production not the text as product in itself.

The source of that more difficult critique, Barrett claims in 'Feminism, and the Definition of Cultural Politics', can be found in a notion of skill. Barrett travels from the England of Charlotte Brontë's *Shirley* to the America of Judy Chicago's *The Dinner Party* to think through existing distinctions between art and other cultural products like soap opera in order to discover what might be a feminist culture. Her premise is that the sex of an author is not a reliable guide either to the meaning of a text or to its feminist potential. Judy Chicago fails Barrett's test because Chicago worked in an apparently hierarchical, dictatorial manner. As with vulgar Marxism, mode of production is all. But Barrett does at least acknowledge that words are ambivalent and contradictory and cannot be read simply for their polemic (Barrett, 1982, p. 41). She is clearly right to attack other feminist critics like Elaine Showalter for separating the activity of reading (consumption) from that of writing (production), but her alternative is perhaps naively simple. Feminist literary criticism should be the identification of 'levels of aesthetic skill in the construction of works of art' (Barrett, 1982, p. 52). While Barrett's notion is an attractive alternative to the élitism of traditional criticism, she leaves open very large questions. What about reader reception? How *do* we judge skill?

At what and for whom? Barrett talks about language practice in some vacuum. Unlike Lillian Robinson, at least Barrett *admits* that value criteria are less important to her, but her notion of skill is a surprisingly idealist suggestion which does not come to grips with aesthetics directly at all. Michèle Barrett then, sees reading not in the formulation of *literary* experience but in deciding what can be saved *from* the terrain of 'literature' for feminist politics. Michèle Barrett has worked hard to link theories of historical materialism with definitions of women in literature. She provides crucial insights into the relation, in particular between the class position of Virginia Woolf and Woolf's system of literary values (Barrett, 1979). It is this insight into Woolf which is my reason for comparing Barrett with another feminist-Marxist (who has worked in America), Gayatri Spivak (Spivak, 1980). The comparison will make clear the different cultural concerns of English and American Marxist-feminism. Reading Barrett and Spivak is like reading accounts not only by two very different critics but as if they were writing about two very different authors. Barrett starts from the question 'What are the consequences for the woman author of historical changes in the position of women in society', and her brief is then to analyse the historical determinants of Woolf's literary/critical production. Barrett gives a very good account of the relation between Virginia Woolf's lack of formal education, her critical reception (or lack of it) by male critics, her domestic isolation and the inevitable effect of these forces on her work. She sees Woolf's writings on sexuality, therefore, mainly in relation to Woolf's other ideas about male belligerence and fascism and the relationship of bourgeois sexual morality to Victorian society. Barrett shies away from Woolf's commitment to female difference, preferring to see Woolf's argument for difference as social rather than biologically constructed.

Sexuality and its multiple forms are precisely Spivak's very 'different' point of departure. Her critique is, like much recent American criticism, heavily indebted to Lacan and Derrida (who Spivak has translated and introduced to American audiences). Spivak's text also illustrates the debt American feminists owe to their disciplinary training in rhetoric and linguistics as undergraduates. Woolf is now translated into allegory and verbal dexterity—a move away from representation and the social creation of art. Spivak attempts to understand *To the Lighthouse* by reading it as the deliberate superimposition of two allegories—the grammatical and the sexual. These are present, Spivak claims, in Woolf's two languages—the language of art and the language of marriage. By an extended pun on the word 'copula', both as a pivot of grammar and as a sexual activity, Spivak makes a Derrida-like business of the different uses and meanings of single words. Hers is not a continuous textual analysis (there is none of Barrett's thorough cultural history) but rather a use of what Raymond Williams would call key words which can represent key grammatical and cultural moments. The difference between English and American Marxist-feminism could not be clearer. English criticism is shown to be illustrative in its welding of social and literary concerns. American criticism is shown to be formalist and assuming an agreed notion of the avant-garde. Both critics offer helpful ways of reading Woolf. By taking a more overtly sexual text like *Orlando* we could (*à la* Barrett) see Orlando's development and gender changes in relation to the literary and historical styles she/he encounters. The critical focus here would be Orlando's attack on Victorian culture and masculinity. Conversely (*à la* Spivak) we could look at *Orlando* as a deliberately uncommitted narrative whose biographer 'slips away' textually to show the difficulty of transsexuality. Since gender difference is *only* described physiologically by Woolf, this reading reveals the sub-text of physical violence as displayed in Orlando's mixture of interrogative and interior analysis.

I would call both feminist readings and have applied the English and American approaches simply as an example of how the two models can balance rather than prescriptively cancel each other out. Of course, there are American Marxist-feminists who also chart the sociology of women's literary culture (e.g. Fox-Genovese, 1980). But the marker that distinguishes English and American Marxist interpretations of literature is their alternative notions of the 'difference' of women's culture.

Where critics like Spivak use psychoanalysis to understand that meaning always lies in the process of the text, Barrett shies away from the nature of discourse. For Barrett and other

English Marxists the text seems to be a 'souvenir' of some superior experience. However, presumably all texts historicise a writer's fantasies rather than simply 'remember' them. If we ignore contradictions in the surface of discourse, we preclude any discussion of the dialectic interplay of conscious creation and subconscious intent. If we read literature only as a paradigm of ideology, we blot out what is literary about literature. English Marxism-feminism so far seems to leave untouched the problem of reading. It gives us no way of thinking about pleasurable response. How do we theorise the untheoretic? How do we decide aesthetically which of our experiences are likely to resist or accept messages? The process of negotiation of meanings, of identification and reassurance is both an internal process in a text and has to do with our own subjectivity. Literary readings are not simply formed by something external.

A way around the problem for English Marxists is to treat the socially situated reader as a discursive construct in the text. This has been one of the strengths of English feminist work on soap operas and the media. This trajectory starts from the desire to examine only genres which are popular with contemporary women of any class. The objective of much of this criticism has been to address the paradox that women's popular culture speaks to women's pleasure at the same time that it puts it into the service of the patriarchal family (Williamson, 1978).

Feminism for Girls provides a good example of this approach (McRobbie, 1981). Angela McRobbie and others detail kinds of discrimination experienced by adolescent girls as constructed in the literary and visual style of the magazines they read. Feminist criticism here is about the reception and subversion of imagery. The approach can be characterised as a semiotic analysis of depictions of reality, or unreality, as modes of signification both for their audience and us as readers. Criticism here becomes an ethnographic rather than literary setting-up of questions about culture and the creation of alternatives. Although feminist work in England on the genre of romantic fiction has enlarged the boundaries of what we can call 'literature', there are weaknesses in the approach as an *explanation* of literary patterning. By describing ethnographically the role of literary culture within women's experience, this criticism often refuses any framework of 'good' or 'bad' representation aesthetically. Meaning, then, can only be the result of a changing interaction between particular verbal forms and socially constructed readers. While the notion of meaning, in this sense, as an ideological force is often very well demonstrated, it ignores the whole issue of literary value.

For English Marxist-feminists, the text alone cannot provide *the* signifying opposition. In the work of the Birmingham Centre for Cultural Studies (McRobbie, 1981), the texts of Michèle Barrett (1982) and Patricia Stubbs (1981), English critics tend to look for themes of family, of public or private rather than fantasy or difference.

Feminists from the Birmingham Centre for Cultural Studies in particular see their responsibility as critics to a constituency of women readers and question the relation between cultural and social practices in terms of the lived experience of readers (Hall *et al.*, 1980). The group took a quite novel concern with 'the popular' in a radically new sense, producing concrete research on ideas of the popular and their interaction with women from different classes. Methodologically this led English Marxist-feminist literary criticism to its more ethnographic approach, moving from the formal text to its lived reception. 'Women, Feminism and Literature in the 1930s' and the study of Barbara Cartland and Winifred Holtby in *Culture, Media and Language* do not consider texts *per se* but look at the process of literary production and the interpellation of, or hailing of, readers by texts. The Birmingham Centre approach, as I shall have to call much of English Marxism, reads popular narratives like Barbara Cartland's *Blue Heather* in a search for motifs (of home and marriage) which can be related to social concerns. The Birmingham Centre has pioneered a collective approach both to research methods in general and to reader groups within literary criticism. It has mapped different cultural practices and aimed to mobilise them. In Britain Marxist-feminism has been interconnected with the reconstitution of 'community' in an active involvement in women's writing groups outside the formally academic, as in the women's groups 'Human Voices' and 'Commonplace Workshop' (Worpole, 1982). Although a radical departure in feminist literary criticism, the movement suffers from anti-formalism.

For example, another way of reading romance texts would be to use deconstruction's view of the text as a set of relations with other texts. This provides as helpful a model for criticism about romance where moral norms are as much to do with readers' *expectations* of form (e.g. four-letter words are added to *Women's Weekly* romances when published as books to attract a wider readership), as with the Birmingham linkage of reader expectation with *lived* experience.

Literature is not simply, however, a practice employing specific 'means' to transform women into something else—a representation. Only in an oppositional practice where reading is the mode of transformation *as well as* its context can we form the ground from which new forms of feminist criticism can develop. What Kate Millett pioneered in *Sexual Politics* was the insight that women's writing is sexually determined. It is sexuality first, not class, which shapes a woman writer's choice of scenes, themes and language.

While the 'culturalist' approach of the Birmingham Centre stays with interrogating the woman reader's concept of literary form, the Marxist-Feminist Literature Collective (MFLC), although no longer writing as a group, did interrogate form for its conception of women. While the overriding concern of the Birmingham Centre is with material production, the 'linguistic' approach of the MFLC focuses on the material means. In 'Women's Writing: *Jane Eyre, Shirley, Villette* and *Aurora Leigh*' the MFLC propose to transform the inadequacies of standard Marxist criticism. They do this by describing the marginality of female literary practice, rather than cultural production, and find representations of that marginality in the situation of female characters. The group looks at two key points of articulation in the nineteenth-century novel: marriage and paterfamilias. The Brontës and Barrett-Browning, the essay claims, by excluding their heroines from conventional family structures, are creating plots which deliberately interrogate the patriarchal ideology of Victorian life. Before we begin to worry that this sounds like the fallacy of author equalling character, the essay becomes more complicated. The location of feminism, the analysis claims, is to be found not simply in what characters say but in what they *cannot* say—in the awkward moments when speech is denied or repressed.

Yet it is actually difficult to imagine each text in the terms the group provide, particularly since they ignore features which might be crucial to feminist criticism like female friendship in *Shirley*. Their notion of women's consciousness is still one of passivity, of woman as victim, with an apparent foregrounding of the 'real'. A more adequate idea of textual moments would be to look at texts as bundles of *discourses*, not silences, bound in different ways. Some discourses would relate to other texts gone before, some would anticipate responses to come. Literary ideology would be less a specific region and more a series of effects.

The problem stems ironically from the very success of English Marxist/socialist feminist history. Contemporary feminism in England is best represented by the work of feminist historians, like Sheila Rowbotham, which predates feminist *literary* criticism. It is feminist historians who have developed new models of women to reconstruct as well as document women's role in the past. In 'The Public Face of Feminism', for example, feminist historians examine suffragette autobiographies since it is autobiographical modes of writing, they say, that pose the question central to feminism: the relation between the 'public' and the 'private' (T. Davis *et al.*, 1982). They claim that a choice of form is as important as a choice of period to feminist history.

By acknowledging 'unwitting testimony' in the writing of women and men, feminist historians often resemble literary critics. As Davis *et al.* do here, they take the gaps, absences and tensions of historical discourse as evidence of repressed feminine consciousness. However, there is one major absence in feminist history—the literary text itself. Imaginative literature is still not being used by feminist historians as source material. By directing our attention towards popular texts and autobiographies, English feminist historians have done an 'unwitting' disservice to literary criticism. Feminist literary criticism needs to read autobiography, popular text *and* literature as vehicles for the production and reproduction of forms of consciousness.

The attempt to treat a text as a more densely orchestrated unity of writing *practices* comes in Mary Poovey's *The Proper Lady and the Woman Writer*. Poovey takes up, where Lillian Robinson left off, by examining a writer's career and ideology as implicated in literary practice. The Marxism of Poovey's feminism is clear in her guidelines for literary criticism. She states that the terms in which femininity is publicly formulated by Mary Wollstonecraft, Mary Shelley and Jane Austen are both part of their familial and economic relationships *and* dictate the way femaleness is experienced. Immediately this gives us a more sophisticated reading of literary style, Where Robinson finds ideology in the social context of the text, Barrett in the production of the text, the Birmingham Centre in the implied reader of the text and the MFLC in the surface of the text, we now have the woman author as a textual construct.

Poovey chose to write about Mary Wollstonecraft, Mary Shelley and Jane Austen, she says, because they represent in literary form a 'critical phase in the history of bourgeois ideology'(1984, p. xv). The French Revolution had presented an explicit challenge to English patriarchy. Poovey's Marxism gives feminist criticism more proof that economic and social conditions exercise a tenacious hold over the imaginative styles of women writers. Her feminism gives Marxism more reasons to read women writers since, to Poovey, it is women above all who naturalise discrepancies in lived experiences (the differences between promises made and the material world).

All, however, is not entirely well. First Poovey has a fairly simple notion of aesthetic value revealed when she prefers Jane Austen to Mary Shelley because Austen could 'resolve' the ideological contradictions left unresolved in *Frankenstein*. Yet often a narrative closure might be compensatory for a woman writer rather than aesthetically valuable. Perhaps more important, Poovey makes an overgeneral use of the term 'ideology', Since her use includes politics, economics and literary practices and institutions, we would ask 'Is there anything non-ideological now?' While her use of ideology is an attempt to escape the social reductionism of some traditional kinds of Marxism, it creates terminological difficulties when we want to distinguish literary practice from literary institution. This is a common weakness in Marxist-feminist criticism. By proposing, as Poovey does, a vague extra discursive reality in some false social totality, 'ideology' becomes an imprecise concept.

The methods of Marxist-feminist literary criticism are

clearly a tricky balancing act. Analysis of women's representation and ideology in Marxist terms alone can become a
substitution for the analysis of differences *between* women and
inherent contradictions in the subject 'woman'. Of course there
is a material world out there, but literature inevitably involves,
to some extent, a subjective perception of it. Marxist-feminists
ignore the fact that material reality in a text can be read too as
real. Clearly feminist criticism has to stress the positionality of
the subject and her history as part of discourse, not external to
it. At the same time, Marxists have to recognise that
representation has its own specificity which must be attended to
not just as caused by history. To take an obvious example of the
difficulty in practice, how do we analyse the Black family as
represented in Black novels by writers like Buche Emechta?
The Birmingham Centre argues that the family is not natural
but a socially constructed institution which they clearly hope
will disappear. But for the Black woman writer in patriarchy,
the family is her site of political and cultural *resistance* to
racism.

A more hostile reaction to Marxist-feminism appears in the
work of radical feminists like Adrienne Rich. Lesbian criticism
and the analysis of myth seems to require a different set of
priorities than those in Marxist-feminism. Rich and others
describe private domains ignored or trivialised in the Marxist
tradition. Radical feminism poses the whole question where we
began, of whether feminist culture can be simply and easily
assimilated into the Marxist notion of ideology, or whether it
requires a new, or modified, critical method. Yet much of what
has been said about Marxist-feminism indicates the absolute
centrality of analysing social along with literary production.
Only a feminist criticism that accommodates both class and
gender could account for textual discourse in its full
complexity.

The attempts to bring together Marxism and feminism
perhaps raise more questions than they answer, but they do
represent a sustained and often very polemical enterprise. In
reviewing the critical work produced in the context of Marxist-
feminism, certain major themes and leading ideas stand out.
Taken together, they indicate the important contribution made
by Marxist-feminists to the development of literary criticism on

the question of women. The practice of group writing in itself represents a quite significant break with traditional critical practice. So too the particular interrelation of literature and history breaks with traditional literary history and its lists of great books across the ages. Marxist-feminism brings in popular romance and the media and proves their formal distinctiveness as specific practices of writing. Marxist-feminism rejects the distinction between knowing woman subject and known woman object—the division between subjective and objective discursive postures. Marxist-feminism offers us the possibility of a more open dialectic between our reading pleasures and the historically precise relations in which we stand. The method it provides may only be a guideline along the way to a future feminist criticism, but it helps us glimpse that future as a more integrated and inclusive practice.

5

MYTH CRITICISM

In the 1940s and 1950s many American women writers began to use myth as a way of generalising personal emotions and feelings. Just as in post-war society the definition of what was prototypically feminine became problematic, so in post-war writing women introduced mythic symbols to defy traditional feminine ideas of feminine passivity in an oblique way. The poet Louise Bogan uses the wild figures of Medusa and Cassandra in her poems 'Tears in Sleep' and 'The Dream' to widen the definition of a 'normal' woman. H.D. (Hilda Doolittle) writing *Trilogy* in 1944 searched through myth and history looking for symbols of archaic rebirth. This enlarged possibility of a woman's life was reflected synthetically by Muriel Rukeyser who, in *Beast in View* (1944), uses the rhyme schemes of myth to express the ambiguities of woman's condition.

On this territory feminist myth critics have camped, building on and strengthening these poets' work with histories of myth and fables. Mary Daly, Adrienne Rich, Annis Pratt, Marta Weigle and critics in the collection *The Lost Tradition*, edited by Cathy Davidson and E.M. Broner, see myth as a key critical genre. Yet a precise definition of what constitutes myth and its function in criticism remains problematic. Women *in* mythology are well documented and discussed but generally from male perspectives.

Yet, ironically, one reason why this mode of feminist criticism might perhaps be more acceptable to the establishment than other types is because of the canonisation of male myth critics like Empson, Frye and McLuhan. The academic tradition of myth criticism, as written by men, is based on their scientifically organised theories of literature which try to use 'external' structures of symbolism.

In his *Anatomy of Criticism*, Northrop Frye amalgamated the empiricist close reading techniques of New Criticism with his sense of 'the archetypal shape of literature as a whole' (Frye, 1957, p. 342). Frye revives archaic doctrines, such as Ptolemaic cosmology, to place criticism exclusively in the realm of transhistorical permanent forms. Building on Frye, Marshall McLuhan made a myth structure, which he calls the global village, drawn from his own misreading of preliterature tribal societies.

These critics created a tradition of male myth-criticism which was very much in vogue in the academic world of the 1950s and early 1960s. Its success depended on a close analogy between Frye's value-free scientism and the social-scientific ideology of the Cold War period. As a tradition it is also racist and patriarchal since it ignores gender and the actual rituals of real ethnic groups. In any case, in Western culture 'mythology', as the classicist Sarah B. Pomeroy points out, has tended to mean what was preserved in classical art and literature and perennially reworked especially in the behavioural sciences. There may be traces of Frye's love of classification in Mary Daly, yet a greater range of myths and their associated ideas of 'womenly' behaviour needed to be found, scrutinised and reinterpreted from a feminist perspective. Unfortunately, mythographers simply do not know very much about women's mythology. Very little can be said with certainty about what verbal, visual and ritual expressions women themselves hold, or held, as opposed to the way women are represented *in* myths as reconstructed by men. But feminist critics, like Daly, Pratt and Davidson, along with some psychoanalytic critics, have begun to depart radically from the male terrain by dealing mostly with myths not generally derived from the Graeco-Roman tradition. To Northrop Frye, Greek and biblical mythologies represent *all* the subsequent principles of literature (Frye, 1963, p. 44). Feminist critics aim rather to analyse structures of meaning in myths from different cultures. A structural analysis sees literature as constituting a message and its value lying in the information it transmits to us. The function of critical analysis in this project is to isolate this message (what Roland Barthes calls a signifying system). In feminist criticism myths are a series of dovetailed stories, from any tradition, whose purpose is to specify and to explain the projected fears, hopes and desires of women and their relationships.

What are these critical concepts which myth critics use, and what values and techniques come with them? Mary Daly's challenge is metaphoric. She contests longstanding conceptions of the feminine with progressive ideas of an alternate women's culture. Annis Pratt examines women's fiction to 'determine if these works constituted a field that could be investigated as a self-contained entity following its own organic principles' (1982, p. viii). The feminist critics represented in *The Lost Tradition*, as the title implies, are trying to explain how and why the mothers and daughters of literature and myth gradually became isolated and lost one another. What unites all these concerns, is the notion of myth as almost a genre of critical writing in itself. Each of these critics is attempting a more precise way of charting and analysing women's past, present and future use of myth and its social and literary function.

The training of myth critics is as varied as their approaches. Although many share a religious background, of Jewish ritual or Roman Catholicism, the stories they choose to investigate are very different. Marta Weigle in *Spiders and Spinsters* concentrates on native American Indian myths using an etymological and lexigraphic approach to document crosscultural explanations. Annis Pratt remains firmly within traditional academic parameters reading nineteenth- and twentieth-century women's novels in terms of Jungian archetypes and imagery. Adrienne Rich (described in detail in Part II, below) and Mary Daly collect psycholinguistic evidence of women's mythical superiority to unite this with their own autobiographies. Critics in *The Lost Tradition* work with the polytheistic myths of the ancient Near East juxtaposing these with the contemporary culture of native American Indians and white women writing today. All these critics, however, do share an approach which is both personal and professional.

This is because myth criticism can offer its writers a comforting structure within which to locate private needs. In the years of the 'feminine mystique' a confusion about sex roles and the status of private life could be answered by the useful metaphors of myth. In the poetry of Sylvia Plath and Anne Sexton, for example, myths provide a structure of meaning represented by the ambiguous mother images they chose as poet daughters uncertain about their roles as poet mothers. Mythological figures could, therefore, be very useful metaphors for each author's mother search and sometime private matrophobia.

In the academic professions myth criticism broke with conventional literary criticism in many ways, while having an ambiguously close relation to the schools of comparative literature in which myth criticism had flourished in the American academic world of the 1960s. The approach offered a radical way of crossing disciplines. Critics could use myth to explain in literature what feminist psychoanalysts were explaining in psychology. In *The Reproduction of Mothering* Nancy Chodorow explores the connection between mother and daughter relations on the formation of the female personality. Because male children have to develop their masculinity in a masculine world, that world is anything which is *not* the mother or the feminine. Therefore the repudiation of the feminine appears, too, in male mythology, particularly in the story of Perseus triumphing over Medusa, the representation of the feminine unconscious.

The female child, on the other hand, has to be both like, and yet different from, her own mother. The mother represents both the childhood the daughter has to reject and, simultaneously, the adult world into which she has to grow. Myths of Medusa, or frequently Arachne, for women reflect this ambivalence and differential evaluation. The psychological dilemmas of women can thus be represented in literature through mythical figures. Annis Pratt's purpose for writing is that 'women find it hard to translate the contents of their unconscious into recognisable symbols and myths' (1982, p. 138).

For Pratt the different psychological experience of men and women writers creates a gendered perception of mythical archetypes. The radical otherness of women's experience she claims is borne out in the more arcane symbolism of their fiction. Pratt chooses Virginia Woolf's *The Voyage Out* as her main example of this mode. Mrs Ramsey, Pratt claims, is using myth to call up 'androgynous powers to fertilise her childish husband' (Pratt, 1973, p. 13).

Similarly, myth criticism provides a different view of philosophy than that which had hitherto informed literary criticism. Although Mary Daly read Aristotle at Freiburg, and teaches Plato and Aquinas at Boston College, she claims that philosophy is too precise to mean anything.[1] The application of precise moral terms or abstract concepts is not possible in myth criticism. Rather than restricting an area of knowledge to empiricism or positivism, myth consists of images and symbols which are vivid but not always intellectually intelligible. Myth narratives aim not to present coherent literary explanations of *all* human problems but to link rituals of daily life with symbols in an appropriate way for women. Literary criticism has used philosophy to get at some formal principles of universability. Feminist critics, however, prefer to raise the everyday actions of women throughout history to the status of myth and therefore necessity.

The real enemy, to Daly or Pratt, is of course patriarchy. One of the problems with early feminist criticism of myth was its need to rely on male theory, particularly the taxonomy of Erich Neumann. In Neumann's (1955) account of mothers and daughters in myth, the narrative manifestations of power relations between mother and child often simply resemble power relations in his own society. Adrienne Rich (1977b) attacked Neumann's theories for reinforcing existing stereotypes. Men maintain a culture's rituals as the translation of their own unconscious fear of women into mythical monsters or, particularly in the Western tradition, into myths of rape and violence to women. Medusa is their traditional symbol of the castrating female, and perhaps part of *feminist* myth-critics' obsession with Medusa can be explained by the internalised gynophobia which all women have as part of our patriarchal inheritance. Dorothy Dinnerstein's *The Mermaid and the Minotaur* catalogues the way women learn these negative attitudes and internalise them.

Feminist critics take Graeco-Roman myths to be masculine constructs whose changing narratives only reflect changes, both ontogenetic and phylogenetic, within the male psyche. The main project of feminist myth-critics is then how to get beyond this patriarchal overlap, perhaps to find that mythology is originally female, or at least to discover the force and outline of early, more specifically female, mythologies. Virginia Woolf's preference for the pre-Greek myths of Egypt and Isis iconography is an early example of a feminist rejecting the patriarchal obsession with Greek myths and their male heroes.[2] This process is one, too, in which many contemporary women poets are currently engaged, such as the Black lesbian poet Audre Lorde and the Navajo poet Leslie Silko.[3] Mary Daly's *Gyn/Ecology* addresses itself to nothing less than a 'vow of derision' against male myths and the language which encodes them. She says that the study of myths is important not to simply *replace* patriarchal myths with feminine versions but to elicit fresh cultural insights by reversing the myths.

What, then, are the main elements of Daly's reversal? As a major work of myth criticism *Gyn/Ecology* is a useful key to analysis of the whole genre. The importance of myth criticism, for Daly, is in its ability to decode literature and culture. She is not intent, in any naive way, to prove that *every* phallic myth has a precedent in a gynocentric one which antedated it, but she shows that every male myth is a reversal of a female tale. Christianity had incorporated Goddess religion and transformed its symbols into a new mythology stripped of female power. By working through 'A-mazing' tales Daly points to the way patriarchy conceals aspects of Greek myth (she cites Apollo's homosexuality) so that it can laud male power. Alternatively, she claims, patriarchy selects particular myths (as the Athena series) in order to create an emblematic woman more identified with male aims. For Daly, the real horror of male aggression is the use of myths, by males, to violate gender boundaries as in the story of Dionysus driving women mad with his femininity. Daly replaces this with female images which can act as magnets for feminist ideas. Daly prefers metaphor because it is spontaneous rather than archetype, which is merely reactive—a 'cookie-cutter' of patriarchy.

The problem with Daly's analysis of patriarchal mythology as an approach is her overdetermined idea of gender assymmetry. To make her explanations work she often reduces women and men to caricatures of themselves and focuses attention away from the structure of male supremacy onto male behaviour as represented in culture. Nowhere is this clearer than in her characterisation of male sexuality as always compulsively violent. (A view of course shared by other contemporary feminists like Susan Brownmiller.)

There are other, stronger reasons for women to use myths. Usually myths need to be read aloud slowly since meanings come more from associations than what is contained on the page. Oral readings bring myths alive, restoring the immediacy of early myth and are collective. It is precisely because myth culture is oral, critics in *The Lost Tradition* claim, that it is likely to be fully understood only by women. In all societies women 'talk-story' (to use Maxine Hong Kingston's phrase) not as mere self-expression but as a way of teaching their children.

Myth is always important to minority groups since it can be a vehicle for expressing the tragic destructiveness of their social reality through analogy or masks. In literature written by Chicana, Black and Jewish women, as Weigle describes, the connections between mothers/daughters, ethnicity and social alienation are often explicit mythologised. It must be tempting for oppressed groups to seek redress in the reclamation of an identity which the larger culture denigrates. Myth provides a psychological way out of the Western tradition while enabling a group to physically remain within. Of course, the reclamation and establishment of a feminist myth must never be seen as an alternative to radical structural change in culture. Hence Mary Daly in *Gyn/Ecology* worries very much about the supposed association of myth-makers with anti-intellectualism. She supports creative criticism in book form since she aims, as other critics, to provide women with a historical past which she describes as a 'feminist journeying'. But Daly proposes a significant alteration to the categories and compartments of existing criticism. Rather than using periods or movements in literature (which Daly understands as specious, intact examples of 'homo-geneous' criticism), she proposes instead that feminist criticism be the 'transmission of our transitions' (1978, p. 23).

Finally, myth can appeal to women more than men in its portrayal of the informal and the private experience of everyday feminine life. Male critics, like Neumann or even Alan Watts, have defined and studied myth as a public means of communication which pertains to metaphysical or supernatural reality. Now a revaluation of the mundane is taking place in feminist

·myth criticism. Weigle lists an ethnography of native American communication patterns, Daly's is a sociolinguistic study of women's vocabulary, Adrienne Rich has given us almost a microsociology of legends, autobiography and poetry about mothers. What had previously been dismissed as trivial, ordinary or gossip have been collected by feminist myth-critics and recreated as wives' new tales.

If there are clear and very powerful reasons for Pratt, Daly or Rich to be interpreting myths, how do they teach us to read mythical signs? What are the main methods and techniques of feminist critics of myth? For most, criticism has a double function. It is both a form of literary appreciation and a form of knowledge. Criticism translates or reconstitutes latent meaning in mythical stories, and it is also, and simultaneously, constituting *new* knowledge about women. So Annis Pratt, for example, examines the narrative devices in the Brontës or Edna O'Brien to point to ambivalences in individual author attitude but also to draw general lessons about the female pysche. Pratt claims that since women writers are alienated from time and space, their plots take on a cyclical rather than a linear form. Similarly, Pratt's own criticism is itself circular. She starts by describing archetypal images as literary forms that derive from unconscious originals. Passion in the modern novel is still 'dark' as a result of centuries of conditioning of women by men. To Pratt, literature is both specifically gendered in form and represents, in a one-to-one way, the psyches of female authors.

This 'unconscious' patterning, Pratt claims, affects the structure as well as characters in fiction. Plots which use a rise-and-fall wave pattern are 'the raising of erotic expectations followed by an anticlimax of patriarchal misunderstanding' (Pratt, 1982, p. 85). And women's narratives will therefore use recurrent patterns which are mythical and can even reject social experience—Pratt cites the rape motif of Daphne and nature myth in *Udolpho*. She concludes that novels by women are replicates of myth using the same pursuit narratives but often involving islands, wells or grottos invaded by men.

Pratt's technique is problematic to begin with since she refuses to distinguish between narrative ideology (which would relate to specific social institutions) and myth archetype. But

Pratt continues to draw her circle by inducing universal categories of fiction from the images, symbols and narrative patterns she examines. 'The structure of the new space novel [Pratt is considering lesbian fiction] itself revolves around epiphanic moments, or peak experiences of erotic or metaphysical vision or both of a better world' (Pratt, 1982, p. 109). So although Pratt describes a very *wide* range of fiction, her criticism remains a series of narrow tautologies. She implies that women writers think differently from male authors because they are socially conditioned to do so. They choose fictional patterns and motifs which enact this difference and persistently use typical themes from myth. From understanding these typical literary themes and techniques, Pratt is saying, we can constitute a body of knowledge about women today. A critique of a whole dimension of literary life is expressed but also reduced to a narrow convention.

It will not do to dismiss myth criticism as locked into a too rigid circle since there are gains to be had from Pratt and other critics. To begin with, her critique is both deconstructive *and* futuristic. Pratt examines masculine and feminine imagery in *To the Lighthouse*, for example, to reveal crucial figures of power and apotheosis pertinent to women's understanding of society. She goes on to replace Jung's archetypes, or extend them, with those more rooted in woman's history. It is crucial that feminist critics address myth since, as we have seen, the process of reclaiming and recreating myths is central to the work of many feminist poets. Audre Lorde in particular makes use of mythological analogies to understand the angry chthonic powers of the goddess figures of prehistory. For both critic and poet women must learn self-love, self-mythologising. So critics and poets often describe female divinities in myth in anthropomorphic terms.

But, although an identification with nature is a persistent theme in women's fiction and vegetation goddesses are among the most prevalent 'culture heroines' of myth, female figures in most of *recorded* mythology are much more likely to be depicted as destructive monsters. And yet, as anthropologist Sally Binford maintains, there is absolutely no valid reason to proclaim a golden age of matriarchy. If the marginality and powerlessness of women is reflected both in the ways women are expected to act, and the ways in which women are acted upon in myths, what could be the ideal myth for feminism?

The answer was to make feminism synonymous with female bonding and contend that the rehabilitation of mother/daughter myths is central to feminism. That feminism and motherhood might be incompatible had seemed almost axiomatic to some earlier feminists. Contemporary feminists now challenge this axiom using myth as a vehicle for their arguments. Adrienne Rich splits the rhetoric of motherhood into two halves which she named 'experience' and 'institution'. The point of this bifurcation is to enable her to attack the institutionalisation of motherhood by patriarchy while celebrating the mythic condition of mothering. Rich writes about literary myths since she believes that the realities of motherhood are obscured by the literary associations brought to it by men. Male cultural icons, she claims, have to be displaced by the creation of a 'symbolic architecture' of feminism. Rich, as Daly, therefore focuses frequently on Demeter and Persephone, or on other mother–daughter bonds in myth. While refusing the idea of an historically specific golden age of matriarchy, Rich describes a number of fertility and goddess myths as artifacts of female primal power.

Through a variety of accounts these critics sought to demonstrate that the power of the Demeter/Persephone myth could be a continuing symbol for women in contemporary society. Annis Pratt, similarly, reads the representation of motherhood in nineteenth-century fiction as expressive of mothers' 'excessive social power' in Victorian society. And the whole of *The Lost Tradition* is an examination of mother–daughter relationships as manifested in the poems and letters of women writers. By exploring the personal and mythological aspects of the intricate and inescapable mother–daughter bond, critics can posit an ideal mechanism for the discovery of female identity.

Motherhood, then, is the one place from which criticism could begin to reformulate the representation of women in myth. Adrienne Rich thinks that the entire construction of women in patriarchy comes from society's need to romanticise or idealise 'mothers' at the expense of the reality of early relationships. Critics in *The Lost Tradition*, by examining difficult mother–daughter relations in the American poetry of Anne Sexton or Sylvia Plath, seek to find in the double faces of mythical mothers 'the source of our own, specifically female, creative powers' (Davidson, 1980, p. 193). In placing the myths of mothering in the foreground in this way critics were able to start rethinking sexual difference, since giving birth is *the* specifically different gendered act.

If motherhood is the main area of knowledge reconstituted by myth critics, Mary Daly's metaphorical journey into Hag-ocracy is another. *Gyn/Ecology* is a territorial examination of the space and architecture of women's prehistory hypothesised as women's future. Daly reads myths as presenting two principles of nature simultaneously. Nature is first a principle of order, giving regulating principles to women's activities. But there is also nature as a principle of creation from which many women may learn some essential truths about individuality. Daly's is a moral rather than a social critique. A social criticism would move beyond order and creativity into contradictions. Daly's is a retrospective radicalism. By characterising prehistory as matriarchy in an order of an avowedly total kind Daly gives us retrospect as aspiration, since she gives us no historical evidence of the roles her goddesses played in the lives of ancient women. We want to ask what variants of myths *were* known to women in particular times and distinguish between those that might reflect an historical period and those that might constitute timeless psychological phenomena. *Gyn/Ecology* is an authentic and moving account of myth, yet it is in other ways unreal. Daly's Hag-ocracy remains an idealisation set against the social disorder of the present and hence evades the actual and bitter contradictions of women's present day social conditions.

Is Daly's work more than a well-known habit of using the past, the 'good old days', as a stick to beat the present? Her notion is of a new women's ecology, a new collective consciousness, both social and literary, which is capable of taking control of an environment in the manner of the myths of prehistory. This is a resonating image of women's power. But it is perhaps not immediately obvious how there could be a radical, socially constituted myth critique founded on the view that society can shape the ways in which mythical features are encountered in actual life. Myths in literature are transhistorical, collapsing history to a set of repetitive variations.

But if feminist critics overemphasise the Utopian root of literature, often male critics—like Frye and McLuhan, as we have seen—use myth as a displaced version of religion to *avoid* socially realisable goals. In McLuhan, myth becomes the fundamental structure of consciousness. He perceives all things in the world, from television to schools, only in their metaphoric dimension. They become significant, therefore, only within McLuhan's schema rather than as a collection of phenomena in their own right. But if male critics seem to be raising the same epistemological problems as Daly or Pratt, there is something much more invidious in the male embarrassment with social changes. Frye uses myths as *laws* of narrative designating the comic, romantic, tragic or ironic as autonomous verbal structures. Not only that, in the writings of Claude Lévi-Strauss, myths are reduced to one key theme: the Oedipus myth. In *L'Anthropologie structurale* he treats the Oedipus legend at great length, yet its *universal* nature goes virtually unquestioned. This critical obsession with laws, and with a fear of women as represented in myth, is far removed from Daly's or Pratt's explanation for the persistence of myths, not as laws but as dynamic symbols of women's possibilities.

Despite Daly's verbal richness there are problems with myth criticism, both in itself and as a model of literature. As literary criticism it is frequently less than adequate. Annis Pratt admires Fay Weldon as a writer precisely because she, to Pratt, 'envisions an extrasocietal solution' (Pratt, 1982, p. 70). Understandably, then, institutional parameters in Pratt's criticism are less significant than personality ones. Novels of marriage all have the same archetypal images and patterns whether written in the American West or the north of England. Pratt's false universality is evident in her idea, for example, that there is a *single* marriage debate covering the entire period of 1870 to 1910 in fiction. She elides the very dissimilar spinsters of Brontë and May Sinclair to prove an archetype of the spinster as modern sister of pre-patriarchal virgins. Pratt's flight from real history is evident since she avoids class or race. Although she *does* treat some Black novels, she finds merely that 'the limitations of racist stereotypes' 'intensify' gender despair rather than the other way round (Pratt, 1982, p. 66). Myth critics treat race and class oppression as patriarchal 'motifs' to be swept away by a women's culture.

If Pratt's racism is an example of the worst feature of myth criticism, there are other less disturbing features which are equally problematic. Myth critics frequently assume that male myths are the enemy by virtue of their maleness rather than the power a patriarchal system lent them. It seems too sweeping for Pratt to claim, for example, that female authors' explorations of alternatives will always be 'bounded by the all-encompassing, ever-present patriarchal enclosure' (Pratt, 1982, p. 67). She is not able, therefore, to answer the question of whether there is, or can be, a specifically gendered social protest novel. This preoccupation by Daly, Rich and Pratt with defining a female sensibility not only leads them to occasional erroneous generalisations about women's writing but implies that literary identity reflects only the intractibility of maleness and femaleness. In advocating a return to a feminine mythical world these writers ignore the extent to which femaleness functions as a *reflection* of any society's given cultural assumptions. This is politics reduced to biology.

The fact, too, that myth critics offer us a normative model of women in myth is a little disturbing. Pratt seems always to find passive women cut off from autonomy, from self-actualisation and ethical capacity if they are in a male literary milieu. Women, in her criticism, are victim figures either succumbing to madness or marriage or frequently both. Fictional heroines, in other words, are acting out in literary strategies the same acting out of real women entering into a 'psychiatric career' in Phyllis Chesler's terms. Women friendship novels (and Pratt looks at May Sarton) result in excessively punitive denouements. Unlike Nina Auerbach's much more optimistic view of women-bonding, Pratt understands a women's space to be *beyond* the social, not functioning through it. This restricts the meaning of any metaphoric image in myth to its *descriptive* context rather than the social context of each fiction. And to some extent Pratt's method is a self-fulfilling prophecy since she treats the same texts under many different heads.

The study of literature for myth critics then becomes too often a meditation on pyschosexual identity, with social history a mere superfluity. The clearest example of this absence occurs in the discussion of native American myths in *Spiders and Spinsters*. The text is imprecise in its generalisations about tribal culture. Aboriginal North American cultures do not offer similar cultural paradigms. As in many cultures throughout the world, men and women in aboriginal North America have separate and complementary cultures. But unlike those in Western religions, myth and ritual in Amerindian religions are often not intimately related. Myths in native American religions are stories and are not usually expressed as part of rituals. To the native Americans, rituals are the primary mode of religious expression. Hence any Utopian or feminist ideology must be extracted from ritual behaviour not myth. The institution-alisation of native American religious practices and the cessation of matrilineal culture came not from some simple male suppression but as a direct result of an economic shift from a mixed to a nomadic economy at the end of the eighteenth century. It should be impossible, therefore, to discuss native American myth and legend without an awareness both of cultural and social discriminations. Due to the influence of feminism, native traditions are being revived which do centre on women. For example, women are dancing in the Lakota Sun Dance (Paper, 1984).

It is obvious from all of this that myth criticism has its problems. It undercuts its own positions. Myth critics are important to any feminist analysis of the culture of sexuality since sexual politics is the base for their analysis. Male myths, Pratt claims, are really prohibitions against women's free choice of sexuality. But it really is not possible to describe patriarchy in a single rhetorical gesture of repressive uniformity. To represent the cultural embeddedness of sexuality criticism must be able to contain at least the following contexts: the social, history, religious differences and ethnic identities. No one of these contexts is causal, nor is the list complete, but they structure the internal and intimate fantasies of characters in the literature of myth. Above all, gender stereotypes can only be eliminated when we recognise the many different styles of thought, feeling and behaviour represented in the language of myths.

In the long run, myth criticism may be most important not so much to feminist criticism but to the future of women's writing.

The creation of *new* myth in lesbian and science fiction novels, as Joanna Russ says, is an uncharted territory of the psychological and physical potential of women (Russ, 1973). Russ herself, Elana Nachman in *Riverfinger Women* and Bertha Harris in *Lover* create apocalyptic communities of strong, witch women drawing on the myths of Amazons and prehistorical matriarchies.

Clearly Daly might argue that in studying a body of myth we are looking less at its narrative contents than at the universal mental operations which structure it. These mental operations are in a way what myths are about; they are devices for women to think with, ways of organising feminine reality. But myths must not become focal points for virtually unlimited powers of rationalisation by offering only a static picture of actuality. This undercuts the crucial gain of myth criticism—the way it refuses a hierarchy of appraisal and the specious normative laws of aesthetics in direct support of women poets.

Women's spirituality and women's involvement in the institutions of spirituality are today subjects of immense concern to feminists. For we are beginning to recognise the profound and often distressing influence religion has on the role of women in any culture. The more we know about our own culture's dominant myths and the more we know about the myths of cultures other than our own, the more feminism will be able to assess its own spiritual experience and what would culturally best express it. In the end, myth criticism can therefore occupy a central position in that critical future as long as it is not hermetically sealed from history.

6

BLACK AND LESBIAN CRITICISM

Black and lesbian criticism has radically transformed the cultural misogyny of early Black studies (as in Robert Bone's *The Negro Novel in America*) and the misrepresentation of lesbians (as in Ellen Moers' *Literary Women*). Lesbian and Black critics make paths that take similar and innovative directions into feminist culture. This is because when lesbians and Blacks speak of developing a new Black or lesbian culture they must *explicitly* refuse the cultural framework of patriarchy. A feminist struggle against the male tradition in literature is hence directly related by them to their struggle against racism and homophobia.

Yet it is hard not to fear when naming a territory 'Black and lesbian criticism' that the very naming is a dangerous ellision of separate concerns. By appearing to give space to Black and lesbian interests in a single and shared section, will the motifs and concerns of their feminism be seen as 'marginally' similar rather than politically central to the feminist agenda? By implication, will the 'real' world of feminist criticism still be a more established area like psychoanalysis? In arguing that most contemporary feminist criticism does not begin to adequately analyse the experience of Black or lesbian writing we also have to acknowledge that it is not a simple question of its absence in college courses; consequently the task is not one of rendering it visible. On the contrary, the *process* of analysing the historical and contemporary position of Black or lesbian writing, in itself, challenges some of the central categories and assumptions of mainstream feminist criticism.

When writing about contemporary Black or lesbian feminist

criticism, however, it is important to remember that the existence of feminist studies was itself an essential precondition for the growth of this area of criticism. While many Black and lesbian critics have attacked the élitism and homophobia of much white feminist teaching, it remains true that a parallel Black or lesbian criticism has come only after the space created by the study of (white) women's literature and culture. And only recently has there developed a body of Black and lesbian feminist theory whose assumptions could be used by Black and lesbian critics. As Jewelle Gomez has pointed out, the construction of a hitherto invisible entity, 'Black Lesbian', needs a 'believable cultural context' (1983, p. 114). Black and lesbian feminism, as a distinct body of theory and practice, is in the process of development.

Like all movements the feminist arguments of the 1960s and early 1970s led to generalisation. Gayle Rubin invented a general term 'sex/gender system' to try to define the oppression of women separately from other social divisions of class or country. But the problem with large definitions of this kind is that they can lead to artificial universalism. To assume that all women irrespective of background have more in common with each other than with men, as feminists did in the 1960s, lead many to generalise from the limitations of their own white experience and ignore the richness of Black or lesbian lives.

Black women and lesbians needed to speak out about *their* own experiences and to point to some of the differences that could make for a distinctive perspective on the meaning of feminist criticism. On the other hand, of course, no critic could posit the notion of a definitive or *exclusive* Black or lesbian criticism. The regional, national or class differences within each cultural tradition are immense. For example, the experience of the American lesbian Adrienne Rich is not at all the experience of Toni Cade Bambara. Each critic's style, themes and mode of address is insistently and recognisably her own. Rich is imagistic, Bambara aggressively direct. But the criticism and writing of Black women and lesbians have features in common which are very different from white feminism. Indeed, they cannot be considered separately since the lives and politics of both are often found in the one person. Because many important critics, such as Audre Lorde or Barbara Smith, are both Black *and* gay, it would be ludicrous not to consider the commonalities rather than differences of culture. Perhaps the most convincing case for writing in tandem about Black and lesbian feminist criticism is that together they demonstrate subtle and innovative techniques for the future of all feminist criticism.

Some of the patterns of Black and lesbian writing derive inextricably from their positions outside mainstream criticism. Both Black and lesbians start by establishing identifiable and separate literary traditions. For both, the critical text in a curious way calls a culture into existence. For example, the controversy among some Black Americans about Ntozake Shange's choreo poem *For Colored Girls* shows how much the Black community wants to read literature as sexual politics (Smith, 1983, p. 290). Without understanding the tradition of lesbian oppression, for example, criticism cannot deal adequately with a literary theme such as lesbian obliqueness. Both begin from a primary commitment to the political over cultural implications of their writing and the connections between the artistic and the political situations of their communities. In America lesbian discourse has been strongly influenced by the visibility of the Black movement of the mid-1960s as much as by the women's movement in which lesbian feminists now represent an avant-garde. The flowering of lesbian poetry in the 1960s came as much from lesbian involvement in Black civil rights as from involvement in white anti-war movements.

Conceptually, both Black and lesbian critics have in common certain critical themes which are a direct result of the kind of political and social experience both share. The way, for example, that both Adrienne Rich and Alice Walker focus on women as victims not just of physical violence but of a kind of psychic violence is not a simple coincidence, nor is their use of a sexual terminology to express profound cultural motifs accidental. The intimidation of colour or sexuality is part of the collective and historical oppression of Blacks and the suppression of lesbian women. Most important, the language and ideas of these critics is nothing like what white patriarchal criticism demands and teaches. This is why it seems to me that for feminist criticism to grow into a full body of work all feminist critics —white, lesbian and Black—must overcome fears of intrusion or of writing as 'outsiders' and provide overviews of, and access to, all outstanding feminist writing, most of which is now firmly located in Black and lesbian studies. Just as when reading Black women authors those of us who are white have to make an imaginative engagement with a different culture, we need to be similarly clear about reading Black writing and what specific pleasures or lessons it can teach us. As a white critic I am making a political gesture when reading Black writing. There are satisfying analogies between Black and white women's oppression. There is a way in which Black writing focuses the problem of estrangement for all women now. But I also have to emphasise the notion of difference without showing that difference as exotic. Just as one of the dangers of anthropology is the way it invites voyeurism, so it is too easy to use Eurocentric models or definitions. In other words, the central motifs of Black and lesbian criticism need to become pivotal to feminist criticism rather than the other way around.

Yet if the objects and aims of Blacks and lesbians are in a certain sense contingent, it seems fair to consider the two groups tangentially rather than meshed together, since the perspectives each offer can therefore be more systematically considered and extend the boundaries of feminist criticism. The fact that Black and lesbian criticism has come into existence only recently is a reflection of a white-dominated publishing industry, but the new features *are* rejecting the narrowly 'literary' focus of the classical tradition by providing dimensions which interrogate every aspect of criticism for whites *and* Blacks, lesbians *and* heterosexuals. Just as there is always more in common between the languages of the oppressed than the oppressor, so too the very existence of oppression must call into question the definition of what is, and what is not, literary. Domination also determines the *mode* of 'oppressed' writing. The effect of domination on writers is to make them, as it were, twice removed; either they use more irony if writing creatively or, in criticism, they prefer to find mixed modes or an historical ambience for any difficult arguments.

It was the burgeoning interest in Black culture during the 1960s that first created critical interest in the past and culture of the Black women. Until the 1960s Black women were misrepresented or marginalised in most critical texts. Anthologies, even one as late as 1979, either did not mention the work of Black women at all or casually dismissed writers like Zora Hurston from an exclusively male hegemony in letters stemming from W.E.B. DuBois. The writings of Afro-American women are simply invisible in the development of Black literary history by males. In *Toward a Black Feminist Criticism* Barbara Smith describes what she calls the 'white racist pseudo-scholarship' of Robert Bone's *The Negro Novel in America* (Smith, 1977, p. 4).Writers like Bone, she points out, not only misunderstand Black women's experience in sexual as well as in racial terms but frequently pretend they do not know that Black women writers even exist. The effect has been twofold. Black women critics have had to spend valuable time reconstructing the Afro-American literary tradition to include women writers. This has left as a secondary task the investigation and eradication of stereotypes of Black femininity and myths about Black women's roles.

The climate has changed. Audre Lorde, Alice Walker, Barbara Smith, Gloria T. Hull and Toni Cade Bambara, among others, are undertaking the total reassessment of Black literature and literary history centring on the cultural importance of Black women writers. In their research they are also discovering the differences and multiplicities of Black feminine style. Alice Walker in *In Search of Our Mothers' Gardens* (1984) seeks out the autobiographies of Black women, describing them as rich and crucial sources in enlarging the field of Black literature. Slave, and religious conversion, narratives are investigated by Mary Washington (1980) in a putting together of the earliest expressions of a Black female identity. Faced with the demands of literary critics to make Black writers describe their experiences in a universal mode, Audre Lorde (1984) creates an alternative 'intuitive' criticism. This criticism is characterised by the abandonment of conventional critical techniques as she returns to the direct language of Black community women. Barbara Smith (1977) has tried to encompass both the aesthetic mode of formal criticism and the political background of Black women's experience in her account of Black lesbian criticism.

But the first job for Black women critics was to prepare bibliographies. A history of Black women's literature could not be created without a search for all available expressions of Black female identity. In *Black Lesbians: An Annotated Bibliography* J.R. Roberts gathers many hidden, and hitherto scattered, Black writings into one collection. She collects the materials both to encourage a holistic approach to teaching and understanding Black lesbian culture but also to make it at last accessible for feminist readers. To this end Roberts brought her materials to the attention of women's studies instructors by publishing interim selections in *Radical Teacher* and other key periodicals. She divides her text into subject sections—literature and criticism, lives, oppression, periodicals and music—in order to enlarge definitions of what might constitute Black lesbian writing. Roberts had found that the bibliographic situation mirrored the denial and invalidation of Black lesbian experience in general. She sought primarily to make this culture visible rather than, as more formal criticism might do, to define and evaluate its content. But by struggling to reclaim a past, Roberts provides a reconciliation between Black women and their cultural heritage. Black feminism had to go on to provide new critical techniques because Black writing was itself often different from that of whites. Black women playwrights, for example, are not easily defined since their plays range from protest to surreal fantasies in a multidimensional way. In contrast to dramas by whites, Black women, for the most part, have great moral courage.

The articulation of that more difficult criticism comes in Barbara Smith's *Towards a Black Feminist Criticism* (1977). The question now was: What does it mean to be a Black lesbian in America? Smith answered by describing lessons of survival which must come, she says, from learning to relate Black life and literature. In her text Smith explores connections between the politics of feminism, the experience of Black women *and* their literature, in order to evaluate Black lesbian writing for what it says about Black lesbian oppression. Before Smith, Black lesbian studies had not been evaluated. She starts her text, 'I do not know where to begin. Long before I tried to write this I realised that I was attempting something unprecedented' (1977, p. 1).

The problem of audience is obviously a major one for the Black critic. Who is she writing to or for? Black academics?

white academics? Black mothers? All women? By incorporating this political theme as part of their own analysis, Black critics help to explain the amazing achievement a Black writer like Hurston made in establishing a literary voice of any sort. Naming names therefore came first, but it was futile to name without creating a new analytic framework for the names of Black literature. Barbara Smith analyses Toni Morrison's novel *Sula* in order to prove her contention that only a new perspective of Black criticism can expose the actual dimensions of many women's texts. If Smith's technique was formal, it could be grounded in difference because of the body of literature established in bibliographies and accounts of lesbian studies (Berry and McDaniels, 1980). Smith's text answers our need to know: What rituals and symbols are essential to Black women's writing? And by what means does she come to speak? Black feminist literary criticism parallels in its own development the socio-aesthetic problems of Black writers also trying to create a literary identity in the midst of racial and sexual antagonism.

If the Black woman's struggle for a literary voice was supported by a past nurturing female community, in contemporary life Black feminist critics also prefer a common Black voice in literature to the (male) notion of single precursors. Toni Cade Bambara, more than most, has refused the meritocratic frame of reference assumed by traditional literary criticism. She says explicitly 'there is not *the* women or *the* experience or *the* profile' (1979, p. 235). Choosing her Blackness over her gender, Bambara in 'What It Is I Think I'm Doing Anyhow' refuses the 'mentorship' of white women writers such as Kate Chopin, who 'hawk' alienation or suicide in the name of all protesting women. But equally she refuses to name an alternative and favoured writer or one who best 'captures' the Black experience. Bambara feels that these questions of choice come from a false frame of reference dominated by solo voice thinking. In order to do justice to the survival techniques (psychic or economic) of Black women in their community, Black critics *have* to adopt an interdisciplinary approach, mixing accounts of songs, writings and oral history. But in so doing they provide a sustained attack on the neutrality of 'universal' criticism.

If the field of Black feminist criticism is charted by Roberts, its culture described by Smith and its innovative techniques are outlined by Bambara, writers such as Audre Lorde and Alice Walker go on to develop its themes. The study of the Black woman in literature, to Lorde and Walker, is much better seen as part of that larger study of expression in Black behaviour. Black feminist criticism requires, they insist, a radical examination of how language operates in Black women's history, how Black women rework it, and how Black women create and support through language what becomes, for them, a flourishing culture. Audre Lorde argues that the issue of Black matriarchy as a 'social disease' diverted attention in the 1960s from the source of Black women's strength. In conversation with Adrienne Rich she stresses the value of nonverbal communication as an energising force beneath the language (Lorde, 1984). This source of energy Lorde locates in the semiotic—in mother-bonding. Lorde's work is a radical reformation of the boundaries of criticism. Indeed, the point of her 'An Open Letter to Mary Daly' is an attack on what she considers as Daly's narrow 'ecology' since Daly restricts herself in the main to white, Judaeo-Christian imagery. Although valuing difference as a dynamic critical focus, Lorde *is* very concerned that white feminists *should* teach Black studies. But this is dependent on the methods of feminist criticism changing. Since Black poems subtly formulate the hidden implications of Black women's lives, that formulation, Lorde suggests, will only be understood critically in hidden 'bubbles' rather than in the linear step-by-step approach of traditional criticism. So grammar, for example, Lorde describes as a 'process', with tenses a way of 'ordering the chaos around time' (1984, p. 95). This is a very original and appropriate perspective for Black literature. Indeed, the psychic history of Black women writers should have a particular significance for critics because writers in the Black female literary tradition have consistently chosen to appear in their own texts in particular ways. When reading slave narratives, for example, we have to deal with their multi-functional nature since they are neither solely literary nor solely history. The teaching writings of Anna J. Cooper, as in *A Voice from the South by a Black Woman of the South* (1892), and the slave stories of Sylvia DuBois and Sojourner Truth are best read in this way.

In 'Uses of the Erotic: The Erotic as Power' Lorde redefines the role of the erotic in literature in opposition to abusive pornography. The erotic, to Lorde, is a life-giving force which can be a source of power, change and creativity. It is our silences, Lorde says, which immobilise us not our differences. This, conceptually, is not far removed from the easy generalisations of much post-war Reichian and libertarian writing. But, for Lorde, the *way* to speak is not in the male mode of documentation or realism. While conscious that feminists (including Adrienne Rich) are suspicious of this apparent return to a place of total intuition, to 'the Black mother in each of us', Lorde fears the documentary can only analyse perceptions not create them. She prefers to use anthropology in her search for an intuitive voice and alternative culture for Black women.

Was it feasible for Black women writers to assert another kind of consciousness? Is the approach too individualistic—the substitution of 'private' psychological needs over the social and historical? The accusation reflects a radical misunderstanding of contemporary Black criticism. There is indeed a real problem about how the history and oppression of Black women is related to their psychology, and one point of Lorde's writings is to make it possible for us to think that relation through in cultural terms. What Lorde is producing, indeed, is an alternative psycho/literary critique which helps eradicate the social model of Black women produced in the 1960s. Several contemporary writers including Adrienne Rich and Alice Walker, as well as Lorde, have described the bond between themselves and their mothers as an alternative and inspirating source of their aesthetic. In sociology, by identifying the institution of the family as a source of oppression for women, white feminists revealed their cultural and racial myopia since at least in Britain it is conservative legislation which works to separate Black families. In literature, by citing allegiance to their mothers, Black American women move closer to African ancestry and away from the white-dominated intellectual context of American academia. Mother myths have a great power and are a continuing part of many African cultures where motherhood is enshrined and traditionally venerated. In criticism the focus permits a writer such as Walker to introduce her autobiography into the critical text, and it helps to eradicate concepts like the 'black exotic' which engender no such live negotiations for American Black women.

Alice Walker's 'mode' of negotiation is to rediscover Black women writers. In her essay 'Zora Neale Hurston: A Cautionary Tale and a Partisan View' Walker describes what reading about Hurston taught her of her own cultural inheritance. When reading Black writers we can capture, Walker feels, all the stories Blacks had forgotten. More important, for Walker, was the positive picture created by Hurston's sense of Blacks as complex, undiminished human beings not as the 'victim' figures so often found in white criticism. Walker is right and it is all the sadder that Hurston's obscurity came as a direct result of the white critical preference for, and acclaim of, Richard Wright's 'protest' writing. For Walker, Black women's intuition that everything is inhabited by a spirit is no stranger than the work of many scientists discovering that flowers have emotions. Against this Black flexibility, white feminist criticism appears somewhat racist and limited. Wittily deprecating the books of Patricia Meyer Spacks, author of *The Female Imagination*, with whom Walker once shared an office, Walker wonders at Spacks' ignorance of Black writing. If the white female imagination refuses to construct theories about (Black) experiences, how can she, Walker ironically asks, theorise about the Brontës in nineteenth-century Yorkshire.

But, although Alice Walker enlarges the terrain of Black feminist criticism by finding out how contemporary themes derive from slave narratives, or herself writing literary criticism as story, as autobiographical narrative, her mode is yet firmly linked to white aesthetics. Her novel *The Colour Purple* uses the schematic simplicity of Conrad's *Heart of Darkness*. Similarly, in some ways Walker's techniques parallel the concerns of the white criticism that she disparages. First Walker has learnt her lessons of feminist criticism from Virginia Woolf. She continually rewrites Woolf by substituting Black for white names in quotations from Woolf. Alice Walker has also edited a collection of Black autobiographies, written by Southern women during a Headstart programme, adding an introductory letter full of her own fears of writing *about* women which is very like Virginia Woolf's earlier introduction to the lives of the Women's Co-operative Guild (Walker, 1984, p. 22). The topics and forms of Walker's criticism also depend on other white forerunners.

Walker's very beautiful account of her mother's garden, which answered for her mother the question of what it meant to be a Black artist, closely resembles Colette's famous paean to *her* mother and the alternative natural resources of French women's culture. But if themes in Black criticism overlap themes presented in the writings of white women writers, Walker *has* isolated an illuminating theme which is that of the Black woman as frustrated artist. Walker's strength comes perhaps less from her focus than from her stance pithily summed up in a comment by C.L.R. James that Alice Walker is 'not seeking to impress white people at all' (James, 1979, p. 259).

What Smith, Lorde and Walker have established is a way of putting aside the limited confines of white feminist criticism and yet creating foci and techniques that could serve the experiences and needs of all feminist women. Simply, Black women cannot be white women with colour. The feminist criticism of white women cannot define or lead Black feminism. In the writings of Smith, Lorde and Walker a dialogue begins which can help feminist criticism reconsider its emphasis on psychoanalysis and literary history and move into an expanded notion of feminist culture.

Just as Black feminists talk about how criticism can function in a positive and visionary way for feminism, so lesbian criticism shares some of that vision. It begins with the same premise: that for lesbians, just as for Blacks, criticism cannot be accommodated in heterosexist male forms. Many lesbian articles are deliberately *not* in traditional essay form, which indicates that, like Black feminism, the field is continually reworking and adapting. Expressing the inexpressible is the aim of Susan Griffin. In 'Thoughts on Writing' she uses a diary form to write criticism about her own 'literature'. Griffin begins the day wondering if the voice of the 'Other' in society (lesbian or Black) takes on in form 'the meaning of the voice of poetry' (Griffin, 1980, p. 115). For Toni Cade Bambara, the use of psychic phenomena is a passport to forms of knowledge for which we, as yet, have no adequate critical vocabulary (Smith, 1983). In other words, that lesbians or Blacks, as outsiders, have some privileged perception (Griffin calls this 'synchronisities'), a larger knowledge not available to those working in traditional modes. Lesbian critics, like Black feminists, had to develop a lesbian literary tradition before they could establish lesbian critical techniques. The perplexing question this task immediately encounters is how to define lesbianism. In this, literary critics were supported by the development of lesbian theory in the early 1970s, at least in America and France. Lesbian theorists Ti-Grace Atkinson and Charlotte Bunch were arguing that lesbians were the new radicals of feminism. A lesbian was a woman who believed in the primacy of women. It was a source, for her, of an alternative model of female identity. More than that, as women-identified women, lesbians were the norm of female experience and heterosexism an abnormal oppression. The logic of this radical theory was clear. Only lesbians could provide a fully adequate women-centred analysis. The theorists gave lesbian literary critics firm objectives. The reality of lesbian experience in literature needed to be uncovered and made part of all women's history.

As before, bibliographies provided pioneering collections of essential value to lesbians researching their literature and wanting to create an alternative canon. Barbara Greir in *The Lesbian in Literature: A Bibliography* provided the first major resource for lesbian scholars and readers. Greir reviewed books for the lesbian periodical *The Ladder* and it was in essays in this and the other feminist journals *Sinister Wisdom, Chrysalis, Conditions* and *Signs* that introductions began to appear. *Conditions* published early interviews with Adrienne Rich who (as we shall see later) offers the most extensive definition of lesbianism as 'woman-identified experience'.

Contributors to lesbian studies emphasised as a first priority the exploration of lesbian literary history. Elly Bulkin in her collections of *Lesbian Fiction* and *Lesbian Poetry* tries to establish a long tradition of lesbian writing starting with Octave Thanet in the 1880s. Bulkin's texts are good accounts, in the periodic mode, of the cultural context and political climate of particular decades like the 1930s. The history of lesbianism receives its most extensive overview, however, with Lillian Faderman's *Surpassing the Love of Men: Romantic Friendship and Love Between Women from the Renaissance to the Present* (1981). As her title implies, Faderman recounts the history of four hundred years of lesbian literature. She 'rescues' many women writers such as

Mary Wollstonecraft and Anna Seward from heterosexuality and ranges across fiction and poetry to include popular magazine stories of the early twentieth century.

Faderman's work earned her many admirers but also a great deal of criticism. The attacks focused on Faderman's wish to detach lesbian culture from the more contemporary definition of lesbianism which centralises sexual contact. Sonja Ruehl and others wanted Faderman to articulate what is *specific* about the experience and oppression of lesbians which, to Ruehl and others, was in the main sexual practice (Ruehl, 1983). But not only does Faderman establish a lesbian tradition by reclaiming past writers, she also enlarges the domain of lesbianism *as* a sexual practice by making lesbian literary history respectable, which makes it possible for more women to think imaginatively about lesbianism. To write lesbian literary history at all requires the exploration of meanings and definitions of a more totalising lesbianism. With Faderman lesbian literary history becomes lesbian criticism since she undertakes that task (inherent in all critical activity) which is to provide clear evaluations and discriminations about writers.

Margaret Cruikshank builds on these critiques and the safe space of burgeoning women's studies programmes in her extensive collection of teaching materials *Lesbian Studies.* The book is an anthology of lesbian perspectives on psychology, sociology and history as well as literature. She demonstrates the range of academic work in lesbian studies but also contextualises that range by showing the connections many contributors made between their lives and work. For Cruikshank the feminist curriculum had challenged the sexist myth of 'woman as Other' but left underexamined the idea of the 'lesbian as Other'. Literature and literary criticism is Cruikshank's main focus because, as she explains, nearly all the sample syllabuses sent to her were for literature courses. The humanities, and hence literary criticism, have therefore played an important role in lesbian pedagogy.

If lesbian criticism begins with establishing the lesbian text, that act is not just an empirical documentation about certain kinds of writing. Lesbian criticism can suggest universal notions about the nature of criticism itself. Jane Rule in *Lesbian Images* gives chronological accounts of the writing careers and relationships of Gertrude Stein, Ivy Compton-Burnett, Violette Leduc, May Sarton and Maureen Duffy, among many others. Yet, although relying on biography, Rule continually makes statements about lesbian history as if it were a series of discourses. Her book is both about models of lesbianism *and* about the concepts and images which encode them. Criticism, like any process of writing, works by difference; but lesbian critics could show difference both as a *concept*, something that can be *thought*, and as a text which 'shows' us something new about the nature of signification.

All literature, for lesbian critics, is continually threatening to break down into sub-text and escape any single meaning which tries to contain it. Lesbian criticism depends for its existence on rejecting the notion of a coherent static interpretation. It moves us, in other words, from realism to a style of thought at once challenging, if ambiguous. By making 'lesbian' a literary construct, criticism could serve as a convenient centre around which to gravitate a series of contradictory but potentially metonymic ideas about women. For example, just as some lesbian writers like Gertrude Stein use cryptic codes to create allegorical meanings, so lesbian criticism can mix dreams and journalism to subvert homophobic vocabulary, as Jill Johnston shows in *Lesbian Nation*.

The primary job of lesbian criticism was to establish a lesbian literary tradition. But, as with Black feminism, when this was accomplished, other foci began to emerge. Many lesbian critics are questioning the rhetorical status of each text in their technical concern with imagery, symbols and stereotypes of lesbians. That development can best be illustrated through an account of lesbianism as represented in *The Ladder*, just as the best sources for Black research are periodicals supporting abolitionism. Appearing from 1956 to 1972 this periodical was the most explicit, and often the only available, commentary on lesbian culture of the period. As the key outlet for lesbian criticism and philosophy it provides a crucial indicator of the way lesbian, like Black, criticism has become more theoretical as it has become more feminist.

At first, contributors to *The Ladder* avoided specifically feminist concerns. Authors typically used male pronouns and assumed that male and female homosexuality were subject to the same cultural or social process. The growing commitment of many lesbians to feminism led, in *The Ladder*, to redefinitions and vocabulary changes in its lesbian criticism (Brown, 1970). Feminism provided a vocabulary of choice. If sexuality could be freely or unconsciously chosen, so too the critical text could move from identifying lesbian in relation to a male world (and therefore a male literary tradition) to a more problematic and exciting account of literary creativity. Lesbian critics were able to attack the language and culture of patriarchal criticism with overtly politicised alternatives. What emerges from *The Ladder* is a clear relation of mode of representation to what can be represented and of both to the larger world of feminist criticism.

The critical strategy was now to invent forms and imagery compatible with this emerging lesbian sensibility. The relation of sexual and textual politics in lesbian criticism and writing liberated texts sometimes (or, for Monique Wittig, always liberated texts) from conventional uses of language. Jane Rule cites many devices used by lesbian writers, from mirror imagery to open endings, by which they could subvert characterisation and replace conventional realism with double meanings. A new technical area was being explored by lesbian writers in order to strip lesbian stereotypes of their power and control in popular culture and literary myth.

It was precisely the outright refusal of patriarchy by lesbian feminists which, to Faderman, forced writers to try stylistic experiments for which she, and other critics, were now providing a more sophisticated criticism. In order that lesbians could identify with positive role models, Faderman says, they need to talk about style. The surveys, by lesbian critics, of alternative narrative techniques in lesbian literature was suggested by the idea that idiosyncratic or *chosen* modes of being needed new ways of describing prototypes or paradigms. Fantasies, kinds of imagery or particular modes of writing could now be identified as lesbian without their authors having ever explicitly written about lesbianism at all. What Rule, Faderman, Cruikshank and others were proving very successfully was the existence of literary configurations which could provide a lesbian typology. Imagery of mirrors or enclosed spaces was related to the growth and decline of particular stereotypes;

lesbian literary histories were establishing the key texts of lesbian culture and paying particular attention to the inter-mixture of the popular with the avant-garde; a lesbian discourse was being defined as having a specific and *different* relation to conventional language.

The lesbian should, to Faderman, choose a different mode to other literary formations. If the coming out story is the lesbian myth of origins, then salient fictional genres such as the novel of development take on a new importance. The descriptions by Cruikshank of the way lesbian writers were using the gothic to escape some of the linear, social restrictions of novel form assume that lesbians were *choosing* to be literary lesbians as they were choosing lesbian sexuality in contemporary life. Lesbian criticism has now described roles, forms and techniques which could be important strategies of resistance for *all* feminist critics in subverting male literary silences.

Lesbian criticism, like the favoured lesbian novel of Utopia, is a vision of the future. Just as fiction writers Alice B. Sheldon (pseudonym James Tiptree Jr.) in 'With Delicate Mad Hands' (1981) and Joanna Russ in *The Female Man* (1975) are creating new forms of sexuality, so lesbian critics are changing the configurations of criticism. Only lesbians, claim Audre Lorde and Adrienne Rich, could transmit, in literature or in criticism a cogent if incoherent image of the feminist women. 'Lesbianism' is as much a textual strategy against the norms of literary discourse as it is a means of subverting sexual stereotypes in everyday life. Lesbian identity is not subsumed into feminism but kept whole within it along with Black or Jew—as a preferred kind of identity.

Black and lesbian critics have engendered along with their new typologies a deep distrust of existing critical and ideological systems. Jane Rule and Monique Wittig, just as Barbara Smith or Audre Lorde, are writers who take very seriously this new relation of politics and literature. Black critics, as lesbian critics, are concerned both with politics in texts and the politics and possibilities of the text itself. A separate Black and separate lesbian identity provides feminist criticism with a cutting edge and innovatory techniques which enable it to move ahead. The ultimate value of both kinds of criticism is that they move outside of classical academic histories of literature by concentrating on racial and sexual imagery from *the point of view* of women-identified women. We begin to see writing in terms of struggles and polarities—of Black/white, lesbian/heterosexual. Instead of some socio-historical *découpage*, Black and lesbian critics prove that authors or texts can be more radically grouped according to affinities than historical periods. Lesbianism and Black studies provide prisms through which we can question white heterosexual academia about its literary categories, about the meaning of its literary techniques and, in particular, about the meaning of the institution of literature itself in its relation to women.

PART II

7

VIRGINIA WOOLF

Virginia Woolf was the first woman writer to write a female aesthetic. Her recognition that literature, particularly its syntax and address, is determined by the gender of the author is what makes her eligible to be called a feminist. The confirmation of that feminism comes in her demand for a new critical tradition for women writers and readers, in her ideas of difference, and her triumphant battle with the techniques of her critic father, among others. Virginia Woolf rewrote literary history to include forgotten women. Any rewriting of history necessarily includes redefinitions of what *is* appropriate literature for history to record. So Woolf charted a new territory where women could relate to women writers of the past by means of a critical language which reflected female experience. The autonomy of women's writing depends on subverting the terms set out by men. Woolf's criticism is shaped by her relation to her father and to writers like Lytton Strachey. The topics, form, even the vocabulary that she uses, come from her assimilation and transcendence of these male critics.

Criticism about Woolf has polarised between those critics who prefer to tie her into modernism and those interested in her sociopolitical concerns.

Until the 1980s Woolf's reputation was established as a writer of artful poetic prose. She was placed firmly within the circles and squares of Bloomsbury as a 'difficult' writer—an artist obsessed with subjective consciousness.[1] This was the angle of vision of *Scrutiny* and Q.D. Leavis. Leavis was careful to conclude that although *To the Lighthouse* is a beautifully constructed work of art . . . The reader is repaid by none of the obvious satisfactions he expects from a novel—no friendly characters . . . He is dimly aware of having missed the point and feels cheated' (Q.D. Leavis, 1979, p. 61). Only the brilliant and trained critic, presumably Leavis herself, could appreciate or even understand Woolf's prose.

Nearer to us in time are critics like Michael Rosenthal, who tells us that Woolf had no serious interest in literary criticism, or Herbert Marder, whose trick is to subsume Woolf's criticism into her novels, where the 'real' locus of art is meant to be. Feminists, like Jane Marcus, counter this paternal perspective by describing how Woolf's literary criticism takes social and political factors into consideration.[2]

Although welcome as a rejection of privileged modes of discourse, this feminist challenge has more to do with changes in our own literary sensibility than with Woolf. There are many feminist critics who prefer to read literature for its messages rather than its aesthetics. The aesthetic and the social interpretations of Woolf's work are two distorting mirrors. Woolf herself faced this dilemma in her writing. Her solution was to create a mixed mode of criticism which can only be successfully read by a woman reader.

It is not generally recognised that Virginia Woolf's criticism encodes in its style the questions she is posing in her content. Although the themes and ideas she discussed—of female friendship and the representation of women—are those that feminists regard as central to feminist theory, it is not only the questions that she wrestled with and answers that she gave us which make Virginia Woolf feminist. It is Virginia Woolf's continuing dialogue with the dead Leslie Stephen, her father, that is the source of her feminism. It is in the very structure of her discourse that she engages in a feminist battle with her father and with her male friends.

Virginia Woolf was intermittently a novelist but continually a critic. She wrote over 500 critical reviews and essays, which are a mixture of autobiography and conjectures on the craft of writing and literary history. She supervised a printing press, the Hogarth Press, making critical judgements about publishing. She financed her novels with her criticism. Even before writing novels, she reviewed for *The Times Literary Supplement*, building up an expert knowledge of literary history in order to write herself into, and free from, the critical past. As we might expect, she developed clear and interesting ideas about the aims and function of criticism.

The First and Second *Common Reader* reveal an astonishing range of reading which encompasses Montaigne, Burke, Jeremy Taylor, Sir Thomas Brown and Lamb, as well as women writers. But the spread of Woolf's literary criticism is not merely there as a series of rhetorical gestures—of proofs to male critics that Woolf understood the conventions. The point of Woolf's reading was to understand literary conventions in order to change them. As *Three Guineas* makes clear, she understood the nonsense of 'neutral' criticism and the book is a defiant exposure of the social and sexual ideology implicit in male conventions. Males were the custodians of critical discourse. Virginia Woolf's task was to understand, to subvert and redefine the female subject in the literary field.

In book reviews she could begin to work out her own criteria of the purposes, aims and methods of literature. Woolf took her criticism very seriously. Both essays and reviews were heavily revised, often going into several drafts before being edited into her collections. Although she did not call her essays 'criticism' until 1927 (when reviewing Ernest Hemingway's *Men Without Women*) one way to challenge literary hierarchies was to be very flexible about what one includes and excludes. As we read through her essays we can see that Woolf selects, and most admires, those critics who were, in some senses, *outside* the academic tradition. Hazlitt's writings she finds exciting because they initiate and inspire rather than prove 'conclusive and complete'. Woolf quotes with glee Hazlitt's comment, ' "You will hear more good things on the outside of a stage-coach from London to Oxford, than if you were to pass a twelve-month with the undergraduates or heads of colleges of that famous University" ' (Woolf, 1944, p. 138). She prefers Butler too, because he was an 'amateur' and had achieved that very difficult task of both freeing himself from the tradition *and* remaining original (Woolf, 1965a, p. 30).

What we have to ask, then, is whether her new areas of enquiry are feminist criticism? Only a minority of Virginia Woolf's writings are directly on women authors. In these Woolf deals directly with questions relevant to feminism. 'What role does class play in creating different categories and styles of women writers?' and 'Are women essentially different from men?' There are two long essays solely about women's writing and lives: *A Room of One's Own* and *Three Guineas*. Yet it would be wrong to assume either that we should read Woolf *only* through the prisms of those, more overtly feminist pieces, or that her feminist criticism is only likely to be found in her writings on women. The crucial question is rather, does Virginia Woolf write a feminist *écriture* which is both ideologically feminist *and* written in a mode which is itself a feminist signature?

But first, what ideas does Woolf contribute to feminist theory? She has a good deal to say about the relation of literature to women's lives. In turn she describes how critical analysis can help women answer questions about our bodies, about our consciousness, and what roles literature and women might take in contemporary and future society. The representation of women, and then definitions of femininity and difference, Woolf uses as organising themes in her search through literature for techniques she could select for a female aesthetic.

Woolf's most condensed and effective metaphor of sexual politics is in *A Room of One's Own*. Woolf describes women as 'looking glasses possessing the magic and delicious power of reflecting the figure of man at twice its natural size' (1945, p. 31). Woolf is not saying simply that men need women as passive spectators (although 'reflect' implies passivity), but that men as well as women are misrepresented. Hence the gender positions in society, and differences between men and women *in* society, are constructed, not essential.

Woolf's critics tend to ignore the complexity of Woolf's point. It occurs in a run-on passage describing men's dependence on women. Woolf's men here are generalised, impersonal patriarchs. Men are 'they', positioned against the precise life-style of the woman narrator enjoying her 'five shillings and ninepence' lunch. The chapter ends with a future of nursemaids who heave coal and shopwomen who drive engines. Just as in her fiction—for example, in *Mrs Dalloway*—'masculinity' is as much a construct as 'femininity', so Woolf says that men and women *do* write in different ways. It was not to be a matter of lexicographical rigidity. Woolf explores the suggestion that women writers—one example is George Eliot—may be unable to effectively characterise men. Men and women may write different kinds of sentences. In 'Women Novelists' Woolf thinks that the sex of an author is clear from the very first words of a novel. Our feminine style is shaped, as Woolf elaborates in 'Women and Fiction', by our values and experience, which are different from men. A woman makes serious what appears insignificant to a man, and trivialises what is to him important. In the essay 'Professions for Women' we can pin down Woolf's ambiguity about 'difference'. She claims women can, and should, write unconsciously and will therefore have the experience 'far commoner with women writers than with men' of the line and imagination running free.

What prevents that unconscious self-revelation is that much female experience—in particular, the psyche and 'passions'— must be hidden. Virginia Woolf's 'ambiguity' might then be more a wish to reconcile these two selves in criticism—a socially constructed woman who yet has some essential femininity. In *A Room of One's Own* Woolf writes about the two selves of real and invented women. The book is a cultural history of the material and psychological constraints of Jane Austen, Charlotte Brontë and Shakespeare's sister. Charlotte Brontë was 'foolish' to sell the copyright of her novel for £1,500 when she could have spent an annual income from royalties extending her social and cultural experience. Yet Woolf argues for a larger sense of what makes a literary tradition than simply that more money for women might mean more, or better, books. Woolf dramatises the argument in her style. The text is full of adjectival exaggeration. Everything is 'prodigiously difficult' for women writers.

Writing is affected by material conditions in several directions. Women, like Shakespeare's sister, could not write because they were deprived of access to education and hence culture. Women are affected differently in different ages. Woolf is careful to show the interaction between historical changes in education and income and the opportunities for women writers. Aphra Behn was an important and significant writer because she was the first to earn money, as well as because she wrote interesting plays.

But, although Woolf consistently describes the social situations of men and women writers, and hence argues that writing is a product of historical circumstances, there are other angles and turns in her ideology. Woolf's compass, deliberately I think, never measures the degree to which literature is grounded in social conditions. Nor is society the base, or even the starting point, for many of her descriptions of writing production. It is because men controlled and dictated the *cultural* values of the everyday life of Charlotte Brontë, for example, not just, or not only, because they subordinated her financially, that she created the twisted Rochester. Material conditions are only a narrow angle in the circle of cultural formation.

Woolf does make a very direct connection between writing forms (or *choice* of genre) and social life but never reduces the one to the other. Women's sensibility, she says, had been educated for hundreds of years in the sitting room. It was a training in the observation of character and the analysis of emotion more suited, Woolf saw, to the production of novels than poetry.

In 'Women and Fiction' Woolf describes her own need for knowledge about the material conditions of the average woman—the number of her children, her housework, her room. 'The extraordinary woman depends on the ordinary woman'. But if knowledge of material conditions relates to the *production* of writing, it does not help us to criteria of value *within* the process of writing. Money might enable a woman to write or not to write, but material conditions alone do not determine what makes her a good or a bad writer.

In *Jane Eyre* and *Wuthering Heights* Woolf hints at an alternative feminist metaphysics which takes us further than her more straightforward feminist economic arguments. Woolf wants Emily Brontë to 'tear up all that we know human beings by, and fill those unrecognisable transparences with such a gust of life that they transcend reality. Hers, then is the rarest of all powers. She could free life from its dependence on facts . . .' (Woolf, 1979, p. 132). To understand what Woolf means in this passage we need to rescue Woolf from sociology and reach some understanding of her aesthetic position.

Virginia Woolf's preoccupation with this theme is evident in the way she continually chose books to review, like *The Tunnel*, which would enable her to develop her ideas about this difficult relation between the material and the creative in women's lives. Relating women's 'transparences' to reality exercises Woolf throughout her essays. In 'Romance and the Heart', for example, she sympathises with Dorothy Richardson. 'We want to be rid of realism, to penetrate without its help into the regions beneath it' (Woolf, 1979, p. 191).

To create a 'sophisticated' and, for us, a feminist criticism, Woolf needed to develop her ideas of realism and emotions both in relation to the material evidence of a writer's everyday life and, more importantly, in relation to the possibility of giving emotions formal significance. How was she to give a gust of life to women's 'unrecognisable transparences' and yet be factually credible? We have to be very careful with the term 'materialism' since our contemporary usage is very different from the meaning that Woolf, and her circle of Bloomsbury friends, understood. Reality and consciousness are not unproblematic categories. Woolf's definitions of critical motifs like 'experience', 'emotions', 'consciousness' can only make sense when read against other discourses of her time.

Women writers, like women readers, would succeed in developing a 'new kind of unconsciousness' only with the support of a coherent aesthetics. Virginia Woolf developed this aesthetics by taking and using terms and techniques from contemporary philosophy. If her ideas about women's nature and material means might be feminist, Woolf describes them in imagery drawn from (male) philosophy. It is G.E. Moore's writings in particular which give a framework to Woolf's architecture. Moore had an impact on all the Bloomsbury writers. In the opening scene of *The Longest Journey* E.M. Forster chooses Moore's example of a table to fictionalise one of the many Cambridge debates about the reality of perception. Moore's influence on Woolf was no less direct; for example, the table image recurs in *To The Lighthouse*, but his ideas took longer to emerge in her work. Woolf's association with Moore lasted throughout her life, from first reading *Principia Ethica* in 1908, to 1940 when she describes looking out of the window at Desmond and Moore 'talking under the apple trees' (Woolf, 1959, p. 332).

Moore's concepts of objects and consciousness recur in

Woolf's essay 'Modern Fiction' and provide her, and us, with a plausible model for feminist criticism. In 'A Refutation of Idealism' Moore states that consciousness (or what he called 'mind') is distinct from objects (or what we might call 'material life'). Neither is dependent on one another, nor can be reduced to one another. Yet there were moments, which Moore called 'diaphanous', when, through introspection, we might become aware of their interaction. People who were unable to become aware were 'materialists' (Moore, 1948). So when in 'Modern Fiction' Woolf attacks Arnold Bennett, H.G. Wells and Galsworthy as 'materialists', what she meant by materialism is not that Wells or Bennett might think culture depended on material conditions but that they, *aesthetically*, were lost in social detail or objects.

The implications for literature and for feminist criticism are clear. Criticism, epistemologically, will describe 'objects' (the social history of women writers or working women). Also, and equal in importance, it will describe the processes of consciousness of those women—their transparences. The linkage between the two is in an aware observer—a heightened and introspective narrator. In other words, Virginia Woolf in her role as a feminist intellectual. Social life and consciousness *are* distinct but art can bring them together. The representation of women's consciousness is tangential to the representation of their social lives. One is not dependent on the other. But the writer and critic has to establish in her *mode* of criticism that she is the right kind of introspective thinker. Hence Woolf's need for a viable literary tradition, for a range of epistemological models to prove her training. And hence Woolf's need for continuing insertions into the very discourse of criticism of autobiographical 'moments' of self-awareness to show us that she has 'seen'. Woolf's final achievement, as a feminist critic, was to negotiate a space for a self-aware woman reader. It was a very difficult position for Woolf to negotiate for herself. It necessitated a dual role for criticism, a continual forwards and backwards journey in the narrator's mind between social reality and the representation of women's emotions. It is against this background that we can understand Woolf's impatience with the critical tradition, with materialist political action, or with stereotypes of feminine or masculine consciousness.

In 1923, looking through her essays to prepare them for the *Common Readers*, Woolf felt that she could devise a new method, 'some simpler, subtler, closer means of writing about books, as about people' (1944, p. 177). It would need a 'theory of fiction. The one I have in view is about *perspective*' (1944, p.83). The novels recapitulate the problem. Woolf continually experiments with perspective, with the aware observer. In *The Waves* soliloquy is mixed with narrative and lyric prose. In *The Years* Woolf uses voices of different generations. *Between The Acts* exemplifies in its structure the impossibility of distinguishing fictions and facts. Woolf continually experiments with viewpoint to give meaning to the simultaneity of experience. It was a deliberately self-conscious technique replicated in the interrogative mode of her criticism.[3] If her criticism is sometimes like the education of 'talk' that Helen proposes for Rachel in *The Voyage Out*, how did Virginia Woolf bring together her ideological and aesthetic notions? In *The Common Reader* and her Introductory Letter to *Life as We Have Known It* Woolf left us the best examples of her critical mode. These will need careful attention, but before turning to those texts we can see that they are peaks growing out of a whole territory of criticism. Woolf's apparent disregard for close linguistic analysis and her dislike of authoritarian criticism means that we have to read her essays impressionistically ourselves. Her style is often epistolary, combining indirection with sudden polemical outbursts. In the Preface to the *Common Reader* (1944) Woolf explained that her choice of title was appropriate for a reader who reads for pleasure and who wants to create 'out of whatever odds and ends he can come by, some kind of whole'.

By writing odds and ends of criticism Woolf hoped to 'escape from the box' of social class and, by experimenting, escape from the straitjacket of literary convention. Woolf wrote about other writers as a way of beginning to write about herself. Her essay on Thomas Hardy may appear to be a conventional assessment of a novelist's career, but her description of Hardy is more revealing as a self-assessment. Woolf admires Hardy because he is an 'unconscious writer' with 'moments of vision' (1944, p.187). In 'How Should One Read a Book?', Woolf says, the trick is to become a writer oneself—to be a fellow-worker and accomplice of the author. Creating a history of literature becomes like establishing friendships—knocking on the doors of particular writers. The 'odds and ends' are not just Woolf's critical mode. They should, she feels, become the way we read. We need to read widely, to include 'rubbish-reading' and to be intimate with those poets and novelists we admire.

There were mistakes, even errors, not so much of judgement but of conservatism. For example, Woolf attacks Olive Schreiner in **much** the way male critics frequently attack women writers. Some of Virginia Woolf's notions might be called regressive. She stays frequently with organic notions of progess and evolution. Writing will change as the 'Duke and the agricultural labourer . . . died out completely as the bustard and the wild cat' (Woolf, 1944, p. 167). Some of her points are still within a liberal ideal of continual social progress.

But the gains compensate for problems. Woolf is constantly searching for new sources of literary form. Madame de Sévigné's letters were one. They created 'a vast open space' in literature (Woolf, 1965b, p. 48). Writers could find creative facts *outside* of literature in biographies, 'the fertile fact; the fact that suggests and engenders' (Woolf, 1965b, p. 169). Yet none of these notions— the idea of mixed modes, the reader in the text, alternative genres—are in themselves particularly feminist. Many could be characterised as modernist. What makes them feminist is Woolf's ability to use them to explore sexual difference.

It seems to me that one of the crucial features of the odds and ends of criticism Woolf collects is precisely her ability to make gender difference both part of the *process* of writing and a part of the social production of literature. It is in Woolf's metaphor of the Duchess of Newcastle, her social freedom and literary style simultaneously represented in her flowing in and out of rooms. It is Woolf seizing on Mary Wollstonecraft's own domestic imagery with her husband only 'a convenient part of the furniture of the house' (Woolf, 1979, p. 102).

Woolf's chief attempt to match apparently random definitions of women to an appropriate syntactical representation of gender is in *A Room of One's Own*. Women should not be defined in terms of some unitary quality, says Woolf, but described as a bundle of contradictory characteristics.

Gender difference was clearly part of the texture of literary form, Woolf says, in her essay on George Meredith. Virginia

Woolf wrote about both male and female writers in order to codify gender difference. She continually explores the gender dimension of language in order to establish a feminist epistemology. When comparing Meredith with Emily Brontë, Woolf describes the interaction of gender, sexuality and literary language. The difference between Meredith and Brontë, Woolf states, is the difference between a male poet-novelist and a female poet-novelist. As a male, Meredith identified each character with one single passion and therefore they become 'abstract' (Woolf, 1979, p. 177). Emily Brontë, on the other hand, could steep her world in passion. Woolf suggests that because Brontë is a woman, she can invest the whole scene and social structure of her fiction with notions of lyrical sexuality. Yet one could qualify Woolf's remarks about gender and the passions by reference to any novel of D.H. Lawrence. Virginia Woolf knew, of course, the work of male modernists and her revisions of this patriarchal, conservative sexuality are most explicit in *Orlando*.

Feminist criticism is not only a matter, however, of understanding how a woman writer writes differently or how she creates a different world. Feminist criticism has to *respond* to women writers in a different way from men. In her essay 'Madame de Sévigné' Woolf is beginning to give us epistemological techniques to build a feminist aesthetics. One is to emphasise the personal pronoun when writing about women. Another is to use a more complex conception of time. 'It is natural to use the present tense, because we live in her presence' (Woolf, 1965b, p.50). Time is not fixed or one-dimensional in woman's work. Only a woman critic, and perhaps only a feminist, would want to be so conscious of the subtleties of feminine rhythm and apparent discontinuities of women's topics: 'Something struck off in a flash'.

What are the mode and manner of Woolf's feminist criticism? The first 'impression' is Woolf's choice of address. In her easy intimacy with us Woolf makes everything reassuringly and carefully significant because she is always asking *herself* 'What is significant?' and 'What does this mean?'. Like the created character of Woolf in her text we cumulatively and heuristically see significance gradually.

A good example in *The Second Common Reader* is the centenary account of George Meredith.

And since the first novel is always apt to be an unguarded one, where the author displays his gifts without knowing how to dispose of them to the best advantage, we may do well to open *Richard Feverel* first. It needs no great sagacity to see that the writer is a novice at his task The style is extremely uneven. Now he twists himself into iron knots; now he lies flat as a pancake. He seems to be of two minds as to his intention. Ironic comment alternates with long-winded narrative.

Here the tone, the mode of address, is the striking feature. We have a vivid representation of Woolf's *own* act of reading as the common reader, common because she uses the everyday clichés of 'flat as a pancake' and 'iron knots'. It seems to me that to read any novel and be able to judge whether or not it comes from a 'a novice' requires a great deal of reading skill and practice. But Woolf reassures us that she, and therefore we, can manage without any recondite critical terminology. Woolf subtly helps us into her own hierarchy of values by using the conditional tense so that we are allowed to make the judgement ourselves. The critic is hesistant (*'we may do well'*), not intimidating. Next follows the dramatised Meredith, all flat as a pancake, and *then* we decide with Woolf, still cautiously, not pejoratively, that it is because 'he *seems* to be of two minds' (my italics).

We could choose any piece of Woolf's criticism and have the same subtle yet incredibly condensed sequence of critical activities. Woolf appears to be secondary, recording only her impressions, yet within a few lines we are all able to judge good from bad writing, early and late style, with some knowledge of critical terms. Of course, it would be difficult to claim the mode as *specifically* feminist since Woolf shares an intimacy of tone with, say, Lamb and Hazlitt, among other early-nineteenth-century essayists. But when Woolf chooses to be intimate *only* with women readers, then she can dramatise in her very style and actively constitute by her work, a feminist audience.

The work of the break came in 1930. It is Virginia Woolf's Introductory Letter to *Life as We Have Known It*. By 1930 Virginia Woolf is in full possession not only of what she thinks is the right *method* for her criticism but also of an imagery with which to sustain it. Where in *A Room of One's Own* Woolf manipulates point of view only by exploiting the passive by the time of 'the Introduction', she could brave a more interesting narrator. Although the whole point of that letter is to enable us as readers, and perhaps the woman she describes, to name and define the value of working-class women's experience, the 'author' herself has great difficulty in naming anything at all. She sees a woman wearing 'something like' a chain, taking her seat 'perhaps at your right . . . perhaps an organ played'. It is all part of Woolf's trick to make us active readers, to force us to take part. However, the technique is not only appropriate as a mode of address to hesitant women *readers*. As Woolf says in 'Jane Austen', women writers like Austen 'stimulate us to supply what is not there. What she offers is, apparently, a trifle, yet is composed of something that expands in the reader's mind' (1979, p. 114). The comment is perfectly apt as a description of Woolf's own critical technique. Because we are introduced to criticism through Woolf's own assumed autobiographical difficulties and interrogative debate with herself, we accept her judgements.

If the mode of address is the first 'impression' we have of Woolf's technique, the second 'impression' is the physicality of her syntax. Virginia Woolf is a very physical critic just as the physiology of the body was to be her fictional motif.

In order to read each woman's life story we have to learn, like 'Woolf the narrator', to make a personal commitment to the writers she describes. Like 'Woolf' we have to cross the barrier from educated consuming middle-class women to a world where women are active workers. Like 'Woolf' we are bound to misunderstand some of their history. We will have shortcomings.

Margaret Llewelyn Davies collected letters and accounts from members of the Women's Co-operative Guild for many years. Virginia Woolf had visited a conference of the Guild in 1913 and, seventeen years later, when asked by Llewelyn Davies to edit the letters for publication, she decided to write an account of her own experience of that earlier meeting as the introduction.

It is apparently a piece of straightforward autobiography. There is nothing wrong or even unusual about criticism becoming autobiography in the context of a political meeting. Much of twentieth-century left-wing writing is autobiographical, from Robert Tressell's *The Ragged-Trousered Philanthropists* onward, and the merit of autobiography is that it leads a writer to an awareness that her activity has inevitable political implications. A question immediately occurs here, because of the *universal* significance which attaches to the factualness, to the documentary evidence, which Woolf is presenting: How does critical form and the overall significance attached to it grow out of the autobiographical moment? And in particular: What makes this feminist literary criticism? Woolf is using one mode to establish another. She makes the particular lives of working women as heard by the narrator 'Woolf' become universal metaphors—take on general significance. The move occurs in two directions. First, the theme of the piece is about speaking out. How do working women speak out about their lives, and how will an intellectual woman in speaking out about them speak freely about herself. Woolf is answering the question 'What is the role of the intellectual woman?' both literally and in the form of her writing. Second, the imagery of the piece dovetails this main theme. One set of imagery is of the body—the women's bodies that they describe in their letters and Woolf sees and 'Woolf's' own body which is located in all possible senses (e.g. physically, socially and historically). The second set is of images of the mind, of the young women with 'minds humming' and our minds at work constructing the passage from facts and 'transparences'. 'Woolf' forces us as readers into the problem of defining experience. The coming together textually of body and mind might be Woolf's answer to her Victorian father's separation of hand and heart.

What is striking is the slow, heuristic growth of 'Woolf' and us, as readers, into the lives of her subjects. And how often and compulsively Woolf repeats this technique throughout all her criticism. The Introductory Letter is exemplary of Woolf's critical mode. Suppose I sketch out a brief chart of the reading process approaching the 'experience' as Woolf wants us to approach experience. It would be a series of notes. But it would help us see how the prose is actualising the experience it is about.

Woolf sets up the essay as a question of how to imaginatively produce experience. 'Woolf' starts with her shortcomings. Her writing will be merely 'a wad of paper' helping 'the table' of text stand more 'steady'. A writing table standing in for the real tables the women will later describe cleaning in their letters. Reader relations are already part of the text. We have to help 'Woolf's' poor memory. 'Woolf' is also addressing the introduction to another woman, Margaret Llewelyn Davies, so 'Woolf' is devised as a mirror of her and, therefore, of our experience. The women are anonymous, 'a figure rose', 'a speaker'. They are constructed in their voices, just as Woolf has to construct her voice for them. The process of their speaking is like the process of writing. Women speak from their pasts and Woolf moves from a past perfect (had come) to a free indirect present continuous.

Each woman is coming to 'speak her mind', a mind which is representative of her home. And how does 'Woolf' see it in her mind? The event is interrogated: 'What was it all about? What was the meaning of it? We have 'Woolf' supplying us with a political context of dates of Divorce Laws, Trades Board Acts. So we are, with 'Woolf', still locked in mental activity, irretrievably cut off from the working women.

How does Woolf move from the universal to the particular? She plays 'Let's Pretend'. She tries to enter the bodily experience of Mrs Giles of Durham City, but it is hard to stand at the wash-tub, when usually 'one sat in an armchair or read a book' (Woolf, 1977, p. xxiii). Middle-class spectators have minds which 'fly free at the end of a short length of capital' (p. xxvii). The women of the heads are asking for meanings; the women of the bodies are asking empirically for eight working hours a day rather than nine. Yet 'Woolf' is dedicated to representing working women. Is the work too difficult? Woolf solves the problem for 'Woolf' by allowing change to develop from *inside* the language. Two elaborate descriptions of working-class lives 'enclose' the passive paragraph of middle-class armchair existence.

We trust 'Woolf'. She still uses a royal 'we' for her implied middle-class readers and controls the text in her role as reporter. 'You asked us to tell you how Congress had impressed us.' Woolf has to continually carry along her readers. This mode of entering into the lives of other women is both political *and* literary as in 'Mr Bennett and Mrs Brown'. In this piece, whatever the complexities of experience might be that Woolf is dealing with, the way in which she represents that experience has to convince us, her urban literate readers. So Woolf chooses a realist mode of pictorial narrative because her implied readers are fiction readers. The organisation of Co-operative women is emblematically represented in 'Woolf's' visit to the offices of Miss Kidd and Lilian Harris who are its officials. The women are from different classes yet co-operation has united them, just as, with 'Woolf', we will join together with working women by the end of the Introduction. The two women's class position is represented physiologically. Lower-class Miss Kidd is heavy and gloomy while Lilian Harris wears a coloured dress and smokes cigarettes.

Yet if 'Woolf' has to be forced out of her armchair into offices and meetings, 'we' readers will also have to work in order to fully share 'Woolf's' and the women's lives. 'Again let me telescope into a few sentences, and into one scene random discussions on various occasions at various places' (Woolf, 1977, p. xxvii). The author is beginning to ramble, secure that her implied reader can sort things out, can engage in the process of construction of those women's lives. 'Woolf' begins to miss the point. Miss Kidd is wearing deep purple, 'The colour seemed somehow symbolical' (p. xxvi) 'Woolf' seems not to know the suffragette colours. We have to start working. Part of the difficulty of Woolf's prose here is the fact that it becomes *scriptible* rather than *lisible*. The narrative runs on in one huge, overlong paragraph. We begin to supply punctuation as we would bring to a play reading the expressions required by the stage directions. Luckily Woolf gives us the odd breathing space. ' "But", we said, and here perhaps fiddled with a paper knife, or poked the fire impatiently by way of expressing our discontent, "what is the use of it all?" ' (p. xxx).

The use of it all are the letters themselves. 'Perhaps it was at this point that you unlocked the drawer and took out a packet of paper' (p. xxxi). The force of working women 'is about to break through and melt us together so that life will be richer and books more complex and society will pool its possessions instead of segregating them' (p. xxx). The quotation elides wealth, and culture, base and superstructure just as we middle-class women will join our 'learning and poetry' to the 'images and saws' of working-class women. The problem of women's language is both content and process of the Introduction. The activity of construction corresponds to what Woolf was trying to do herself in her criticism, trying to open up language to some collective voice.

Perhaps Woolf should have ended here. But there is a final coda. Woolf worries that the implied reader might still be locked into existing literary conventions. 'The writing, a literary critic might say, lacks detachment and imaginative breadth' (p.xxix). But we are immediately overwhelmed by Woolf's three examples of working-class narratives. The first is Mrs Scott, who can describe physical detail very beautifully. Mrs Burrows, the second, was saved from starvation through women's friendship. The third is Miss Kidd herself, raped by a male employer. The narratives are emblems of sexual politics and feminist discourse. The Introduction has its own uncompromising logic.

At the end the organic vocabulary is firmly brought back from humanism and tied in to feminism. To help ease the physical hardship of working bodies, women need their own physical space. Woolf does not describe the Co-operative Guild as an economic organisation but as a room, a physical space where women can argue and dream, just like the physical space of writing for Woolf.

If we are queasy about the 'thick-set and muscular' working women, the vocabulary is there for a more radical feminist intent. Vocabulary like the mode of address matches Woolf's ideology. Working women, Woolf claims *are* only bodies without the vote, and yet purposefully, if paradoxically, by joining in a co-operative body they might collectively create a new political form. The questions Woolf deals with ideologically have their appropriate representation syntactically in her discourse.

It is the same technique in her fiction. *Orlando* is about the difficulty of communicating, between sexes, between classes and across centuries. Related to this are sub-themes of exclusion and inclusion (of gypsies or prostitutes) tied to notions of ownership and power. The sociosexual message is duplicated in the difficulty of the narrator to communicate, and Orlando to write, a difficulty shared by other writers who appear as characters in the text. Yet the novel is a fantasy not a naturalistic narrative of sociosexual and cultural problems. It is a mixture of transparences and facts. Woolf uses a physiology of the body in her syntax and characterisation to stand for her intellectual ideas. First, the 'body' of the narrator intervenes awkwardly between us and the narrative, changes his point of view and gender, and finally disappears forcing us to the 'physical' job of discovering the truth about Orlando for ourselves. But, in addition, we are never simply detached from the text, looking *at* it as a series of events, because Woolf bombards us with the smells and sensations experienced by her characters.

It would be impossible to float above *Orlando* like the detached groups of Elizabethans floating past Orlando on ice blocks down a melting Thames. That highly metaphorical passage is perhaps the best example of Woolf's ability to match syntactical form to social ideas. However, Woolf does not rely on single passages. The whole narrative of *Orlando* is constructed around physical contrasts of summer and winter, of sub-worlds of violent sailors against an icy court, of the earthy mixture in Orlando of 'Kentish earth with Normandy fluid'. The physical is crucial to gender identity. Sexuality and difference are presented physiologically in terms of clothes, voice-tone, the size of 'huge men' or strange bearded Russian women.

In her criticism it is the very specificity of physical detail that enables Woolf to see and understand absences, the trade-mark of contemporary feminist criticism. For example, in 'Jane Austen' Wolf describes Austen's anti-physicality—her devices for 'evading scenes of passion' and of Austen's need to approach in a sidelong way to Nature (Woolf, 1979, p. 118). Alongside her physical presence as a narrator, and her body syntax, the form of poems, like the bodies of poets, are physiologically described. The lines of Donne's poetry are metamorphised into the 'obscurity of his mind', which is the 'thickest of thorn bushes', where his rage 'scorches' (Woolf, 1979, p. 76). Although novels, Woolf says in *A Room of One's Own*, do start in us all sorts of physical emotions, it is these emotions that enable us to understand their structure. The architectural structure of a novel is made, not by *objects* 'by the relation of stone to stone, but by the relation of human being to human being'. Woolf (particularly in 'De Quincey's Autobiography') writes long descriptions of summer evenings and her own emotions, not solipsistically, but to stress the significance of detail in De Quincey's work. De Quincey, Woolf says, used sunlight and flowers to make us 'explore the depths of that single emotion. It is a state which is general and not particular' (Woolf, 1944, p. 102). Physical imagery is not used by Woolf simply to naturalise herself, us as readers, or her readings. Nor is it used in any idealistic sense. Being in a critical scene is the first step of reading, and therefore her sentences are full of varied pauses, consonances, assonances and perceptual stimuli. When writers use physical detail it is their way of encapsulating in a familiar image more difficult general ideas to which we will be able to respond emotionally via the image. Woolf's topology of the body is a form of criticism which I think can only successfully be read by women. It was precisely because Woolf herself read for emotions that she could make feminist judgements in *A Room of One's Own*. Sitting in the British Museum cataloguing male notions of female difference Woolf refuses to read male texts in an 'efferent' way for scraps of information she could take home. She reads them emotionally for their tone and point of view and could therefore find out about men's anger and its source— disgust at women's increasing refusal to physically reflect men (Woolf, 1945, p. 31).

The point is here (and elsewhere in Woolf) that there are two aspects of her critical discourse; the 'bodily' language which, without sinking into essentialism, is feminine in the sense that Woolf is using a female iconography of the body; and the 'abstract' politics of sexuality that the language is addressing. What makes Woolf a feminist critic, it seems to me, is that she trusts and allows the 'bodily' language to reveal sexual politics. She does not cheat or shuffle away into a rhetoric of general argument 'in case' her emotional iconography is inadequate. The narrator is finding her source of knowledge in her own female body just as men, she claims, are misrepresenting women and their bodies. The real problem for Woolf, beginning to write criticism at the turn of the century, was that the Victorian age, as she tells us in 'A Man with a View', was the age of the professional man. Biographies of the time 'had a depressing similarity'. The great men were 'very joyless' and distanced, 'strangely formal and remote' (Woolf, 1965a, p. 29). Nor was the critical tradition any better. Criticism was part of academic ideology, an ideology Woolf scathingly attacks in *Three Guineas* for leading directly to political violence. Woolf saw that it was also tied to sexist notions of gender. She wanted in *Three Guineas* to give one of her three guineas to women to buy petrol and matches to burn down men's colleges.

H.G. Wells was one such professional man. His characters are poor dummies crudely moulded, whose defects he has covered up with 'rouge and flaxen wigs' (Woolf, 1965a, p. 93). Wells was a poor writer not only because he was male or because he was bourgeois but because he had forced literature into the service of male, bourgeois ends. 'He has run up his buildings to house temporary departments of the Government' (Woolf, 1965a, p. 93). If women give in to this authority, the vision becomes too masculine or it becomes too feminine (Woolf, 1979, p. 48). Not only that, but women would soon cease to write at all.

To defy the father, open the gate in Jane Austen's park, and walk through into the promised land of feminist criticism, Woolf needed maps. She read and found help in some male critics, as Hazlitt or Butler, and she made paths using some conventional critical steps. It is tempting to claim all Woolf's techniques as unique to feminism. But in order to find the source of her *real* uniqueness and her feminism we have to start by putting her back in her historical moment.

In an interesting essay on Virginia Woolf, Barbara Currier Bell and Carol Ohmann select one of her techniques in particular to bring Woolf into their feminist fold. 'She pushed, for example, a certain kind of biographical criticism to its frontier' (Bell and Ohmann, 1975, p. 55). Bell and Ohmann are careful to note an affinity with Leslie Stephen and Hazlitt but still feel that Virginia Woolf overtook her predecessors only in the skill with which she practised.

We have to stop for a moment. Certainly as part of Woolf's general attack on the literary tradition, she redefined the techniques of criticism to include all kinds of hitherto miscellaneous skills. Her essays, as we have seen, are clear working examples of a mixed mode of biography and literary analysis. But there's a kind of fallacious circularity in Bell and Ohmann's argument. To them Woolf uses biographical criticism. She likes writing about and for women. Because male critics scorn her, and because she is a woman, therefore her criticism is feminist. This is very dubious logic. Obviously biographical modes of writing have played an important part in the development of feminist consciousness, both then and today. This is because they provide an interesting way for women to pose questions about public and private authority in literary texts. But before we can really say how much of an insight the technique gives us to the sexual politics of literature, we have to ask 'Was it *new*' before 'Is it feminist?'

Virginia Woolf's contribution to feminist criticism can only make sense when read against contemporary male critics who share her techniques. A reading of kinds of biographical criticism which were currently available can give us interesting insights into those representations of women available in critical texts. Any account of Woolf's uniqueness has to come from placing her work against other constructions of masculinity and femininity in critical texts of the period. The battle against this 'authority' is the striking feature of Virginia Woolf's literary criticism. The refusal of 'the father' was Woolf's 'anxiety of influence'. One writer very close to Woolf was the biographer/critic Lytton Strachey. Strachey, unlike other critics, according to Woolf in her diary, preferred Woolf's criticism. 'And he said the C.R. [Common Reader] was divine, a classic, Mrs D. [Mrs Dalloway] being, I fear, a flawed stone' (Woolf, 1959, p. 79). Lytton Strachey was a well-known man of letters in the Georgian period. His key work *Eminent Victorians* went into fifteen editions between 1918 and 1926. Virginia Woolf, on the other hand, is considered to be first and foremost a creative writer of modernism. Those looking for contrasts between male and female criticism could easily find them by distinguishing between Lytton Strachey, the popular explorer collecting specimens of Victorian life, and Virginia Woolf, the feminist philosopher of the psyche. As we come to examine her criticism more carefully, however, we begin to see that the tension she was exploring in her criticism between private and public is a tension shared by Strachey. There are continuities in the criticism of that period which we need to know about in order to understand the discontinuities and Strachey and Woolf's eventually very different constructions of femininity.

Choosing Strachey, a gay male critic, to compare with Woolf might seem to pose its own problems about gender. But to raise the question of male and female difference by comparing two homosexual critics can intensify and finally establish gender difference in writing. The very juxtaposition of homosexuality and criticism obliges us to confront the definition of what is and is not feminist criticism. It also obliges us to determine the locus of sexual politics within criticism and its part in feminism.

It is not surprising that their criticism is similar. Strachey and Woolf were friends and professional colleagues throughout their lives. They were constantly in correspondence, not only about writing but also about their more private experiences. They shared the same political point of departure. Both were writing about aspects of the collapse of Victorian life. Woolf attacks the militaristic male professions in *A Room of One's Own*. Strachey attacks Victorian bureaucracy in his life of Florence Nightingale, and Victorian Christianity in his life of Matthew Arnold. Both made biographies of individual lives to be microcosms of social history. Both were writing about inclusion and exclusion in Victorian life, about insiders and outsiders.

In *Three Guineas* Woolf designs an 'Outsiders Club' as an alternative to male hierarchies and professional codes. Matthew Arnold's whole philosophy, according to Lytton Strachey, is about outsiders and insiders and their codes of behaviour. 'He would treat the boys at Rugby as Jehovah had treated the Chosen People: he would found a theocracy' (Strachey, 1928, p. 193). And both Woolf and Strachey understood the success of Victorian theocracy to depend on the naturalisation of masculine ideology: for Woolf, into the feminine psyche, for Strachey a displacement represented at Rugby in the way boys were conditioned to discipline each other.

Not only did Woolf and Strachey share positions and topics, their criticism also shares a sub-text of implicit sexual politics. The sudden violence of men to women in *A Room of One's Own* is matched by Strachey's inability to contain Florence Nightingale within the syntactical discourse of his text. Nightingale controls her supporter Sidney Herbert by 'something feline . . . then the tigress has her claws in the quivering haunches; and then – !' (Strachey, 1928, p. 149). Lacking a public expression of their homosexuality, Woolf and Strachey reveal it privately in vocabulary and syntax. Metaphors of power leap almost out of context. The technique enabled both writers to break through the confines of nineteenth-century criticism.

Often their figures seem the same. This is Strachey's description of Florence Nightingale late at night writing her letters: 'She would fill pages with recommendations and suggestions, with criticisms of the minutest details of organisation . . . piled up in breathless eagerness' (Strachey, 1928, pp. 134–5). It might also be Mrs Ramsey with her recommendations about cows' milk at the dinner party in *To The Lighthouse*.

But Strachey remains at the ideological level of Mrs Stephens. Although he attacks Matthew Arnold in terms of his own, personal agenda of liberal humanism, there is a great difference in the way Arnold appears in Strachey's text *because* he is male. Even when Strachey presents feeble men, their weakness is not on the basis of their *gender* but on the basis of their class or individual personality defects (as with General Simpson's alcoholism). Arnold strides into the text at the moment of his public power (as Nightingale, a woman, enters only through her childhood). Arnold has power syntactically since Arnold's own thoughts have a certain space in the text. There is a consistent tone throughout the chapter. The attack on Florence Nightingale, however, is confused. It has spaces and gaps and reveals that more ambiguous notion of femininity that Strachey is handling. In the figure of Florence Nightingale Strachey is ostensibly attacking Victorian constructions of the public woman. Ironically, he describes how, in spite of her expert knowledge, she was not allowed to appear in public before the Army Commission. Strachey is apparently asking the same questions of history as Virginia Woolf: 'What can women represent?' and 'What role is there for women in public life?'. But, although Woolf can kill the Angel in her house, Strachey constructs an exaggerated myth of femininity.

Nightingale, in Strachey's text, is a good shopper, buying shirts, towels and toothbrushes on her journey to Scutari. Strachey translates her into an ideal domestic science teacher. He imposes on Nightingale germ theories current at the turn of the century, not those actually contemporary with her,[4] in order to fashion Nightingale into a new Mrs Beeton. Only two problems are described at Scutari: the dirt and lack of domesticity. In order to solve them Strachey's Florence Nightingale introduces the middle-class virtues of thrift, orderliness and, above all, *privacy* (by buying the soldiers dressing gowns). 'Femininity' is here the Victorian Angel made into a social planner. Nightingale's sanitary reforms are not described medically but merely as the upgrading of familiar household tasks. The barracks becomes a gigantic family with Nightingale at the centre creating punctual meals and 'the necessary elements of civilised life—materialism, order and cleanliness.

The question of women is addressed but answered by a new male fantasy. 'Femininity' as domestic order incarnate is how Strachey replaces the Victorian Angel. Not only is 'femininity' constructed as domesticity and mediation, it exists only in relation to men (like Woolf's vivid metaphor of the looking glass in *A Room of One's Own*). Nightingale could work in the Crimea only with the support of a male Member of Parliament, Sidney Herbert. She lacked the public authority, Strachey claims, which belonged to the successful politician and therefore displaced her need for authority by manipulating her other family, 'her "cabinet", as she called it' (1928, p. 150).

Strachey has no worry about his 'New Woman'. Luckily for men, his Nightingale is an empiricist—never at home with a generalisation.

If the events of Florence Nightingale's public life can be contained within the framework of domestic science, the events of her private life and psyche break through Strachey's narrative control. It is Nightingale's 'hysteria' and Strachey's use of Victorian psychology which finally expose the contradictions in liberal male 'femininity'.

Sickness is a kind of 'malingering' by Nightingale. Like Weir Mitchell's theories of hysteria, which were used to treat Virginia Woolf, Strachey thinks Nightingale *plays* the invalid. Hysteria is episodic, not organic, in Nightingale's life and therefore becomes a 'choice' of neurosis in the usual Victorian elision between hysteria and femininity.[5]

But the psychoanalytic milieu was changing. Freud's *Three Essays on Sexuality* (1915) and essays on hysteria (1905) were published by Woolf's Hogarth Press. Freud understands hysteria to be repressed sexuality with neurosis as the negative of perversions. Hysteria is therefore conditioned by a loss of object or love, with the loss of love playing the same role in women's hysteria as the threat of castration for men.[6]

Strachey's aim, however, is to demonstrate that the *working* woman will become a hysterial formation. His Florence Nightingale wears out men. She kills off helpers Sidney Herbert and Arthur Clough in her battles with bureaucracy.

The discourse of male Bloomsbury has constructed a liberal woman. But the new liberal woman in these male texts is not free. She must still be controlled if not by society's norms then by the author for his own psychosexual ends. The versions of 'femininity' that Strachey is prepared to give us are ambiguous. They hide the real terror for Bloomsbury men: a woman who enjoys working more than she enjoys personal friendships. Even worse is the woman who only enjoys other women. In the end Florence Nightingale's brain 'grows soft' because she 'indulged in sentimental friendships with young girls' (Strachey, 1928, p. 173). Strachey quotes Nightingale talking to God. ' "He comes to me, and He talks to me", she said, "as if I were someone else" ' (Strachey, 1929, p. 17). We might say the same about Strachey's 'femininity'. Lytton Strachey's liberal refusal of conservative authority could not be an adequate guide for Virginia Woolf's attack on patriarchy. Like all relationships, however, that of Virginia Woolf's to male authority is more perdurable. If she was able to upbraid her male peers, she found her male parent a much more difficult project. Woolf had also to exorcise the contribution of her female relatives to the making of nineteenth-century patriarchal ideology.[7] But the question of Woolf's literary relationship with her father Leslie Stephen is a question which takes us into one of the deepest dimensions of her life of criticism. While it is untrue that Virginia Woolf is the only female writer having to battle against a famous writing father, in their battle there is an important sense in which the personal and the political becomes the heart of feminist criticism.

If Woolf was to develop her feminism she would need to reject these bad fathers of literary criticism. But first 'when one hasn't had a good father, it is necessary to invent one' (Bloom, 1973, p. 56). And Virginia Woolf 'invents' her father in her essay

'Leslie Stephen'. She writes about his criticism that 'to read what one liked because one liked it, never to pretend to admire what one did not—that was his only lesson in the art of reading' (Woolf, 1978, p. 74).

Bloom's 'anxiety of influence' is the fear and attraction writers feel for their predecessors. He divides poets into 'precursors' and 'ephebes' or revisers, and he defines revision as *purposeful* misinterpretation. Bloom traces kinds of poetic misprision in the life-cycles of Keats, Wordsworth and other poets. Using Freudian notions of the Oedipus and sublimation, Bloom explains that a 'strong' poet makes *use* of his precursor in the tropes and imagery of his poem in order to violate or usurp his poetic father. Bloom's model of literary history is itself intensely patriarchal since he talks only about dynamics between fathers and sons. Feminist critics[8] have rightly called attention to the absent daughter in Bloom's text and the way that female writers can experience the literary authority of predecessor 'mothers', as I described in Chapter 3. But Woolf's father did spend his life trying to set her rhetorical standards. Stephen was her main teacher until he died when she was twenty-two. Woolf could not publish until nine months after her father's death. Virginia Woolf's anxiety of influence is a continuing revisionary struggle in her criticism, and it was only long after Stephen's death and her own success that Woolf could praise him, as the quotation shows, for having been what she herself had become. Bloom's concise terminology can be the vocabulary of the story of Woolf's contest for power. Bloom suggests that his analysis of patriarchal poetics can be applied equally well to criticism. 'Poets' misinterpretations or poems are more drastic than critics' misinterpretations or criticism, but this is only a difference in degree and not at all in kind' (Bloom, 1973, p. 94).

If we pursue Bloom's enchantment of incest in the criticism of Leslie Stephen and Virginia Woolf, we can understand her real victory over patriarchal authority. Virginia Woolf fought Leslie Stephen on his terms and won. Reading and rereading their criticism together is like hearing two voices in argument. The argument took in gender definitions and notions of appropriate literary forms and readership—the terrain of feminist criticism.

In her memoir Woolf explicity acknowledges her intellectual debt to Stephen. The Woolfs built their library on the nucleus of books that Virginia inherited from her father.[9] She preserved them with brightly coloured paper. 'Fear of the father' is revealed in the way she made no marks in the books which were his but wrote occasionally in her own. Even her marginalia resembles Stephen's practice—both marked cant by 'O'. He influenced her choice of topics. Woolf focuses on the same writers that Stephen does. They both wrote about De Quincey, George Eliot, the Brontës, and Hazlitt, and they both wrote about the same aspects of literary form—on autobiography and historical narrative. There are other features of Stephen's criticism connecting him with Woolf. Both Woolf and Stephen are very accessible critics. Stephen writes engagingly, becoming strongly autobiographical, like Virginia Woolf, to put the reader at his ease with literary terms and values.

Woolf often paraphrases her father word for word. About De Quincey Stephen wrote 'He has one intolerable fault, a fault which has probably done more than any other to diminish his popularity . . . He is utterly incapable of concentration. He is . . . the most *diffuse* of writers' (Stephen, 1917, p. 230; my italics). Here is Virginia Woolf on De Quincey: 'Strange that De Quincey failed to be among the great autobiographers of our literature . . . Perhaps one of the reasons . . . was not the lack of expressive power, but the superfluity. He was profusely and indiscriminately loquacious. *Discursiveness*—the disease' (Woolf, 1944, p. 104; my italics). Virginia Woolf was far more in debt to her father than simple source-hunting or allusion-counting reveals. But as Bloom suggests, poetic influence need not make poets less original; as often it gives them strength. In juxtaposing Woolf's essays with those of her father we can hear the creation of a feminist voice and read the creation of a feminist poetics.

Stephen wrote his essay on De Quincey fifty years before Virginia Woolf, but they are asking similar questions about literature and asking them often in the same way. Like Woolf, Stephen introduces De Quincey as if he is walking through De Quincey's landscape. Both father and daughter are very physical critics, fascinated by the details of De Quincey's daily life and prepared to take him on his terms rather than only on theirs. Stephen's metaphors are congenially domestic. The difference between Swift and De Quincey is 'the difference between the stiffest nautical grogs and the negus provided by thoughtful parents for a child's evening party' (Stephen, 1917, p. 237). Rhythm is crucial to both critics. Woolf thinks De Quincey works on us 'as if by music—the senses are stirred rather than the brain' (Woolf, 1944, p. 101). Her father thought, too, that De Quincey is best read as a musical composition. But Woolf has to create a different De Quincey for a different purpose. She has to find in writing, forms of expression to interest a woman reader, rather than the male implied in Stephen's text; and forms that will help the creative woman writer, herself, rather than the moral philosopher, her father. Stephen assumes we share his social class and education: 'If any reader will take the trouble to compare De Quincey's account of a kind of anticipation to the Balaclava charge at the battle of Talavera, with Napier's description of the same facts, he will be amused at the distortion of history' (Stephen, 1917, p. 229). We will understand the military references. The judiciary supports the military. Stephen interrogates De Quincey like arguing with a clever undergraduate. And, like a tutor, Stephen gives a bad end of term report. De Quincey is not a 'sound or original thinker' (p. 237).

The moment Woolf's 'revisionary swerve' from Stephen comes when she prefers De Quincey's expressive language, which Stephen so disliked. Woolf defends flaws and distortions in writing as a strength not a weakness. 'For page after page we are in company with a cultivated gentleman who describes with charm and eloquence what he has seen and known—the stage coaches, the Irish Rebellion . . . then suddenly the smooth narrative parts asunder . . . and time stands still' (Woolf, 1944, p. 106). Woolf sees that the 'narrative parts' at moments when women appear. The self-consciousness which Stephen found so disturbing, Woolf seizes on because it reveals a masculine evasion. To understand the distortions in De Quincey's portrait of the prostitute Anne is to know more about the historical misrepresentation of women.

As Bloom suggests, 'A poet antithetically "completes" his precursor, by so reading the parent-poem as to retain its terms but to mean them in another sense, as though the precursor had failed to go far enough' (1973, p. 14). Woolf has deliberately misprised Stephen to win over literature to feminism. But the battle would clearly be fiercer in their arguments about women rather than men writers. In the essays Virginia Woolf and Leslie Stephen wrote about George Eliot they both choose to write about the interaction of gender and literary form. And whereas in her essay on De Quincey Woolf swerves from her father only at the end in order to displace him, Woolf struggles to possess George Eliot by incorporating Stephen's argument point by point. Their essays are like a dialogue, with Woolf directly confronting each of Stephen's statements. Woolf's fear of being 'flooded', as Lacan would say, arises because in writing about Eliot she is dealing with the identity of the woman writer.

Stephen starts by describing Eliot's career. He praises her for holding back from writing to 'store emotions' like a good housewife. Woolf, rather, points out how *late* George Eliot came to writing in terms of her need for self-identity. Eliot's forte, Stephen suggests, is her ability to catch the vanishing traces of rural life. He prefers the earlier to the later novels because they have mathematical plots set in vivid country landscapes. By imprisoning Eliot in her earlier agricultural scenes, Stephen is doing what Virginia Woolf deplores: 'Confine George Eliot to the agricultural world of her "remotest past", and you not only diminish her greatness but lose her true flavour' (Woolf, 1979, p. 159). The heroines of Eliot have to be rescued for feminism. Stephen thinks Eliot's heroines are misconceived. Dorothea, he feels, is a failure because she ought to have realised she was mistaken about men. As many men do, Stephen interprets the actions of female characters only in so far as they relate to men.

It is obvious that Woolf would disagree. But she works within *his* framework using *his* terms. Woolf deliberately inverts Stephen's criticism of Dorothea. It is precisely a heroine's *doubts* about the ordinary 'tasks of womanhood', that *are* her search for truth. It is a battle of sexual politics. Virginia Woolf is calling for fiction to incorporate political demands. Dorothea's exaggeration which upsets Stephen is there, Woolf claims, because her demands *are* 'incompatible with the facts of human existence' (1979, p. 159). Woolf's feminism is her understanding that Dorothea's suffering is the pivot—the linkage of emotional form with social life. Stephen, as the archetypal Victorian critic, desperately wants to keep them apart. Women who strain beyond domesticity, he concluded, should join the 'Social Science Associations' not write novels. Calculating the syntactical relationship between a writer and her work is a source of continual tension in Woolf's criticism. Her negation of Stephen's notions of that relation is the 'daemonisation' in their contest to possess the Brontës. Stephen takes a canoninic approach to the Brontës by looking at them in the context of intellectual history. Charlotte Brontë is a failure not only because she was 'not familiar with Hedges or Sir William Hamilton' (Stephen, 1926, p. 5) but because that lack of knowledge is revealing of the enclosed and impoverished cultural life she led. The omissions, Stephen suggests, ultimately create mannerisms in her fiction. Her characters are not, as they should be, representatives of the cultural life of their times, but are autobiographical, even 'rather unpleasantly Ossianesque'.

Woolf subverts Stephen's arguments in a series of 'revisionary swerves'. Her essay is an antithetical use of Stephen's worst fears. To Woolf, Brontë's 'diseased mind' is a protest against cultural exclusion. Woolf writes into her text a language of taboo. Brontë becomes Woolf herself fighting Victorian authority in the discourse of her novels. So we read Brontë 'not for the exquisite observation of character but for untamed ferocity perpetually at war with the accepted order of things' (Woolf, 1979, p. 130). Woolf makes a complicated distinction between the surface design of the text (where Stephen remains) and its sub-text; and, too, with what emerges from this in 'some connection which things in themselves different have had for the writer' (p. 130). The enclosed world of the Brontës, which Stephen dismisses, is to Woolf, a source of creativity. The textural constraints which are its fictional expression are important, Woolf feels, because they were chosen not imposed. 'For the self-centred and self-limited writers have a power . . . Their impressions are close packed' (p. 129). Virginia Woolf frees Brontë from Stephen's paternalism. Defences are now strengths. Woolf, like Charlotte Brontë, is protesting against authority not only in the social *content* of her criticism but through its discursive form.

Though he was a biographer, Leslie Stephen did not respect autobiography. People who 'confess' were, he thought, 'full of dubious self-love' (Stephen, 1926, p. 233). As usual, he tries to set standards, involving the reader not as an actor in the text but as a listener at a lecture. The aim of autobiography is moral improvement since the 'peculiar interest of the autobiography is in modification of character' (Stephen, 1926, p. 243). The hidden sub-text of Stephen's essay, and why it might interest us, is that the essay *on* autobiography becomes *his* autobiography. Stephen's misrepresentation of 'femininity' is finally exposed: 'It requires a certain moderation of character to be satisfied with a history instead of a wife and Gibbon is so great an historian because he could accept such a substitute' (Stephen, 1926, p. 250). Stephen is clear. Women inhibit any great intellectual endeavour.

The return of the dead is in the third part of *Three Guineas*. Woolf examines cases of 'infantile fixation', of fathers controlling their daughters' lives and sexuality. It is the educated man's daughter, she feels, who can best testify about the powerful and subconscious motives of men. Woolf's piece becomes, like Stephen's essay, a revealing autobiography in itself. The third example of infantile fixation which Woolf chooses to describe in the case of Mr Jex-Blake. This is the father threatened by an intellectual daughter, a case, Woolf suggests, which 'explains much that lies at the root of Victorian psychology' (1982, p. 151). There is more space in Woolf's text for *this* daughter's battle against her father than for those daughters battling to marry.

Only by the time of *Three Guineas* could Woolf let the power of the fathers flood into her text so dramatically. Although in her novels the power of patriarchy is certainly dealt with earlier—in the figure of Sir William Bradshaw in *Mrs Dalloway* or the quasi Leslie Stephen figure in *To The Lighthouse* — it is in criticism that Woolf wins possession of discourse.

Virginia Woolf invented a new feminist form for a new reader. The reader becomes an active feminist in the Introductory Letter to *Life As We Have Known It*. We helped 'Woolf' produce that piece of criticism (our implied reactions are 'Woolf's' interrogatives) and thanks to us 'Woolf's' shortcomings are redressed. Many of Woolf's questions in that text, as elsewhere, contain complicated aesthetic ideas. 'What is appropriate style for women?' and above all, 'How do women read, and what is the use of it all?' In her criticism we readers find answers through a comprehensive feminine imagery of our bodies, our cooking and our minds. In some greater sense we *want* to read to join Woolf's community of women.

Having said this much about the kinds of form observable in Virginia Woolf's criticism, what can we say about the collection as a whole? Virginia Woolf was customarily modest about her aims. In *A Writer's Diary* she describes *The Common Reader* as 'a test' to 'beat up ideas and express them now without too much confusion' (1959, p. 83). Clearly, both in terms of the number of literary experiments she tried and the number of essays she wrote, no single point can hold all her criticism together.

It has to be said that there are ambiguities. Virginia Woolf seems occasionally to have an unproblematic concept of the uniqueness of artists. In *A Room of One's Own* art becomes an 'instinct'. She slips occasionally into an evolutionary concept of feminism and art. In 'George Eliot' Eliot is reaching beyond the 'complexity of womanhood' to 'the strange bright fruits of art and knowledge' (Woolf, 1979, p. 160). This has danger signals for feminists wary of those who think feminist politics are merely a stage towards an ungendered Utopia.

The ambiguities come, I think, from the continuous tension, for Woolf, between saving Shakespeare's sister and standing by Mrs Brown. Between negotiating a new critical path through literature and opening that path to general women readers, Woolf's quest for form became a brilliant protest against her literary 'fathers'—both a protest against their construction of femininity and against their tradition of criticism. The persistence of her struggle in close association with the development of an innovative discourse make her an exciting feminist. Virginia Woolf makes her ideological engagement with feminism have meaning from within and through a feminist aesthetic.

8

REBECCA WEST

Rebecca West began writing criticism when the suffragette movement was experiencing an often violent political reaction to feminism. At the age of nineteen, Rebecca West wrote for *The Freewoman*. The following year, in 1912, she became a reviewer and political journalist with *The Clarion* and she was an active suffragette. Although her literary career is amazingly long, since it spans fifty years, the aesthetic and ideological themes of her first reviews are the feminist constants of all her writing.

Some of Rebecca West's best writing is in her literary criticism. Indeed, it is her most continuous activity since, for more than twenty years, she wrote no novels at all. West trained in languages and linguistics but she produced philosophy, political journalism, psychoanalysis, biography, travel sketches and legislative proposals.

We may well wonder why such a productive writer—a feminist who could influence 1930s American psychoanalysis *and* women writers like May Sinclair—has not fed directly into subsequent feminism. The answer is that she did not write for an exclusively feminist audience, nor did she develop in one specific genre. She addressed ideas which were surfacing in the 1920s and 1930s but were not then being incorporated into the literary tradition. To some extent, Rebecca West is being resurrected by Marina Warner and Jane Marcus, but *the extent* of her ideas and techniques has not, as yet, been adequately analysed.

Yet the collections of essays in *The Strange Necessity* (1928), *Ending in Earnest* (1931) and particularly 'Woman as Artist and Thinker' are some of those prophetic works whose hour is yet to come. Even *Black Lamb and Grey Falcon,* which is superficially a guide to the Balkans, represents a huge attempt to understand the relation of political violence to culture on the eve of the Second World War.

It is West's critical method which is one particularly appropriate to current feminism. She writes in a personal voice, continually moving between topics and disciplines and always to focus on the role of women in culture. The combination of her concerns is unusual either for literature or for feminism.

West's writings map out an area across disciplines. She does not pose a dichotomy between culture and society but recognises that relations between the cultural representation of women and society, whether in a novel or in our daily lives, are always interconnected. It is difficult to place Rebecca West easily into a critical tradition. Her list of favoured writers is very wide from St Augustin to Mark Twain (Warner, 1981). Similarly, her concepts are drawn from disparate disciplines— from biology, politics and psychoanalysis.

Today we might be more interested in her conclusions than in the evidence she gathers to support them. Men, West claims, are often life-denying or authoritarian and have imposed their nature on politics and art. Her first book, *Henry James* (1916), which could be called the first book of feminist literary criticism, describes how James like other men, sees women only as 'failed sexual beings'.

West's deductions are as controversial today as they were in the intellectual milieu in which she first wrote—the world of H.G. Wells, Kipling and Huxley. But in some respects her criticism is best read against the techniques and ideas of that world if only to clarify its uniqueness. Above all, West echoes our current preoccupation to replace patriarchal discourse with one drawn from psychoanalysis.

There is one feature of current feminist criticism of which West's career is a prime example. Since West wrote, often, for the practice of the moment rather than to construct a consistent aesthetics, it is difficult to know what aesthetic criteria we should use in evaluating her work. However, because Rebecca West was a cultural polymath, we must not assume that she had *no* precise ideas about the role of criticism. To West, the central function of criticism is to create an enabling environment for feminist ideas. West often uses her literary reviews as an occasion for a free-ranging discussion about women. For example, West attacks August Strindberg, who 'had a stroke of luck. He went mad', as a pretext for an attack on marriage and its often disastrous effect on children (Marcus, 1982, p. 54). She uses Strindberg emblematically, as it were, rather than simply aesthetically.

West thinks that criticism stimulates social change. The main problem for the woman writer, as West puts it when reviewing Ellen Key, was 'how this emotional revolt against war is to be turned into an intellectual attack on it' (Marcus, 1982, p. 340). In other words, how could Rebecca West make criticism a political as well as an aesthetic activity.

She often writes, in a strikingly similar way to George Eliot or D.H. Lawrence, about the moral function of literature. West is a moral critic because she is interested in developing emotional and moral values—in substituting feminist attributes of love and co-operation for male aggression and authority.

Throughout her criticism Rebecca West is judging what is significant about male power and the linguistic means by which it is maintained, and, as a corollary, what new concepts of women will best help her woman readers. There are a number of feminist themes here. Themes of difference, of authority, of the relation of ordinary women to extraordinary writers or, as West calls them, 'heretics'. Although Rebecca West dislikes propogandist texts, which had what she called 'the "*so* simple" attitude', her writing has a clear feminist framework (Marcus, 1982, p. 73). The framework held, and weaves together, political ideas with literary criticism. West wrote to expose the basis of male power that male propaganda tried to conceal. Her ability to expose politics, however, is determined by her critical skill in linguistically analysing political rhetoric. Although her writings, therefore, do not form a seamless web, it is impossible to separate out her more overtly journalistic pieces from her literary criticism since her literary skills are evident in both and are the reason for the clarity and precision of her political attack.

To West, feminism is of crucial importance to literature since she names it so frequently in her reviews. It is identified, it has a space in a direct way. West uses the label 'feminist' in final paragraphs, like a flag which writers need to salute, although she, herself, with irony, claims not to be able to define 'feminism': 'I myself have never been able to find out precisely what feminism is; I only know that people call me a feminist whenever I express sentiments that differentiate me from a doormat or a prostitute' (Marcus, 1982, p. 219). Her agenda is to reform the Victorian status of woman, and she writes about a myriad of associated concerns—the Personal Service Association, the role of the Labour Party in relation to the demands of the WSPU, the economic exploitation of working-class women. There are articles on communal kitchens, cheap lodgings and the impact of National Insurance legislation on women servants. However, the *way* she writes political essays is as if they were literature. If her aim is ideological, West's essays are frequently imagistic and end in some compelling metaphor or allusion.

In 'Women and Wages' Rebecca West addresses the 'ladies of Great Britain', 'we are clever, we are efficient, we are trustworthy, we are twice the women that our grandmothers were, but we have not enough devil in us' (Marcus, 1982, p. 104). Here West has a feminist purpose but not yet an appropriate critical technique. Where Woolf in *Life as We Have Known It* is an initially disengaged narrator won over by the physical presence of working women, West is curiously abstract. Although West might be called a radical feminist since she encourages women teachers to leave the unsympathetic NUT and 'form a union of their own', she lacks the personal detail of actual women. They remain 'ladies' in the abstract. This may be due, in part, because Rebecca West was writing in *The Clarion* for a socialist audience. It may also be due to West's moral perspective. West's early reviews have a consistent high moral tone. The terminology is judicial, full of 'oughts' and 'must'. West is always trying to test the 'norms' of political life against her sense of a normal woman. Attacking the Criminal Law Amendment Bill, West both spells out the implications of the law and ridicules it syntactically. Because women prostitutes were defined in the bill as 'outside' society, West prefers to isolate males outside civilised life: 'I think we ought to treat procurers as tigers ... But the procurer is an immutable specialised type, whose energy has been concentrated by degeneracy' (Marcus, 1982, p. 123). West's use of terms from biology, we shall see later, has much to do with the scientific writing of H.G. Wells. Here they point up, rhetorically, the *abnormality* of 'normal' political events. Male politicians, West is saying, had begun to 'normalise' the abnormal by endorsing physical violence against women demonstrators and capitalist violence against women workers.

The relation of ordinary to extraordinary West describes in her criticism as pairs of opposites—of outsiders and conservatives, of statism and small-scale alternatives. In her fiction West uses colour contrasts; for example, the black and white imagery in the short story 'Indissoluble Matrimony'. One of the qualities Rebecca West most admires in other authors is their ability to make these contrasts. Talking to Marina Warner about the writer A.L. Barker, West said 'She really tells you what people do, the extraordinary things that people think how extraordinary circumstances are, and how unexpected the effect of various incidents' (Warner, 1981, p. 152). In the interview, she links this theme to ideas of normal and abnormal sexuality and the need for more flexible definitions of femininity.

Edwardian males approached the Woman Question in order to codify women into the natural scheme of things. H.G. Wells, and Havelock Ellis had no hesitation in applying the results of their biological studies to human society. All social functions, they suggest, could be typed and ordered in some reference to evolution with women, and childbearing, having a defined space.

To overcome male typologies West needed the flexibility of literature. She began to describe social events more symbolically. Within the *idea* of each piece, Rebecca West mixes description with metaphor, to make the political an emblematic drama. Probably the best example of her feminist criticism is her very moving account of the suffragette Emily Davison. The piece starts quite informally with an everyday cliché: 'I never dreamed how terrible the life of Emily Davison must have been' (Marcus, 1982, p. 178). At first we read this as the usual glib sympathy from one socially secure women to another less fortunate. But Emily Davison was a well-educated woman who had been a journalist and teacher. She was not unfortunate or ordinary. Yet 'She led a very ordinary life for a woman of her type and times. She was imprisoned eight times; she hunger-struck seven times; she was forcibly fed forty-nine times' (Marcus, 1982, p. 179). West, by making an extraordinary woman be treated as the suffragette norm makes us realise how 'abnormal' is that normal treatment. The 'terrible' was the norm of Davison's life—of 'horror', 'tormentors', 'infamous' and 'sacrifice'. Gradually West as narrator succumbs herself to the atmosphere she has created:

> I felt a feeling that is worse than grief. It was the feeling that one has when one is very ill and has not slept all night. There comes an hour in the early morning when one realises that one will not sleep again for a long, long time; perhaps never. So now it was not only England had passed through a hot restless night of delirious deeds. But England has murdered sleep [Marcus, 1982, p. 182].

What are the causes of the excitement we feel on reading the passage? There is nothing exciting in merely being told that political violence keeps one awake at nights. Rebecca West's style is effective for several reasons. The most obvious is the mixture of concrete verbal particulars: 'forty-nine' force feedings (not fifty—that would be too rounded, too easy), with the moral abstractions that the particulars are meant to suggest. It is effective too because West uses a common ideogram of illness/sleep. She continually sets up a tension between the moral abstractions that she wants us to carry away from her pieces and other language processes in her text. The key to her success is the match between syntax and topic.

West is most insistently feminist in her battle with the concept of men as rational individuals. Men use their power over women, West feels, to prevent any disruption to the 'natural' process of their political institutions, Parliament or the army. Against this male hegemony West places an alternative conception of female identity in writing. The name leads her into a psychoanalytic critique of male and female novelists.

The essay 'Nonconformist Assenters' from *The Court and the Castle* is an account of psychological patterns in male novelists. By identifying with the rich, West says, Henry James's novels reveal a desperate male need for an ordering, centralising intelligence. Kipling was worse. He regresses to a more ancient spartan discipline. Males are too retrospective, West is saying, too much in love with the past. Although male writers might be displaced from a country or from received notions of the avant-garde, this does not affect their concern for order. Conrad, for example, could constitute his 'court' anywhere since it was a group of itinerant peers. Male texts, to West, are about the creation and re-creating of authority. If West uses psycho-analytic criticism to point to defects in male writing, in her essay on Charlotte Brontë West's description of psychosocial en-vironments *redresses* what deficiencies male critics find in Brontë's novels. The piece is a psychoanalytic case study of family relationships. West examines Brontë's texts for documentary evidence of the character traits of their author. To West, Charlotte Brontë's childhood need for protection is emblematic of women's general dependence upon men. Rebecca West reads the Brontës within a Freudian perspective, taking their childhood to be a source of the Brontë's adult experience of cultural oppression. Male critics who find *Jane Eyre* naive miss the point. Charlotte Brontë, West says, is radically exposing our own infancy in the emotional writing of her text. West links Charlotte Brontë's career to psychical formations occasioned by childhood as they are reconstructed as identity crises in the novels. Any defects are then more from her poor attempts to translate these crises inappropriately. 'She had become a panic-striken adept in the art of negotiation' (West, 1978, p. 435). For example, the artificiality of women's *social* negotiations make women writers, like Charlotte Brontë, choose inappropriate *character* encounters in their plots. Rebecca West uses psychoanalytic criticism to make fascinating and very apposite distinctions between male and female writing in a way crucial to feminist criticism.

Rebecca West writes again and again of the link between the exploitation of women and other forms of political power and social disorder. When asked about her first encounter with fascism Rebecca West surprises her interviewer by choosing one in her childhood rather than later visits to Nazi Germany. The first encounter was 'a lot of boys, who stopped my sister and myself and took her hockey stick away from her. The thing was they weren't doing it as robbery but it was fun and good fellowship' (Warner, 1981, p. 130). Men are fascists, not just the Nazis. This male instinct leads, she claims, to the creation of the state and professionalism, 'I find the whole idea of a professional army very disgusting still. Lacking a normal life they turn into scoundrels' (Warner, 1981, p. 131).

Where West's training in literature is so very helpful is because it helps her make linguistic connections between the abstract and the everyday. Men distort history by a process of abstraction, mainly of women. To restore women to history West has to use a mixed mode of cultural and literary criticism. In other words, through her own critical mode she attacks the seamless abstract of male tradition.

As we might expect, all her reviews tell the same story. Writing about Granville-Barker's *The Marrying of Ann Leete*, Rebecca West notes that Granville-Barker's solution, for his heroine Ann, of 'going "back to the land" . . . is the easy solution that would appeal to a very young man. It is the solution that fascinates the child-like minds of Chesterton and Belloc' (Marcus, 1982, p. 23). Male infantilism restricts women's development. What was needed was a healthy association between organisms and their surroundings that Rebecca West called process. Part of the problem of containing men, West suggests, is defining the difference of women. Her articles may appear short, polemical pieces but they contain a series of quite careful definitions of women which West felt could be helpful to women trying to understand their roles in society and literature. From her knowledge of biology West understood that women were only different from men in 'the disposition of the reproductive tissue and the resulting modification of physical structure' (Marcus, 1982, p. 163). This is quite a sophisticated judgement to be making when West wrote it in 1913. Like contemporary feminist anthropologists, for example Shirley Ortner,[1] West is saying that gender dispositions are not genetically created but socially or culturally constructed. To West, difference is a physiological characteristic, but how does West's knowledge of biology interact with her ideas about literature? It appears in her criticism, in her careful character-isation of women. West is alarmed by categories of femininity. In a long correspondence with Mrs Hobson in *The Freewoman* West attacks Hobson's repressive scheme of women and domesticity: 'Mrs Hobson believes that there are varieties of women separate and immutable—the slattern, the housewife, the muddler, the manager—as distinct from one another as the lion from the cockatoo. Untidiness and laziness, like all the "beastliness" of the poor, are largely accidents of environment' (Marcus, 1982, p. 39). West is easy with terms from biology and psychoanalysis and can use them as metaphors rather than accept the stereotyping made by conservative women or men.

Men and women are, she says, dynamically different in sensibility. In *Black Lamb and Grey Falcon* West invents a marvellous phrase for the difference between male sensibility and female sensibility. 'Idiots and lunatics. It's a perfectly good division' (Warner, 1981, p. 125). Asked if she thought the sensibility was innate or produced by culture West replied 'Oh, I really can't tell you that. It's awfully hard. You can't imagine what maleness and femaleness would be if you got back to them in pure laboratory state' (Warner, 1981, p. 125).

By refusing to categorise women as *essentially* different from men in anything other than reproductive physiology, West is not less of a feminist. She recognises that men use arguments about difference to subordinate women. West does not want to work with men: 'sometimes it seems rather a questionable ideal—to work among common men, to be sucked under into the same whirlpool of sterile activity' (Marcus, 1982, p. 23). What she wants is to give women writers male advantages.

In 'And They All Lived Unhappily Ever After' West reviews the novels of Edna O'Brien, Penelope Mortimer, Doris Lessing and Iris Murdoch. West thinks their novels represent the general social position of the woman writer. She asks, does the 'elegant sufficiency of women novelists' in the period of the 1970s help us 'make up our minds' whether the feminist pioneers were right in their dreams? The pioneers hoped that if women gained the vote, earned their own livings and developed their minds they 'might also be luckier in love than their mothers' (West, 1978, p. 460). West finds no evidence, in the work of O'Brien or Murdoch, that those hopes have been fulfilled. Women characters in these novels are victim figures, and West 'finds oneself muttering as one reads, "Come now, it cannot have made all that difference to you that he is not around." But that is what the book is about, excessive grief' (West, 1978, p. 461).

For West, the essential issue is the sexual power of men, and she uses the review to attack women novelists who cannot deal with it adequately. West's pessimism, here in the 1970s, is still shaped by her earlier suffragette world with its demand for positive women role models in literature. Rebecca West focuses on the seduced and the betrayed in contemporary fiction as if arguing an earlier (but still very relevant) case for the literary expression of affirmative feminism. West finds contemporary women writers fairly alien because they refuse to make moral *and therefore* artistic judgements. Rebecca West is a cultural critic puzzled by any woman writer who abjures her moral role. The key is in her style. Because she is a moralist West writes very directly: 'A cell is more honest than a forsaken bedroom; it always made it clear that one would sleep alone' (West, 1978, p. 460). West's own epigrammatic tone frees her from restraining literary conventions. Although when asked: 'Interviewer: "Are there any advantages at all in being a woman and a writer?" West answered "None, whatsoever", (Warner, 1981, p. 135).

The critical tradition, West says, misrepresents the woman writer. Writing again in 1932, about Charlotte Brontë, West isolates herself from other critical positions of the time in order to respond more sympathetically to women:

> A school of criticism . . . has imported into this country its own puerile version of the debate between romanticism and classicism which has cut up the French world of letters into sterile sectionalism, and trots about frivolously inventing categories on insufficient bases, rejecting works of art that do not fit into them, and attaching certificates to those that do. [West, 1978, p. 438]

The vituperation is almost Johnsonian. West appears to be the typical English amateur distrusting continental poetics. But she is more concerned about the inadequate *process* of criticism. Criticism, to West, is lost in a classifying formalism. It is overly concerned with categories and genres which particularly inhibit the more diffuse linguistic terrain of the woman novelist—in this case Charlotte Brontë. 'Towards literature we preserve the attitude that the eighteenth century adopted towards nature when it called the Alps "horrid and undisciplined", and turn our steps away' (Marcus, 1982, p. 313). By representing literature as a particular organisiation with specific laws and devices, West says, criticism was inhibiting the ability of readers to read. Literature is no longer being read for ideas nor as a reflection of the social reality of women. Yet the canon alone could not explain the misrepresentation of women. Explanations were also to be found, outside it, in popular culture. Reviewing *The Considine Luck*, West points out that in popular novels the heroine is a puppet. The reader 'paints her wooden cheeks with the flush of his sensuous dreams' (Marcus, 1982, p. 42).

To West, criticism and popular culture share a continuity: they provide the unreal with a structure of meaning. It has been a function of both, West implies, to involve a meaning process that women must exist in a man-controlled world.

It is in her later essays, above all in *The Strange Necessity*, that Rebecca West raises more general questions about the role of art. Her questions, in that book, are the vexed questions that are central to all criticism: 'Why does art matter?' and 'Why does it matter so much?' Art matters because it has a relation to living people and their need for 'information of one sort or another about the universe' (West, 1978, p. 378). But this still begs the questions 'Why does art matter so much?' and 'Why do we feel so emotionally about great works of art?', which West goes on to answer.

A simple answer is that since art is an analysis and synthesis of experience, it predicates continuity—that life will go on, at least in print. This in itself should give us pleasure. But West works harder, moving away from art-as-reality principle to art-as-pleasure principle. She makes an explicit analogy between the experience of art and sexuality: 'It overflows the confines of the mind and becomes an important physical event . . . Is this exaltation the orgasm, as it were, of the artistic instinct . . ? (West, 1978, p. 379).

West uses here one of the primary and most resonant metaphors provided by female sexuality to assess the creativity of art. West's use of sexual tropes is a conscious attempt to obliterate aesthetic distance—to escape the confines of critical language. The technique has hints of a much later critic, Herbert Marcuse in *The Aesthetic Dimension*. It is as if West and Marcuse make the same intellectual journey—West moving feminist criticism on from its dependence on positive heroines and Marcuse moving Marxist criticism from its dependence on working-class heroes. It is notable not that West so closely presages that later work but that Marcuse cannot provide any answers that West had not already given.

As a male, Marcuse, like West's modernist contemporaries, represents sexuality as the masculine post-coitus where Eros 'appears in the brief moments of fulfilment, tranquility—in the "beautiful moment" which arrests' (Marcuse, 1978, p. 65). West reappropriates biology for metaphors of female creativity. Her language is revealing. It is full of tropes—of 'embraces' of 'leaping of the blood'. Sometimes this becomes merely organic. For example, writing about *Daisy Miller*, West says 'there were discernible in it certain black lines which, like the dark veining in a crocus that foretells its decay . . .' (West, 1916, p. 47). But Rebecca West tries to celebrate the darker patterns in heroines—the repressed, the submerged world of female sexuality. She is sensitive here, and throughout all her criticism and fiction to the current of sexuality that swirled beneath polite society and might hopefully rush through. Rebecca West's most consistent feminist technique is her use of physical tropes. When she describes a writer's prose it is always full of colour and 'smell' and 'taste'. Sometimes the terminology is specifically sexual. Barker 'embraces logic like a lover . . . To avoid the ordeal of emotion that leads to the conception is the impulse of death' (Marcus, 1982, p. 21). Why did Rebecca West use physical metaphors? The importance of metaphor as a form lives in its potency. Metaphor shakes our bearings on the question of how we stand in relation to 'objective reality'—to make us lose our fix in the position of what is 'out there' in 'reality'. It puts the significance of a situation in its most compelling form. West can fault Strindberg, for example, because his physical metaphors were not potent but too intensely autobiographical.

As we have seen (in 'Virginia Woolf'), sexual tropes are a language of taboo. Rebecca West seems to use taboo words to clear her mental space in what Harold Bloom calls the act of 'kenosis'.[2] In *The Anxiety of Influence* Bloom describes kenosis as the act of swerving away from the 'anxiety of influence' of earlier writers by the use of breaking-devices. 'Taboo' words are breaking-devices. What is dramatic about West is that she is a woman critic using sexual metaphors against men to reveal their 'sex-antagonism' to women.

But what *is* more problematic for a woman critic is defining female experience itself. To West literature provides the exciting experience 'which if left in a crude state would probably make one feel that life was too difficult' (West, 1978, p. 379). This attitude towards literature is a valuable advance on seeing it simply as the 'expression' of artistic objects. But it leads directly into another difficulty. The idea that literature is good for women if it manifests a concrete feel for women's experience focuses attention on the text often at the expense of its cultural and historical context.

There are ambiguities, then, in West's writing, which it might be worth pointing to if only to clear away our own confusions about the concept 'experience'. First West claims that women need a full experience of life, otherwise they cannot write: 'For want of emotional experience Jane Austen's imagination never developed virility' (Marcus, 1982, p. 48). Lack of 'virility' is a rather unfortunate term for a feminist critic. It also suggests the 'expressive' fallacy that the novel equals the convictions of the writer. Another problem occurs in West's reviews of Virginia Woolf. To West, Woolf's best novels 'are those which deal with material familiar to her because she had lived it. *To the Lighthouse, Mrs Dalloway,* and *Between the Acts* were descriptions of people and events not only known but well known to her' (West, 1978, p. 407). West is assuming that 'people' and 'events' are existing prior to and independent of Virginia Woolf's conception of them, as if Woolf's writing was simply a reflection of Woolf's life. But 'experience' *per se* is not an adequate criterion of literary value. Novels are not simply 'good' because they are about the experiences of the author. West often describes novels as if they were case studies of real women. She liked *The Price She Paid* by David Graham Phillips because he created a typical woman: 'This condition of things seems to Phillips typical of what marriage may become ... Besides, Mildred the heroine deserved nothing better. She is doing no work' (Marcus, 1982, p. 77). Rebecca West often takes actions and characterisation in the novel to be real events. In her later criticism West develops her ideas more problematically. In 'The Event and Its Image' she defines the difference between an event and experience: 'Not everything that happens to us is an experience. It is an event. But an experience is an event which affects one so that it tests one, and one tests it . . . to modify one's philosophy in the light of the added knowledge it has brought one' (West, 1962, p. 189). 'Experience' of the novelist then is not a naked reflection of her reality but is, simultaneously, the expression of life *and* a moral judgement about it. Only in this way can 'experience' be incorporated into literary form as an image. This seems to me quite an interesting position and one directly helpful to feminist criticism. It begins to answer questions about what makes fiction 'true' for women and how we look for evidence of that truth. By 1962, then, West is easy with the complexities that her earlier criticism perhaps simplifies. Yet, having said that, if we return to her first book, *Henry James*, we find West handling difficult questions about the representation of experience in literature. She asks why did James find the representation of femininity so fruitful to his art, and what analysis of the myth of femininity is he presenting which is of use to us? West is very certain about types and categories of women, their ages and behaviour. There is no hint in her text of James' more problematic concept of 'femininity', which made him put female children at the centre of his fiction. West's stance is very much this: What can James teach 'our generation' about women? First, West says, his heroines are attractive women with whom we can identify. With Milly Theale in *The Wings of the Dove* 'one's knowledge of her grows into love' (West, 1916, p. 103). To West, being able to identify with characters is a way to test the artistic value of novels. What is particularly revealing, here, is West's linkage of James' ideas with his syntactical expression of them. West finds femininity to be in James' method. It is part of his very style: 'In those days when his sentence was a straight young thing that could run where it liked, instead of a delicate creature swathed in relative clauses as an invalid in shawls' (West, 1916, p. 41).

West establishes, as early as 1916, a possible 'feminine' linguistic practice. *Henry James* contains many other examples of what became West's standard techniques. She uses domestic imagery and most consistently those images of houses and domestic interiors, thinking that although James had built 'comfortable' houses the 'furniture' of the novels is meagre because this 'is neither made nor sold in his country' (West, 1916, p. 30). West's extended or condensed analogies work illustratively and are always appropriate to her subject. What *is* surprising in such an early book is West's interrogative tone and conceptual handling of the terms of 'culture' and 'emotions'. Finally, she takes issue with James because he is conservative and allows that conservatism to distort his characters. West dislikes what she understands to be Henry James' jocular treatment of social history because West wants art to deal with the *whole* ideology of women. James, to West, cannot adequately represent women because he represents women not as human beings but as cramped innocents, which is 'as ridiculous as a heaven where the saints all go about with their haloes protected by mackintosh covers' (West, 1916, p. 54).

Critics writing about West assume that the variety of her criticism inhibits her from entering a specifically literary perspective. Peter Wolfe thinks her 'no literary critic *per se*' (Wolfe, 1971, p. 25). Even her defenders, like Dale Spender, praise West's irreverence' at the expense of her scholarship (Spender, 1983, p. 46).

Yet is it by developing a wide-ranging number of concerns— from the media, politics and travelogues—that West, like feminist literary criticism today, escapes the paternal tradition. But why did West speak in such a variety of voices by using the languages of biology, psychoanalysis or sexuality? There are hundreds of articles, several novels, short stories, lectures and speeches. All daring, exciting examples of West's provocative views. To circle back to our beginning she was, because she wanted to be, a cultural polymath. But why the intensity? If we are looking at Rebecca West's criticism as the study of the life-cycle of the critic-as-critic, then we need to look for influence. I think we have to sketch out another line which should help us read West more accurately. It is not chronological or even heuristic. Since the line is tenuous, perhaps I should draw it as follows. Cicily Fairfield needs a writing pseudonym and becomes Rebecca East. At the Academy of Dramatic Art she acts in *Rosmersholm* and 'Rebecca East' becomes Rebecca West. Ibsen's *Rosmersholm* is a play about artists and the role of language. It is a play in which the events are in the *minds* of the characters psychologically rather than materially present on the stage. The character 'Rebecca West' establishes her identity as a woman by bringing down the reactionary patriarchal Rosmersholm.[3] The 'real' Rebecca West is surrounded by patriarchs. Her father is a well-known war correspondent and ballistics expert. To become a writer against *that* writer? And to become a pacifist travel correspondent? It would need a great deal of practice, of constant writing. Rebecca West's most intense imagery is from ballistics. She often uses the exaggerated tropes of physical action. Working women are 'hot-eyed battalions, in luxury-lusting armies' (Marcus, 1982, p. 184). Women are projectiles, with Emily Davison the emblematic missile, 'her pyrotechnic intelligence blazing the brighter through a body worn thin by pain and the exactions of good deeds' (Marcus, 1982, p. 178).

The negation of the father is never possible but in writers' *intensity* of rhetoric is 'their brief moments-of-moments in which truly they are liberating gods' (Bloom, 1973, p. 103). Freud, too, writes about the energy of refusal in Ibsen's *Rosmersholm.* He traces Rebecca West's motivation to guilt about her incestuous relationship with her father and the way she repeats that relationship with Rosmer. Freud's phrase 'the reproach of incest' might be a metaphor for the real Rebecca West (Freud, 1951, p. 329). West had other 'fathers'. One was that defender of Victorian values Herbert Spencer, Mr Fairfield's favourite philosopher. Spencer has to be written out: 'he produced a quotation from Herbert Spencer—who was ever undone by his love of classification—to the effect that all women are morally and intellectually deficient' (Marcus, 1982, p. 152). Rebecca West breaks with Victorian anti-feminism, while remaining partly mortgaged to its language. For example, West's resolutely 'organic' approach to her objects of study resembles Spencer's idea of natural order. But Spencer's impact on West arrives indirectly through the scientific ideas of H.G. Wells. It is *this* patriarchal milieu that West had to counter. Indeed, West had to orchestrate her writing around H.G Wells' demands on her and on their son. Even after they separated and while she was writing *Harriet Hume,* Wells made West ill from his constant demands (Ray, 1974, p. 184). West's relationship with H.G. Wells breaks through, autobiographically, into her criticism in two ways. First, the secret of West's role as unmarried mother of Wells' son keeps being 'revealed' in her text in her obsessive concern with other unmarried mothers in fiction or in life. Second, H.G. Wells' scientific language influences West's terminology. Scientific ideas of biological 'nature' are of course crucial to that feminist problem of 'essentialism'. Therefore, to understand West's notions of sexuality and the feminine, and her contribution to the 'essentialist' debate, we need to sketch out the contemporary scientific ambience of H.G. Wells and Rebecca West.

Rebecca West was an established critic by the time she reviewed H.G. Wells' *Marriage*. She found 'Mr Wells' mannerisms are more infuriating than ever in *Marriage* (Marcus, 1982, p. 64). To West, Wells generalised from one unfortunate type of woman who West felt would be disappearing by being 'sifted clean through the sieve of work'. The tone of West's review made Wells want to meet her. Wells, as his letters reveal, is always as interested by West's style as much as by her person. Rebecca West is disguised as the character Amanda in Wells' *The Research Magnificent*, and *Babes in the Darling Wood* was Wells' answer to West's *Return of the Soldier*. Their relationship was, then, as much intellectual as sexual. West learnt from Wells' writing and conversation the organic animal language that she uses again and again in her criticism. She was 'Panther' to his 'Jaguar'—nicknames which stood for the withdrawal from polite society that their 'wild' relationship entailed. But they were at odds about the role of art. Wells dismisses Rebecca West's style because 'It is no good whatever for a philosophical discourse' (Ray, 1974, p. 179). The difference, between them, to Wells was that 'you have a richness. I am simplicity' (Ray, 1974, p. 191). But the difference also may have had to do with Wells' masculine materialism. After his death, Rebecca West realised that her relationship with Wells had made her the 'victim of a sort of sadist situation' (Warner, 1981, p. 134). But the tenor of much of her literary and political comments come directly from their relationship. For example, the Home Secretary is 'a very dangerous criminal' because he refused to allow a prisoner to marry his girl-friend to legitimise their baby (Marcus, 1982, p. 142). Ibsen is a very moral writer to West because when Nora Helmer leaves home 'her feeling of responsibility to her children was not lost, but intensified'

(Marcus, 1982, p. 378). Both West and Wells are influenced by an evolutionary or deterministic philosophy of life process but both are trying to establish a basis for a more active concept of freedom of will. H.G. Wells wanted freedom for Mr Polly and Rebecca West wanted freedom for feminism. The traces of Wells are in the way West often writes about working women as if they were a *species* to be catalogued 'dazed with overwork and underfeeding: quite obviously an inferior species' (Marcus, 1982, p. 187). West combines this imagery with the idea (derived largely from H.G. Wells and T.H Huxley), that we can *influence* the evolutionary process rather than emulate or be subdued by it. In the future, West 'saw some bronzed and travel-scarred pioneer . . . Women struggling to maintain a parasitic sex' (Marcus, 1982, p. 192). West's future is optimistic but still part of her contemporary (male) scientific framework which erupts constantly in her metaphors of 'microscopes' and 'parasites'.

What was valuable for Rebecca West was an introduction, through reading H.G. Wells, to a general scientific milieu. What was not valuable, and had to be discarded, were the concepts of femininity that this milieu endorsed. In *First and Last Things* Wells writes about 'The Case of the Wife and Mother', 'Sex' and 'Personal Love and Life'. A woman must 'consider herself an unrecognised public official, irregularly commanded and improperly paid. There is no good in flagrant rebellion' (Wells, 1933, p. 172). To Wells, men's relationship with women resembles the bourgeois role of England with her colonies. Love is 'an impoverished capital that has no dependent towns' (p. 198). Although he discusses alternatives to marriage, Wells is very hesitant about them: 'It is perhaps advisable to point out that to discuss those possibilities is not the same thing as to urge the reader to hazardous experiments' (p. 188). In any case, such a partnership can work only if the male's life was 'insured'. Wells argues in a patriarchal trajectory from capitalism to fascistic biologism. Love, he says, is 'a synthetic force in human affairs, the merger tendency, a linking force, an expression in personal will and feeling of the common element and interest' (p. 163). Finally, gender is biologically determined. 'If for example, it is for the good of the species that a whole half of its individuals should be specialised and subordinated to the physical sexual life, as . . . woman have tended to be, then certainly we must do nothing to prevent that' (p. 184). H.G. Wells habitually places a great faith in scientific method as the only effective means of organising society. Wells thinks the role of a woman is for her to voluntarily contribute all her powers to the developing life of the species. The quotations reveal Wells' patriarchal attempt to interweave a would-be scientific rationale with a mystical philosophy. He endeavours to justify his ideas scientifically with a Darwinian terminology of 'experiments'. Since the framework of Edwardian science derived from Spencer and Huxley, was capable of supporting such fascist and patriarchal doctrines, West clearly would have to discard all her 'fathers'.

The vexed relation between women, sexuality and creativity Rebecca West addresses in a long essay 'Woman as Artist and Thinker'. The essay was commissioned by the American psycho-Marxist V.F. Calverton and Samuel D. Schmalhausen[4] for a symposium which includes pieces by Charlotte Perkins Gilman and Havelock Ellis. The book gives us some understanding of what was considered to be radical ideology in the 1920s and 1930s, and it is interesting to see the context in which Rebecca West wanted her work to appear. The introduction sets the agenda and tone of the collection. The starting point of each essay was to be the institutional conspiracy of men against women: 'A general religious conspiracy coupled with a more specialised intellectual and political and educational collusion' (Schmalhausen, 1931, p. xvii). And the concept which informs that central theme is one 'essentialism': 'Are there still differences between the sexes that no condition of equality can ever remove? (p. xvi).

The symposium was West's best opportunity to deal directly with the connections between sexual oppression and creativity. The book provides West with an American psychoanalytic forum and spoke to an audience away from the Darwinian stringencies of British intellectuals. 'Take an X-ray photograph of a child of ten and you will see the white lines where already decay has begun to establish itself' (West, 1931, p. 379). West's vocabulary is still from that Darwinian source. She speaks of 'performance' and 'factors' in the environment'. Then Rebecca West's rhetoric undergoes a kind of osmosis. She displaces

Wellsian science and turns instead toward metaphor and sexual imagery. West's objective is to determine how best to encourage the natural development of the woman artist. She needs, West asserts, psychological autonomy in order to project her sexuality into her art, since sterility will 'cut down the performance of women to a negligible fraction of their potentialities' (p. 374).

As she travels deeper into her topic, West's own voice emerges. She disengages from organicism and also, more importantly, from the association between feminism and materialism made by the editors. West's interest is now anthropological. Why in different kinds of social systems, she asks, do more men than women become insane? If sexuality *is* crucial to creativity, how does that experience relate to art and to women's nature? To West, the 'experience' of women can never be measured or quantified since it is in 'their desire for art and thought' (p. 371). Women's art itself is different, 'different in essence', from that of men and West's terminology subtly readjusts to the metaphoric and imagistic in order to accommodate this 'uncontrollable' experience. 'It becomes plain that women do not carry a knife as they go through life, but a box' (p. 381). Her conclusion is feminist. Since intellectual life was dominated by the 'neurotic' males, 'it is against them that women must defend themselves' (p. 382).

West is purposefully seeking out the significance of gender to art and struggling to define a more authentic criticism for women. By placing West's account against one of her 'neurotic' male contemporaries, we can judge the extent of that displacement of male neuroticism. Havelock Ellis, in his contribution to the symposium, addresses the same problem of 'essentialism'. Unlike West's adequate discourse of sexuality, Ellis describes biological symptoms as a coherent set of distinguishing marks which infallibly characterise women. In his essay 'Women's Sexual Nature' Ellis finally asks only for 'precise and statistical studies, on a large scale' (Ellis, 1931, p. 233).

To West, women's experiences are controlled not by their innate biology but by a masculine fantasy of the feminine. At a trivial level, West, like Virginia Woolf, links working women's diet of milk puddings and boiled eggs to the enforced asceticism of working women's lives. More importantly, she describes how the physical and sexual oppression of the working class mother acts as a scapegoat for capitalism. West also finds that contemporary feminist descriptions of sexuality were not any more adequate than those of patriarchy. She attacks Christabel Pankhurst's 'coarse description' of venereal diseases when 'the body loves beautiful things—like sunlight and the sea and swift running—and this thing against which we are fighting is not a beautiful thing' (Marcus, 1982, p. 207). Men's historical abuse of women, West says, might better be addressed in the language of literature.

West matches her ideology with a discourse of sexuality in her short story 'Indissoluble Matrimony', published in 1914. We could read the story as a key modernist step from James to D.H. Lawrence's association of the psyche and nature. But, more importantly, the story encapsulates all the themes of Rebecca West's later career of criticism. The main narrative is an account of the attempted murder of a wife by her husband which may, or may not, be a self-created nightmare in his mind. The story is more than simply an early example of modernist narrative technique. A hint is to be found in the way West describes the feelings of George and Evadne: 'But this sense of the earth's sympathy slipped away from them and they loathed all matter as the dull wrapping of their flame-like passion. At their wishing matter fell away and they saw sarcastic vision. He saw her as a toad squatting in the clear earth' (Marcus, 1982, p. 280).

Rebecca West uses metaphors of physical appearance and sexuality to stand for subconscious thoughts. It is the same imagery as in her criticism—a metaphoric language of sexual politics. West does not explicitly describe levels of consciousness but represents them in imagery. The narrator is able to enter the unconscious, not just the subconscious, of each character through her perception of psychical and sexual emotions. The man is weak and unimaginative, the woman physically strong—a good swimmer and of mixed race. Sexual power is the motive force of their relationship and characterisation. Evadne is a feminist, and West connects Evadne's verbal dexterity as a public speaker with her physical strength. Sexuality is inter-connected with the political ideology of each character as it is, or should be West is suggesting, of living people.

Rebecca West wrestled all her life with problems of creativity and with feminism. For a radical like West, the solution to these problems was to create a psychosocial discourse for criticism, one whose generic origins could not be determined by male definitions. In rejecting her Victorian fathers and her Edwardian peers West demands a new feminine consciousness both for literature and for society. In her more overtly feminist pieces she continually links the conventions of writing with the conventions of politics. West's interest is always in how they (men) distort the world and how we (women) can re-create it. If West's criteria of value are frequently organic, it does not mean that she remained in a humanist project but that she aims for a more inclusive world-view. She writes almost like an anthropologist seeing culture as the whole way of life of a society, its beliefs and its attitudes as expressed in all kinds of structures, rituals and gestures. The certainty of judgement is there in the way West always wants criticism to take a moral stand.

Rebecca West writes better, because she writes more clearly, in the essays about women. She knows what she wants to say. A good example is the essay on Mrs Pankhurst from *The Post-Victorians*, which attempts to bring public and private strands together—to link the private themes of Mrs Pankhurst's life, like her French education, with the public events of her politics. West's mixture of psychoanalysis and feminism enable her to contextualise the difficult problem of Mrs Pankhurst's nationalism by relating it to her childhood conditioning. West's ability to mix disciplines enables her to deal openly with Mrs Pankhurst's 'sublimated sex-antagonism' (Marcus, 1982, p. 248).

In keeping with the age of psychoanalysis in which she wrote, West can describe male uniformity as conformity, a loss of individual identity, and therefore diversity can be the special individuality of women. West believes passionately in a creative originality which springs, not only from rational, conscious mental knowledge, but from an imaginitive feminine unconscious. Rebecca West's feminism comes, in large part, from her artistic exploration of possible forms of belief of which modern women are the inheritors of a burnt-out male theosophy. As she says: 'The woman who is acting the principal part in her own ambitious play is unlikely to weep because she is not playing the principal part in some man's no more ambitious play' (Marcus, 1982, p. 85).

9

ADRIENNE RICH

All criticism is influenced by the cultural tradition in which it is formed. More than most feminists, Adrienne Rich has a firm sense of her particular position in contemporary feminism. In her criticism Rich delineates a variety of feminist ideas which she calls her 'Revision', or rewriting, of patriarchal culture. They include many notions crucial to contemporary feminism. Calling herself a radical feminist, Rich offers fresh definitions of women's oppression, of male violence and racism and creates an alternative libidinal, women-centred, criticism.

For contemporary feminism the concept of *difference* is central. Like Julia Kristeva and Mary Daly, Rich uses psychoanalysis and anthropology to show a feminine subject as constituted differently from a masculine subject. The question of motherhood, in *Of Woman Born*, has been an extraordinarily fruitful topic for Rich since she understands that mothers, not just women, are *the* repressed subject in patriarchy. In *On Lies, Secrets and Silence*, and later essays in *Signs* and elsewhere, Rich takes that relation between reproduction and sexuality into a more radical definition of difference. In posing a sexuality independent from men, Adrienne Rich has developed complex arguments about the differences *between* women, as well as between women and men, and thus is challenging many normative values even in contemporary feminism.

Adrienne Rich *is* however a literary critic, as well as a writer of theory. The problems of a text as a signifying practice are as much her daily experience in poetry as they are the focus of feminist literary criticism today. Adrienne Rich is a notable exception to the Anglo-American empiricist tradition of literary criticism in the way that she mixes autobiography, myth and literary criticism to offer her reader moral judgements as an evaluation of authenticity in literary readings. Rich is therefore central to any understanding of feminist literary criticism since she grounds her thoughts on the relation between women and textual production in a challenging libidinal theory of radical feminism.

Radical American politics in the 1960s provides the background to Rich's criticism. When protesting against American involvement in Vietnam Adrienne Rich, along with Denise Levertov, began to question and rethink the role of literature through reflections on her own 'colonialised' experience as a woman poet and mother in patriarchy: 'I became a mother in the family-centered, consumer-orientated, Freudian-American world of the 1950s' (Rich, 1977b, p. 25). Rich always translates her autobiographical experiences into those generically appropriate for other women. The problem she describes in *Of Woman Born*, and talks about later, is one of definitions: 'Defining what would be a radical feminist force, or a very radical thrust in the States, has never been done' (1981, p. 15). Introducing her first collection of poetry, *A Change of World*, W.H. Auden found Rich's emotions to be among the 'typical experiences of our time' (Auden, 1951, p. ii).

In *On Lies, Secrets, and Silence* Adrienne Rich says her aim is 'to define a female consciousness which is political, aesthetic and erotic, and which refuses to be included or contained in the culture of passivity' (1980, p. 18). It is an enormous feminist project. Making a deliberate continuum of her life, her creative writing and criticism also makes Rich an unusual user of autobiography. As Estelle C. Jelinek has shown, women autobiographers rarely describe their professional lives and are often reticent about dealing directly with their feelings (Jelinek, 1980, p. 13). Adrienne Rich violates this regressive tradition of female writing just as she flouts the patriarchal constraints of literary production.

Rich cannot develop a female aesthetic without definitions. Describing her sterilisation in *Of Woman Born*, she is unhappy with the terminology: 'Nothing is removed from a woman's body ... Yet the language suggests a cutting—or burning-away—of her essential womanhood, just as the old word "barren" suggests a woman eternally empty and lacking' (Rich, 1977b, p. 29). Rich's frequent use of inverted commas is part of her care with definitions and qualifications.

Rich prefers a criticism drawn from her own domestic landscape. The formulation of women's experience, for Rich, is determined by the basic language at women's disposal for analysing and describing their adventures to their own understanding. Domestic events can give rise to specific feminist questions and are frequently articulated by Rich in the form of these questions. Yet Rich *is* concerned with generative ideas of moral value to women.

Each new set of questions Rich forms into a shaped critique organised around a particular theme—as the concept of 'motherhood' in *Of Woman Born*. But it would be wrong to treat her texts in isolation one from another. She often tries out new areas of investigation in relatively simplistic ways, within the context of a critique centering on another theme. Adrienne Rich's criticism is therefore best analysed as a continuum (rather than self-contained achievements) and as a radical mixture of polemical and introspective writing.

Adrienne Rich is a good feminist critic because she links her two main subjects—women's emotions and culture—to the realities of their contemporary history. Just as through the 1960s these two subjects moved closer together in her poetry, in her criticism they are a collage of feminist ideas. In her best writing, politics and the personal life are a mixture of mimesis and determinism. A recurrent scene in her criticism is the vignette of herself: 'In a living room in 1975, I spent an evening with a group of women poets, some of whom had children . . . We talked of poetry, and also of infanticide' (Rich, 1977b, p. 24). The pattern is one of relationships between herself and another, or group of women, formed to cope with the cultural realities of women's lives.

Rich's main technique—the autobiographical journey into feminism—provides a structure for much of her literary criticism. In the essay on Emily Dickinson, for example, Rich seizes on images of Dickinson *in* contemporary life as much as images *in* Dickinson to get across her feminist points. Rich finds on an envelope 'an engraving of the poet as popular fancy has preferred her, in a white lace ruff and with hair as bouffant as if

Part II

she had just stepped from a Boston beauty-parlor' (Rich, 1980, p. 163). Rich's problem, the critic's problem, is to include her reader—the buyer of contemporary stamps—as a potential critic who will share Rich's disgust with Dickinson's misrepresentation. Rich is helping us understand how to be makers of a criticism which is *relevant* to us today.

Feminist criticism, then, could provide contemporary women with an understanding of their repression, and Rich's role as a feminist critic, as we have seen, is to provide definitions: 'Feminism is the place where in the most natural, organic way subjectivity and politics have to come together' (Gelpi, 1975, p. 114). Adrienne Rich therefore set about collecting and introducing women writers who, for her, stand out primarily as images of resistance as much as images of literary achievement. Over and over she evaluates and celebrates the writings of Dickinson, Wollstonecraft and de Beauvoir, among others, not only for their literature but also for their ideas. These writers Rich chooses because they are writers who make the representation of women central to their literary texts. For Rich, women's writing can provide a mythical re-evaluation of women's lives to counter the violence and depersonalisation of patriarchy. In *The American Poetry Review* Rich translates the American bombing of Vietnam into a symbol of American patriarchal society at home:

> The bombings, for example, if they have anything to teach us, must be understood in the light of something closer to home, both more private and painful, and more general and endemic, than the institutions, class, racial oppression, the hubris of the Pentagon or the ruthlessness of a right-wing administration: the bombings are so wholly sadistic, gratuitous and demonic that they can finally be seen, if we care to see them, for what they are: acts of concrete sexual violence, an expression of the congruence of violence and sex in the masculine psyche. [Rich, 1973, p. 10]

Adrienne Rich's use of run-on punctuation prohibits an elided quotation, but the punctuation reflects Rich's two central convictions. One, that contemporary patriarchy is, like the syntax, out of control, as it is out of touch with women's daily lives; and two, that individual acts of male sexual hostility are part of a much larger repression of women's sexual identities, just as America itself suppresses other colonised groups. Sexual

180

repression is like war—a confirmation of the split between female and male psyches. In her criticism Rich pursues this split by investigating its origins in prehistory and their representation in the psyche. In effect, she conducts a historical examination of the psychic life, as I will argue later when dealing with *Of Woman Born*.

The form of Rich's investigation is why it is particularly hard to respond to her only in terms of conventional literary techniques. Her style has to be read as part of theory. An example from very early in her career will show what I mean. Rich was invited, with other poets, to evaluate a recent poem by an important contemporary poet who could then write a commentary in response. Rich, together with Donald Justice and William Dickey, wrote about Karl Shapiro's 'The Bourgeois Poet'. Her piece is very revealing, not only as an accurate account of Shapiro's failings, but, more especially, for what it tells us about Rich's own future development as a critic: 'It seems to me that the poem as a whole is going to be a moral experience if it is anything. For a poet, in any case, language is always a form of moral behaviour' (Rich, 1964, p. 194). Literature is potent, then, for Rich, in so far as it *creates* experience, not just describes or reacts *to* experience. She does not react to Shapiro in terms of explication *de texte* but reads Shapiro (as she was to read all subsequent literature) for moral lessons.

What Rich needed was a literary theory which, while preserving attention to literature as an aesthetic object, would make something a good deal more radical and feminist out of it. She found the answer in an idea which could provide her with an agenda for her criticism.

Re-vision—the act of looking back, of seeing with fresh eyes, of entering an old text from a new critical direction—is for women more than a chapter in cultural history; it is an act of survival. Until we can understand the assumptions in which we are drenched, we cannot know ourselves [Rich, 1980, p. 35]

In 're-vision' Rich discovers nothing less than a way of defining the 'essence' of feminist criticism. It is worth getting at the precise notions Rich incorporates since re-vision is the central technique of her criticism. The run-on which Rich is making here is instructive. Re-vision is first historical—'looking back', cataloguing our inequities and rewriting the past. It remains 'cultural' but is always psychic—an analysis of our deepest 'assumptions'. Revision would help 'the girl or woman who tries to write because she is peculiarly susceptible to language. She goes to poetry or fiction looking for *her* way of being in the world' (Rich, 1980, p. 39). This is very like Virginia Woolf trying to create a criticism and a literary tradition that can respond to contemporary women.

By the time of the Foreword *On Lies, Secrets and Silence* Rich's rhetoric is more elaborate: 'To do this kind of work takes a capacity for constant active presence, a naturalist's attention to minute phenomena, for reading between the lines, watching closely for symbolic arrangements, decoding difficult and complex messages left for us by women of the past' (Rich, 1980, p. 14). Criticism, for Rich, is a life-long activity, an almost obsessive noting of patriarchal instances which eventually takes women outside institutionalised education. The rhetoric Rich employs here is more akin to Foucault's use of 'archaeology'—a topographical exposure of moral values encoded in linguistic forms.

Adrienne Rich took the term 're-vision' from the American poet Robert Duncan, who first uses it in *The Artist's View* in 1953. It is instructive to compare Duncan's original conception with Adrienne Rich's very different usage. The comparison highlights, I think, that more fundamental difference between 'male' and 'female' writers' conceptions of literary activity. This is Robert Duncan:

ON REVISIONS. In one way or another to live in a swarm of human speech. This is not to seek perfection but to draw honey or poetry out of all things. After Freud, we are aware that unwittingly we achieve our form. It is, whatever our mastery, the inevitable use we make of the speech that betrays to ourselves and to our hunters (our readers) the spore of what we are becoming.

I study what I write as I study out any mystery. A poem, mine, or others, is an occult document, a body awaiting vivisection, analysis, X-rays.

My revisions are my new works, each poem a revision of what has gone before. In-sight. Re-vision [Allen, 1960, pp.400–1]

Duncan, like Rich, uses organic imagery, but he is calling up a very masculine world. Both poets start from a notion of perception, but Duncan's concern is only to turn inwards, rather than Rich's open self-examination. Rich's 'looking back' is a method for her readers to share; Duncan, on the other hand, is *hunted* by his readers. Duncan's revision is the uncovering of his own dead past—a 'body awaiting vivisection' with new poems merely 'spores'. Patriarchy is not only in the vocabulary—of 'mastery' and 'hunters'—but is inherent in the very tropes of Duncan's rhetoric. Revision, to Rich, is not this self-exhumation but rather a way of seeing afresh to live afresh. Criticism, to Rich, is part of an intrinsically open and unresolved verbal and moral activity. The criteria for good criticism become the degree to which it participates in developing *all* women's experiences, not merely the development of the poet's personal experience. Rich's main task was to find a new language. The woman writer's need to find or reinvent vocabulary in which she can give power to her originating voice has been the central challenge for all committed nineteenth- and twentieth-century women writers: 'If the imagination is to transcend and transform experience it has to question, to challenge, to conceive of alternatives' (Rich, 1980, p. 43)

One way is to validate the linguistic enterprises of women. Rich is constantly introducing and supporting the work of other women poets. The new language she needed would be one spoken by and for other women in order to bring into existence a community of women readers. It is from this sense of a women's community that her critical method develops. The desire to convert everyday experience into a women-centred mythos leads Rich to explore the conversational and autobiographical aspects of spoken as well as written language.

The phenomenon Rich wishes to describe—this female community—makes great demands on her vocabulary. Her essays are full of powerful images from the domestic 'journalism was part of the strategy—like asbestos gloves, it allowed me to handle material I couldn't pick up barehanded' (Rich, 1980, p. 40). The vocabulary matches the message. Women's daily physical activities yield metaphors more vibrating than traditional poetic images. Similarly, Rich shapes the physical space of her essays with colons and dashes to create juxtapositions in order to disrupt normative forms. Adrienne Rich writes criticism in a language both discursive and generative. She refuses the old rhetoric of pattern and resolution. For example, many of her recent essays are in note form as 'On Separatism'. The refusal of that articulation is most complete in her descriptions of women-centred systems of thought acting as catalysts in an open-ended process of knowledge.

Even in an early essay, on the women poet Anne Bradstreet, Rich's motifs are clear. The piece is a straightforward account of a poet's evolution. Rich does not say that her gender is *always* the significant parameter of Bradstreet's style, since many of Bradstreet's techniques might be common to any colonial poet male or female. But Rich is feminist in the way she chooses to locate the quality and *value* of Bradstreet's techniques precisely in those poems specifically about her life as a woman with other women and children. Rich chooses the arrival of Bradstreet's life in her poetry as *the* moment of value since it is then that 'the web of her sensibility stretches almost invisibly within the framework of Puritan literary convention' (Rich, 1980, p. 31). Rich tells us that the more intimate poetic details of Bradstreet's life—her childrearing and sickness—are a triumph rather than a trivialising confession. The word 'web' has become one of most generative terms in literary feminism. Placing women's experience at the centre of critical attention gives Rich a basis for a fresh figurative language.

A sense of identity with other women stirs Rich more than any other experience (after childbirth). In the 1974 version of her *Selected Poems* she altered the pronouns of protagonists to women. She describes many different kinds of female groups, from the Cambridge women in *Of Woman Born* to the more theoretical examination of Elizabeth Stanton and Susan B. Anthony's friendship in *On Lies, Secrets and Silence*. Rich describes these groups to prove that feminist culture must come from an alternative feminist intellectual tradition based on friendship: 'To name and found a culture of our own means a real break from the passivity of the twentieth-century Western mind' (1980, p. 13). The creation of a women's culture is the only necessary antidote to the passivity of individualism. Hoping that the community of women will replace the violence of patriarchal society, Rich believes that women must explore their collective experience in order to transcend the isolation of their lives.

Rich's call for a separate, female-identified physical and semantic space brings Rich close to the feminism of writers like Mary Daly or Luce Irigaray. But although Rich describes the space as fundamental to feminism, it is not necessarily an *essential* constituent. This is because Rich, unlike Mary Daly, for example, is prepared to examine in more detail the inter-relationship between socialisation and psychical patterns. And Rich's plans for alternative models of social institutions are her best contribution to that more expansive feminist critique.

In 'Towards a Woman-Centered University' Rich outlines her idea of a women's community: 'If a truly universal and excellent network of childcare can begin to develop, if women in sufficient numbers pervade the University at all levels . . . there is a strong chance that in our own time we would begin to see some true "University" of values emerging from the inadequate and distorted corpus of patriarchal knowledge' (1980, pp. 154–5). Rich uses Virginia Woolf's three basic techniques—subvert from within, be selective and validate women's personal experience—but moves ahead of Woolf into strategic planning. The full account reads very like Catherine Beecher Stowe or Dolores Hayden's architectural models of women's communities. By very carefully itemising needs, Rich is occasionally taken over by minutiae, but there is a thoroughly optimistic feeling about the account—one that springs from Rich's animating sense of identity and direction, the feeling that each woman is travelling a path along with others. Rich is very close to anarcho-feminism in her intuitive attraction for the idea of local and organisational pluralism.

In a later review in *Ms* Adrienne Rich clarifies this anarchist impulse and ties in her notion of women's culture more closely to literature: 'This new culture, created and defined by women, is the great phenomenon of our century. I believe that in any genuinely human retrospect it will loom above two world wars, and several socialist revolutions . . . Women's art, though created in solitude, wells up out of community . . . and, by its very existence, it strengthens the network of the community' (1977a, p. 106). To Rich, it is the art/politics matrix of women's networks which will ultimately prove to be *the* most significant political and cultural event in our time.

Why writing is so important for women, Rich is saying, is

because it is a bridge between women. For herself, criticism provides Rich with the opportunity to take the typical stance of the divinating American—a Whitmanesque mission of the critic as seer. Poetry is 'where I existed as myself' (Rich, 1977b, p. 31). But it is in her criticism that Rich speaks out most fiercely. It is criticism which is continually the challenge since it is where Rich is most consciously hostile to misogyny. The 'I' in criticism is there so directly because Rich wants 'us' as readers to identify with her feminist world: 'I have hesitated to do what I am going to do now, which is to use myself as illustration . . . Like Virginia Woolf, I am aware of the women who are not with us here because they are washing the dishes and looking after the children' (1980, p. 38).

Rich, by 'using' herself autobiographically, can appeal to a wider audience than with a more academic literary criticism. Her criticism, however historical in reference, proceeds in a tone of intimate revelation, as if Rich understands that the political is most manifest in the language with which we explain ourselves to friends.

'Teaching Language in Open Admissions' tells us of the day-to-day life of a woman teacher and writer. Dates are given, names and events are all listed. But the personal account of her teaching very quickly leads her to conceptual questions about the use of Standard English as a weapon of colonialisation. Just as Virginia Woolf 'learnt' from working-class Co-operative women, so Rich 'learns' from her students. Both are outsiders, Rich as a lesbian feminist and her students as Blacks. It is worth observing that Rich talks in the piece about white female and Black *identity*, not about feminist or Black values. The sense of value is something very different. It suggests the comparative, the competitive. Adrienne Rich knows what feminism is, and she shows how it can be expressed. Literature can express it through a full awareness and valuation of psychic crises—birth, pregnancy and death. This is why Rich's notion of feminist process is convincing and is not just vaguely 'evolutionary', because she has a very precise notion of what she means.

What determines the success or failure of this enterprise, for Rich, is whether she can stake out a territory *within* literature. It will need to be a territory free from centuries of masculine connotations and associations, but a territory where literature is reappropriated, not destroyed. In conversation with the Gelpis, Rich framed the task as a question:

> What I am asking myself is not, if we have a political programme what kind of poems would poets be taught to write, but if we were in an altered state of consciousness, if we were free of the past, of the stereotypes, of the projections, of all the ways in which women have been used as aesthetic objects, what kind of poetry would we have then? . . . I cannot think of a single male poet . . . who hasn't misused and abused actual women' [Gelpi, 1975, p. 116]

Rich focuses on three problems: changing the language, developing a new perception of the psychic origins of conscious actions and rewriting the myths that have misrepresented women. There are several techniques which she perfects as a critic. The first is to look at male opinions through a kaleidoscope of feminist prisms. Male views are made to seem odd and single-minded in contrast with the multifarious offerings of women. Second, throughout her criticism Rich is fascinated by psychoanalysis. The essay 'Jane Eyre: The Temptations of a Motherless Woman' is a good example of this. Rich presents Jane as a paradigm of a Victorian woman's 'choice' to be either hysteric or scapegoat. Rich, metaphorically, describes the space of Thornfield Hall as an emblematic version of Jane's psyche. And in *Of Woman Born* she describes how 'for centuries women have felt their active, creative impulses as a kind of demonic possession' (1977b, pp. 69–70).

Any analysis centred around the theme of repression is psychoanalytically orientated. But Rich uses psychoanalysis to bring to literary criticism a particular conception of symbolism. It takes her in the direction of a study of emotions, religion, fantasy and, above all, of myth where the human response is a constructive, not passive, activity. That study is most fully developed in *Of Woman Born*, but passage after passage elsewhere in Rich begins with the personal experience or mood and moves to the generic, the mythical.

But the rewriting of myths is Adrienne Rich's particular contribution to feminist criticism. *Of Woman Born* takes key myths and puts them against Rich's autobiography and her account of the way women are moulded in contemporary culture. By analysing the historical paradigms of consciousness, Rich can expose how women's feelings and options have always been moulded by male assumptions.

What Rich does is to work out possible modes of women's myths, verbally, to achieve imaginatively what could not at that point be achieved in actual social relations—hence her interest in hypothesised primitive events. But every major advance in thinking, every new insight, springs from a new type of symbolic transformation. Myths are the first version of general ideas and are both metaphysical and psychical.

Phyllis Chesler's *Women and Madness*, which had a great influence on Rich, puts the tension more explicitly: 'My theology may be viewed as the psychology of modern history. It seems to represent the interaction of biology with later culture' (1972, p. 24).

Chesler, like Rich, reformulates the basis of myth. Both place great emphasis on the way culture connects with the individual psyches of women. Rich makes the same links: 'Madness, i.e. eruptions, disturbances of the unconscious, have had a very political meaning for women all along' (Gelpi, 1975, p. 114). *Of Woman Born* contains quest patterns and primitive archetypes, although Rich always balances the primitive past with our contemporary experience. This is because Rich understands the primitive may be the *only* set of experiences women are likely to share in civilised life. We menstruate, we give birth and we lactate.

Thus Rich is not writing an elegiac myth in *Of Woman Born*. She does not investigate eternal moments in women's past history but breaks with that idea of an essentially unchanging reality. She describes myths of birth and menstruation to help us more fully understand our contemporary culture and thus change it. Rich's stories are not something superadded to particular elements of day-to-day life. She refuses to see myth and life as independent modes. Unlike classic masculine myth-makers—Mailer and Pynchon are examples—Rich does not try to organise culture through one totalising framework. Rich is prepared to be multivarious. She seeks the source of metaphor in physical events or sometimes in anthropology. The different directions of her quest are what gives *Of Woman Born* its real originality and energy.

The book has become *the* classic text of feminist literary criticism. But it is important to see that Rich *starts* from reproduction, since some contemporary feminists try to deny the link between reproduction and sexuality altogether. But neither does Rich accept that the link must be made in the essentially heterosexual world of patriarchy, because she *substitutes* maternal love for marital relations. Rich is a very original critic because she was writing, as she herself explained, at a time when motherhood was a 'still relatively unexplored area for feminist theory'. *Of Woman Born* argues the case for a clearly confirmed tradition of female power. This power Rich locates in motherhood which men have mythically mis-represented. Rich carefully distinguishes between motherhood as an institution creating a dangerous schism between the public and private lives of women, and motherhood as a crucial experience *for* women. Rich interweaves her own story as a working mother into the text, using herself as an example of culture. Maternity, not marriage, is the centre since her maternal emotions have infinitely more space than the events of her marriage—even than her husband's suicide. The book is about maternal experience and its relation to women's culture. Rich paraphrases mythological versions of motherhood and treats them historically—putting them into a notional chronology of the writing out of women's power by male rationality. Rich shows how history constructs women's psyche—like constructing the notion of passive suffering as a universal female destiny.

Yet, by being mothers, women can counteract patriarchal definitions of femininity with their creativity. This is the agenda in *Of Woman Born*—Rich's proof that when becoming mothers women enter into a more complex territory of emotional experience. The book is as interesting for its absences as its argument. Unlike other feminists, Rich is not setting out on an imaginary quest for her *own* mother, as, say, do Margaret Atwood in *Surfacing* or Agnes Smedley in *Daughter of Earth*, but creating *herself* as mother. The book is about self-identity as well as psychic reconciliation. *Of Woman Born* ends with an interesting analogy between the physical relationship of mothers and daughters and its replication in the lesbian couple.

Why did Adrienne Rich need to write a cultural rather than

purely literary criticism? The answer lies, as she herself demonstrates, in a bankrupt masculine intellectual tradition. So Rich, single-handed, supplies us with a new tradition in an enormous spread of readings—through Rilke, Malinowski to psychoanalysts Chodorow and Chesler. But she goes further to supply us with a new critical technique. *Of Woman Born* crosses disciplines and mixes modes—of the diary, paraphrased narrative and historical quotations. It is full of visual and literary images. The technique is a coefficient of her theme. Telling stories of our past is traditionally the principal method mothers use to educate children. One problem with Rich's argument is her overuse of simplified contrasts. The primitive is too often seen as a possible refuge from civilisation. But since the book is about definitions, we should expect an epigrammatic style. Rich is in the business of giving a conceptual analysis even if she does sometimes try to define matriarchy as everything which is not patriarchy. She is very good at organising structurally around themes like the history of forceps, and if we are oppressed a little by her blinkered world, Rich does describe mothers, not in a static, iconographic fashion, but as real functionaries—the makers of acts and beliefs.

Rich is also presenting a very different myth of mothers than that described by Simone de Beauvoir and Julia Kristeva, who, to date, have presented the most systematic accounts of motherhood (see Ch. 3, above). The force of Rich's feeling and her indisputable social facts undo some of the harm done, conceptually, to mothers by de Beauvoir in *The Second Sex*. There are moments of similarity, mainly in the strong argument in both that the whole construction of motherhood is irredeemably harmed by marriage, although de Beauvoir prefers to find harm in an economic, not psychic, context. Pregnancy, to de Beauvoir, depersonalises the woman by enslaving her to the species. She locates motherhood only in a social context of abortion and contraception and accepts, unproblematically, psychoanalytic half-truths like the tenuous link between pregnancy and psychic abnormalities (de Beauvoir, 1972, p. 516). There is none of Rich's *repossession* for woman of the genius of her own body.

Adrienne Rich seems closer to the more contemporary French theory of Julia Kristeva. According to Kristeva, women desire children from their own fathers: 'She becomes, she is her own mother' (Kristeva, 1980, p. 239). Also, *Of Woman Born* is, in a sense, Rich's answer to her father—the medical professor. Both Kristeva and Rich think that when men make artistic representations of mothers they are representations of archaic memories of maternal seduction. Kristeva, however, is interested primarily in the *pre-symbolic* function of maternity (the semiotic depends on its maternal articulation). She does not, like Rich, look for a contemporary female discourse using symbols based on the maternal body. *Of Woman Born* is autobiographical as, say, Thoreau's *Walden* is autobiographical. Both have heroes in the process of writing a book, of writing themselves, of making themselves into emblems. In *Of Woman Born* Rich was able to provide a logically complete account of the reality of motherhood *and* a future dependent on it.

When feminists speak of 'difference' it is usually in the sense that Rich outlines in *Of Woman Born*, that of women's difference from men. That book is Rich's attempt to define women's feelings and give them some meaning (the maternal) in order to make the sense of difference valid. The change to defining 'difference' as lesbian identity is the work of Rich's key essay 'Compulsory Heterosexuality and Lesbian Existence'. As Rich suggests in her conversation with Marlene Packwood, lesbian identity is a necessary part of radical feminism: 'I think it has to be about transformation. And that's where I see lesbianism and feminism having very common ground' (Rich, 1981, p. 14). Feminist writings on sexuality up to that point had focused largely on the relation between reproduction and social controls. Adrienne Rich builds on de Beauvoir's thesis that women are originally homosexual, but she moves on from de Beauvoir to focus on elements like desire and fantasy which would be the special contribution of lesbian criticism to feminism. She was stepping into an area riddled with contradictions. What enables her to talk about 'difference' with coherence is 'a kind of clarity that we get from being that extra degree an outsider' (Rich, 1981, p. 14). Rich's notion of 'lesbian' is both historical and literary:

> Lesbian existence suggests both the fact of the historical presence of lesbians and our continuing creation of the meaning of that existence. I

mean the term *lesbian continuum* to include a range—through each woman's life and throughout history—of woman-identified experience; not simply the fact that a woman has had or consciously desired genital sexual experience with another woman [Rich, 1983, p. 156]

Rich wants to separate lesbianism from the gay movement in favour of making it part of general female experience. This would be for heterosexual feminists a more congenial, as well as more fruitful approach. Rich does not condemn heterosexual relationships *per se*, since she believes that patriarchy has, for too long, imposed arbitrary sexual dichotomies (lesbian *or* heterosexual) which have no meaning. The eradication of false dichotomies is, as usual, part of Rich's critical aim. She inverts our 'normal' way of thinking by asking if the *faux naïf* and very resonating question, 'If women are the earliest sources of emotional caring and physical nurture . . . *why in fact women would ever redirect* [to men]' (1983, p. 145). The future for feminist criticism, Rich concludes, is to delineate, more subtly than hitherto, all the forms that lesbian existence assumes. She does not ask us to find the lesbian continuum necessarily in ourselves but rather to help unveil and describe the cultural mystification of lesbian spheres.

This has important consequences for feminist analysis. When Rich talks about the construction of lesbianism she means a psychical and literary construction. The taking up of 'lesbian' or 'heterosexual' positions, she rightly sees, reproduces oppression. 'Lesbianism', as representation, depends on the ever-present heterosexual order of reality. But by greatly *enlarging* the categories of 'lesbianism', and hence redrawing its system of representation, Rich can set up contradictions, overlaps and distinctions which may alter patriarchal ideology.

'Compulsory Heterosexuality and Lesbian Existence' experimentally seeks to give feminism a new dynamic. The redrawing of sexual maps is, of course, the central project too of contemporary male critics like Michel Foucault. Both Foucault and Rich are writing about images of male power and the way it operates. For both, sexuality is the entry point to understanding the controls and regulations of capitalism. It is the key to unlocking power since it provides the link between otherwise disparate discourses. Where Rich differs from Foucault is that she does not assume that the *main* characteristic of sexuality as it occurs in patriarchy is the way it uses confessions to codify practices. To Rich, the main characteristic of contemporary sexuality is male violence. Lesbianism, she feels, is especially hated in patriarchy and personified by men as *the* feminine evil. And therefore, unlike 'lesbianism' in Foucault, for Rich lesbians do need, intensely need, to create separate defined spaces of existence—of difference.

The essay has provoked a great deal of debate among feminists.[1] There are problems in any account grounded in 'Men the problem, Lesbians the solution'. Rich implies that only heterosexual relations are distorted by power differentials. This prevents a recognition that lesbian relations might be equally corrupt by power inequities. Another vulnerable feature is Rich's description of sexuality as if it is a driving force constituting some 'essential' truth of the human individual. It is an ambiguous jump for such a writer to take, who was analysing anthropology so satisfactorily in *Of Woman Born*. Surely the central triumph of feminist anthropology has been to prove that 'human nature' is a cultural *construct*.

But in a heightened form Rich has written out for us the cultural-linguistic struggles of lesbianism as a whole. For this reason Rich is sometimes verbally aggressive, even simplistic, since her situation after all is objectively violent. The essay is a clear statement about the meaning of language as social practice and the role of lesbian criticism. Rich has enlarged the techniques of feminist criticism. Lesbian identity cannot have meaning unless there is a culture to sustain it. It is impossible to use the word 'lesbian' without also using imagery, definitions and concepts. So lesbian criticism is about the construction of a viable, cultural language. Lesbian criticism can concentrate on notions of masculinity and femininity and their representation in literature and clarify the arbitrary assignation of gender. It can associate more directly with the languages of ethnic or minority groups. It can evoke a community whose vitality is genuinely erotic. Rich quotes another lesbian poet, Audre Lorde: 'as Audre Lorde has described it, [the energy] omnipresent in "the sharing of joy—whether physical, emotional, psychic", and in the sharing of work; as the empowering joy' (Rich, 1983, p. 158). Rich's addition of libidinal work to Lorde's libidinal leisure puts her into an anarchist line stretching from Fourier. It is a potent and productive notion of critical process.

It is also a major ideological advance in feminist criticism. Lesbian criticism has grasped the point that sexism and racism are totally interdependent. Rich writes continually about the connections between sexism, racism and homophobia. In *Of Woman Born* she describes the continuum of Black and white women's lives.

> Neither the 'pure' nor the 'lascivious' woman, neither the so-called mistress nor the slave woman, neither the woman praised for reducing herself to a brood animal nor the woman scorned and penalised as an 'old maid' or a 'dyke', has had any real autonomy or selfhood to gain from, this [male] subversion of the female body (and hence of the female mind) [Rich, 1977b, p. 35].

What is being argued here is that the construction of sexual difference is created by male violence into a series of dehumanised and meaningless definitions. Rich is in danger of freezing the antagonistic relation between women and men into a mutually exclusive idea of sexuality. Yet having said that, at least Adrienne Rich *is* focusing on the connections between sexuality and race at a time when few others were so bravely outspoken. And she was prepared to make that focus an important part of all her writing.

By the time of her *Spare Rib* interview, Rich is seeing the issue more problematically: 'When we really begin to understand fully how race and sex are enmeshed we will understand things about both of them that we don't yet understand' (Rich, 1981, p. 15). Rich does understand that the concepts of racism and sexism are inadequate. Only by examining the workings of particular practices in past and contemporary culture can we get at the unexpected character of sexual difference. The difficult problem, for feminist criticism, is how to analyse the effects of difference in everything from social policy to artistic practices. Criticism has to be about sexual politics to be feminist *and* it has to be about culture. ' "A Woman Is Talking to Death" is both a political poem and a love poem. I mean, that it is a political poem to the extent that it is a love poem, and a love poem in so far as it is political' (Rich, 1980, p. 251). This immediately gives feminist criticism a more complicated job. It cannot easily separate out kinds of poetry into discreet genres.

Critical techniques must deal with the interdependence of modes of discourse—of 'love' and 'politics'. Feminist criticism can do this if if uses particular language practices from lesbian criticism—like those of eroticism, or taboos. In her 'Twenty-One Love Poems' Rich is in the business of describing a semiotic of eroticism. Her poetic articulation of the erotic power of lesbianism is connected to her critical concept of difference as a dynamic force. For Rich 'difference' is the source of eroticism and dialogue between women and therefore new ideas for criticism. As a lesbian critic Adrienne Rich is able to remind American feminist criticism that linguistic power comes from our bodies—as mothers or as lovers. Clearly the acculturation of libidinal images can be self-indulgent if merely experiential. But Rich's vocabulary is revealing. She does not describe pleasure in idealist terms since she links it continually to the cognitive—to 'intelligence' and to 'thinking'. We might ask whether Rich can continually offer the larger relation between herself, her body and women's bodies—her story in the strictly political sense. The poems always provide an answer. 'Twenty-One Love Poems' is a good example of how Rich can create an erotic world whole and close to, and in, our everyday world. The representation of erotic experience was also right from the beginning of her career a sure criterion of 'good' art. As Rich noted in her review of Karl Shapiro, language is 'potent because it is created as experience, not as a reaction or defense against experience' (1964, p. 192). This is very different from, say, Kristeva's concept of the semiotic, where meaning is from *non-verbal*, pre-linguistic elements of the female body. Rich is closer in kind to an earlier feminist, Mary Wollstonecraft, who Rich often cites. The character Mary in Wollstonecraft's novel *Mary* enlarges her experience precisely through studying the physical world in order to combat (male) medical maltreatment of her woman friend. Should we see the privilege accorded by Rich to the 'creative imagination' as Romantic? Is her image of the literary work and women's culture offered as a mysterious organic unity, in contrast to the alienated world of patriarchy? In fact, it is odd coming to Rich's descriptions of emotions from current English literary criticism with its anti-Leavis, anti-humanism bias. It is hard not to scorn the least taint of organicism. Certainly Rich has a very romantic notion of childhood. *Of Woman Born* continually praises the sensuality of children and babies as some kind of immaculate truth against the harshness of social life. Yet Rich does treat emotional experience materially. For example, she ties the negative, emotional experience of some eighteenth-century mothers—their depression and anxieties—directly to the male medical practice of cross-infection.

We must, in any case, be very careful with the terms 'romance' or 'organic'. They are too often casually applied to denigrate any critic not measuring up to the textual ambiguities of post-structuralism. Rich has indeed explicitly rejected the American Romantics' belief in the poem as a performative act detached from social action. Her position, as we have seen, is inseparably bound up with her feminism, where poems are politics. Rich wants to create a new libidinal imagery for women in a world of a new communal shape. Her criticism is not only *about* a feminist erotics but also tries to enact it syntactically in images drawn from biology and domesticity. The blending of emotions, of autobiographical confession, of history and social events in Rich's poetic structures is sometimes extraordinary. She makes a fresh inventory of women's needs in order to include the love of magic, bodily action, the seriousness of art and the characteristic activity of dreams.

Sometimes Rich reads like a conduct book for feminism. Her essays often contain catalogues of good resolutions for a feminist New Year. She is a very moral writer, but one who *does* identify a feminist language as absolutely central to the act of living as well as to the art of writing; central to the identification of woman, to the relation between women. Thus Rich's literary criticism does not exist in a separate compartment from her other ideological enterprises.

> If we conceive of feminism as more than a frivolous label, if we conceive of it as an ethics, a methodology, a more complex way of thinking about, thus more responsibly acting upon, the conditions of human life, we need a self-knowledge which can only develop through a steady, passionate attention to all female experience . . . If this is so, we cannot work alone [Rich, 1980, p. 213]

All the themes are here. Knowledge is generated by a women-centred 'passionate' women's community. Feminism is not just an account of women's topics but 'a way of thinking', a whole mode of address of those topics. Rich's criticism is a criticism about the origin of criticism. So she is not talking only about discrimination against women but about discrimination against feminine knowledge and experience. For Rich, feminism means depending on the direction it takes—two very different things. In the one case, it is something very concrete, an emotional sisterhood with contemporary women. In the other, it is an almost pantheistic celebration of female history. Sometimes the quality is uneven. Sometimes Rich degenerates into noisy rhetoric. But the core of her work will bear comparison with the best criticism in her notion that any miscarriage of the symbolic 'difference' of women aborts our freedom.

NOTES

1. Feminist Criticism

1. P. Bourdieu and J-C. Passeron, *Reproduction in Education, Society and Culture* (Sage Publications: London, 1977). Bourdieu is specifically writing about class not gender controls but provides a crucial analysis of the masking of such controls by pedagogic institutions.
2. This is the main argument of T. Eagleton, *The Function of Criticism* (Verso: London, 1984).
3. The process is very well described by B. Doyle in 'The Hidden History of English Studies'. in *Rereading English*, ed. P. Widdowson (Methuen: London, 1982).
4. Cited in D. Spender, *Women of Ideas* (Routledge & Kegan Paul: London, 1982).
5. S.S. Lanser and E.T. Beck, 'Why Are There No Great Women Critics?: And What Difference Does It Make?, in *The Prism of Sex*, ed. J.A. Sherman and E.T. Beck (University of Wisconsin Press: Wisconsin, 1979).
6. The definition is from S. Kofman, 'Enigme de la femme', in *Diacritics*, Summer (1982).
7. I describe Woolf's point in detail in the Chapter 7' 'Virginia Woolf'.
8. D. Spender in *Man Made Language* (Routledge & Kegan Paul: London, 1980) provides a good general survey to this field.
9. M. Foucault characterises the rise of the bourgeoisie in these terms in *La Volonté de savoir,* (Editions Gallimard: Paris, 1976).
10. H. Marcuse, 'Marxism and Feminism', *Women's Studies, (1974), 3.*

2. Pioneers

1. Wilhelm Reich described a subject in therapy as a 'character' whose physiology and neurosis were the result of a 'characteriological repression of his sexual instincts dictated by capitalism' (W. Reich,

Sexual Revolution, Vision Press: London, 1972). Reich's ideas were very influential in the 1960s.

2. P. Boumelha builds on Millett. In *Thomas Hardy and Women* (Harvester Press: Brighton, 1982) she describes Hardy's debt to Darwin and his account of sexual selection based on a fixed polarity of male and female characteristics at the level of physiology.

3. Language and Psychoanalysis

1. It is useful to refer here to the work of Pierre Macherey. Macherey claims that literary texts have double meanings – their overt ideologies and their absences, the 'not-said' of these ideologies. Literary criticism (and his own examples are Jules Verne, Borges and Balzac) must demonstrate how texts are distorted by absences. P. Macherey, *A Theory of Literary Production,* (Routledge & Kegan Paul: London, 1978).

2. This has links with an Althuserian interpretation of base/superstructure. In 'Ideology and Ideological State Apparatuses' Althusser describes how an individual's 'culture' is simultaneously a complex system of practices made up of everyday acts, and even art and the semiology of dress. L. Althusser, *Lenin and Philosophy,* (Monthly Review Press: New York 1971).

3. See the journal *Enclitic* for some valuable analysis of psychoanalytic writings.

4. This is explained in more detail in 'Virginia Woolf' and 'Rebecca West'.

5. The best introductory account of Freud/Lacan remains J. Mitchell, *Psychoanalysis and Feminism,* (Penguin: London, 1974).

6. Lacan describes the mirror stage in structuralist terms. That is to say the child by 'agreeing' her reflection might agree with Saussure that she is 'She' only by being different. She is never in control of her language of representation.

4. Marxist-Feminist Criticism

1. The most useful introduction to Marxist literary criticism remains T. Eagleton, *Marxism and Literary Criticism,* (Methuen: London, 1976).

5. Myth Criticism

1. Mary Daly has described her antipathy to aesthetics in an analogy with Oppenheimer's construction of the atomic bomb. Both avoid social

effects in an obsession with technical expertise. (In answer to a question, Institute of Contemporary Arts June 1984.)

2. A fuller account of Virginia Woolf's involvement in Egyptian iconography appears in E. Haller, 'Isis Unveiled'. in *Virginia Woolf, A Feminist Slant*, ed. J. Marcus (University of Chicago Press: Chicago, 1983).

3. Audre Lorde has pointed out, however, that women poets are not always well served by feminist myth critics. In 'An Open Letter to Mary Daly' in *This Bridge Called My Back: Writings by Radical Women of Color*, ed. C. Moraga and G. Anzaldúa (Persephone Press: Watertown, Mass., 1981), Audre Lorde attacks Daly for describing Black women only as victims rather than as a source of wisdom.

7. *Virginia Woolf*

1. The collection of essays in *Virginia Woolf*, ed. C. Sprague, (Prentice-Hall: Englewood. NJ, 1971) have revealing titles. 'The Novel as Poem' and 'The Novel of Sensibility' are examples of a blinkered search for metaphor and metaphysic in Virginia Woolf's writings.

2. It is disappointing that Michèle Barrett, as a feminist making the first (and very useful) feminist collection of Virginia Woolf's criticism in *Virginia Woolf, Woman and Writing* (1979), introduced by Michèle Barrett (Women's Press: London), should take this unproblematic position.

3. Naomi Black notes Woolf's mixture of the social and the imaginary in her political activity. *See* Naomi Black 'Virginia Woolf: The Life of Natural Happiness', in *Feminist Theorists*, ed. Dale Spender (The Women's Press: London, 1983).

4. The role of domestic science and its relation to an ideology of femininity is discussed in Barbara Ehrenreich and Deidre English, *For Her Own Good* (Pluto Press: London, 1979).

5. There is a very useful account of the history of medical treatment of hysteria within an American context in Ehrenreich and English above.

6. Juliet Mitchell (1974) *Psychoanalysis and Feminism*, (Penguin: Harmondsworth) discusses these ideas of Freud's as concepts within psychoanalysis as a system of thought particularly in Chapter 7, 'The Castration Complex'.

7. Virginia Woolf's debt to the Stephen women is described by Jane Marcus in 'Thinking Back Through Our Mothers', in *New Feminist Essays on Virginia Woolf*, ed. J. Marcus, (Macmillan: London, 1981).

8. The model is one used by Sandra M. Gilbert and Susan Gubar, *The Madwoman in the Attic* (Yale University Press, New Haven, 1979) in relation to nineteenth-century poetry (*see* Ch. 3). Woolf's satiric fondness for Victorian fathers is noted by Jane Marcus in 'Enchanted Organs, Magic Bells: Night and Day as Comic Opera', in *Virginia Woolf*, ed.

R. Freedman (University of California Press: Berkeley, 1980), pp. 97–123.

9. Note Virginia Woolf's recurrent associations of libraries with moments of crisis. *In a Room of One's Own* these moment become 'defined' only in libraries; here the review is entitled 'In a Library', and the relation is of course to Leslie Stephen, *Hours in a Library,* (John Murray: London, 1917–26).

8. *Rebecca West*

1. In 'Is Female to Male as Nature Is to Culture?' Shirley Ortner established that the meanings attached to biological needs are gender based *and* arbitrary. Her argument is that there is nothing more intrinsically natural about women's physiology than men's, and that the attributes we assign to gender categories are culturally conditioned. S. Ortner, 'Is Female to Male as Nature Is to Culture', *Feminist Studies,* I:3 (Fall, 1972).

2. Harold Bloom describes kenosis as a 'breaking device similar to the defence mechanisms our psyches employ against repetition compulsions'. H. Bloom, *The Anxiety of Influence,* (Oxford University Press: Oxford, 1973).

3. Ibsen's *Rosmersholm* is probably cited in more feminist reviews of the Edwardian period than any other play. In *Rosmersholm* the socialist-feminist newspaper is called *The Lighthouse;* so *To the Lighthouse?* (but that is another story).

4. V.F. Calverton played a crucial role in American intellectual life in the 1920s and 1930s. As founder of the *Modern Quarterly* he brought together Marxism and psychoanalysis. The journal was co-edited by S. Schmaulhausen, author of *A Mental Hygiene Inventory.*

9. *Adrienne Rich*

1. *See,* for example, Cora Kaplan, 'Wild Nights: Pleasure/Sexuality/Feminism', in *Formations of Pleasure* (Routledge & Kegan Paul: London, 1983). Kaplan usefully compares Wollstonecraft and Rich in an interesting essay about sexuality. However, Kaplan makes two unjustifiable attacks. She claims that Rich totally condemns hetero-sexuality and, second, that Rich presents only abstract women. The first claim, as I have demonstrated textually, is untrue. The second is particularly unfair since Rich 'enters' her text *only* via the texts of other writers, all carefully referenced, interspersing academic theories with student quotations in her usual vivid and accessible fashion.

BIBLIOGRAPHY

This list comprises the periodicals, books and articles cited, as well as some of those consulted in the preparation of the book. The Bibliography is by no means an exhaustive list of publications on feminist criticism but is intended to be an extensive and helpful guide for the student.

An annotated guide to that wider field is in preparation. *See* Maggie Humm, *An Annotated Bibliography of Feminist Criticism*, (Harvester Press: Brighton, forthcoming).

Allen, D.M. (ed.) *The New American Poetry* (Grove Press: New York, 1960)

Andermatt, V. 'Hélène Cixous and the Uncovery of a Feminist Language', *Women and Literature* 7 (1979)

de Beauvoir, S. *The Second Sex* (Penguin: Harmondsworth, 1972)

Bambara, T.C. 'Commitment: Tony Cade Bambara Speaks', in *Sturdy Black Bridges: Visions of Black Women in Literature*, ed. R.P. Bell *et al.* (Anchor Press: New York, 1979)

Barrett, M. *Women and Writing* (Women's Press: London, 1979)
Women's Oppression Today (Verso: London, 1980)
'Feminism and the Definition of Cultural Politics', in *Feminism, Culture, and Politics*, ed. R. Brunt and C. Rowan, (Lawrence & Wishart: London, 1982)
et al. 'Representation and Cultural Production', in *Ideology and Cultural Production* (Croom Helm: London, 1979)

Beauman, N. *A Very Great Profession* (Virago: London, 1983)

Bell, B.C. and Ohmann, C. 'Virginia Woolf's Criticism', in *Feminist Literary Criticism*, ed. J. Donovan (University Press of Kentucky: Lexington, 1975)

Berry, L. and McDaniels, J. 'Teaching Contemporary Black Women Writers', *Radical Teacher* 17 (1980)

Black, N. 'Virginia Woolf: The Life of Natural Happiness', in *Feminist Theories*, ed. D. Spender (Women's Press: London, 1983)

Bloom, H. *The Anxiety of Influence* (Oxford University Press: New York, 1973)

A Map of Misreading (Oxford University Press: New York, 1975)

Brown, R.M. 'The Woman Identified Woman', *The Ladder* 14 (1970), 11/12

Bulkin, E. *Lesbian Fiction* (Persephone Press: Watertown, Mass, 1981)

Chesler, P. *Women and Madness* (Doubleday: New York, 1972)

Chodorow, N. *The Reproduction of Mothering* (University of California Press: Berkeley, 1978)

Cixous, H. 'The Character of "Character" ', *New Literary History* 5 (1974), 2

'The Laugh of the Medusa', *Signs* 1 (1976), 4

'Castration or Decapitation', *Signs* 7 (1981), 1

Cooper, A.J. *A Voice from the South by a Black Woman of the South* (Aldine Printing House: Xenia, Ohio, 1892)

Coward, R. 'Sexual Politics and Psychoanalysis', in *Feminism, Culture, and Politics*, ed. R. Blunt and C. Rowan (Lawrence & Wishart: London, 1982)

Cruikshank, M. *Lesbian Studies: Present and Future* (The Feminist Press: New York, 1982)

Culler, J. *On Deconstruction* (Routledge & Kegan Paul: London, 1983)

Daly, M. *Beyond God the Father: Toward a Philosophy of Women's Liberation* (Beacon Press: Boston, 1973)

The Church and the the Second Sex (Harper Colophon Books: New York, 1975)

Gyn/Ecology (Beacon Press: Boston, 1978)

Pure Lust (The Women's Press: London, 1984)

Davidson, C.N. and Broner, E.M. (eds.) *The Lost Tradition: Mothers and Daughters in Literature* (Frederick Ungar: New York, 1980)

Davis, T. *et al.* 'The Public Face of Feminism', in *Making Histories*, ed. R. Johnson (Hutchinson: London, 1982)

Delphy, C. 'No Right to Choose: A Materialist Feminism is Possible', *Feminist Review* 4 (1980)

Dinnerstein, D. *The Mermaid and the Minotaur* (Harper & Row: New York, 1976)

Dijkstra, S. 'Simone de Beauvoir and Betty Friedan: The Politics of Omission', *Feminist Studies* 6: 2 (Summer 1980)

Eagleton, T. *Marxism and Literary Criticism* (Methuen: London, 1976)

Ehrenreich, B. and English, D. *For Her Own Good* (Pluto Press: London, 1979)

Eisenstein, Z. *The Radical Future of Liberal Feminism* (Longman: London, 1981)

Ellis, H. 'Woman's Sexual Nature', in *Woman's Coming of Age*, ed. S.D. Schmalhausen and V.F. Calverton (Horace Liveright: New York, 1931)

Evans, M. 'Views of Women and Men in the Work of Simone de Beauvoir', *Women's Studies International Quarterly* 3 (1980)

Faderman, L. *Surpassing the Love of Men: Romantic Friendship and Love Between Women from the Renaissance to the Present* (William Morrow: New York, 1981)

Falk, N.A. and Gross, R.M. (eds.) *Unspoken Words* (Harper & Row: New York, 1980)

Felman, S. 'Women and Madness', *Diacritics*, Winter (1975).
  'Turning the Screw of Interpretation', *Yale French Studies* 55/56 (1977)
  'Rereading Femininity', *Yale French Studies*, 62 (1981)

Fox-Genovese, E. 'The New Female Literary Culture', *Antioch Review* 38 (1980)

Freud, S. 'Those Wrecked by Success', in *Essays* (Hogarth Press: London, 1951).

Friedan, B. 'An Interview', *Social Policy*, November/December, (1970)
  The Feminine Mystique (Penguin: Harmondsworth, 1982)

Fromm, E. *The Fear of Freedom* (Routledge & Kegan Paul: London, 1960)

Frye, N. *Anatomy of Criticism: Four Essays* (Princeton University Press: Princeton, 1957)
  'The Developing Imagination', in *Learning in Language and Literature* (Harvard Cambridge, Mass. 1963)

Gardiner J.K. *et al.* 'An Interchange on Feminist Criticism on Dancing Through the Minefield', *Feminist Studies* 8 (1982), 3

Gelpi, B.C. and Gelpi, A. (eds.) *Adrienne Rich's Poetry* (W.W. Norton: New York, 1975)

Gilbert, S. and Gubar, S. *The Madwoman in the Attic* (Yale University Press: New Haven, 1979)

Gomez, J. 'A Cultural Legacy Denied and Discovered', in *Home Girls*, ed. B. Smith (Kitchen Table Press: New York, 1983)

Gordon, L. 'The Struggle for Reproductive Freedom: Three Stages of Feminism', in *Capitalist Patriarchy and the Case for Socialist Feminism* ed. Z. Eisenstein (Monthly Review Press: New York, 1979)

Gornick, V. and Moran, B.K. (eds.) *Woman in Sexist Society* (Basic Books: New York, 1971)

Greer, G. *The Female Eunuch* (Paladin: London, 1971)

Griffin, S. 'Thoughts on Writing', in *The Writer on Her Work*, ed. J. Sternburg (W.W. Norton: New York, 1980)

Hall, S. *et al. Culture, Media, Language* (Hutchinson: London, 1980)

Hardwick, E. 'The Subjection of Women', *Partisan Review*, May/June (1953)

Heilbrun, C.G. *Toward a Recognition of Androgyny* (Harper Colophon: New York, 1973)

Hole, J. and Levine, E. *The Rebirth of Feminism* (Quadrangle: New York, 1971)

Holtby, W. *Virginia Woolf* (Academy Press: Chicago, 1978)

Horney, K. 'The Dread of Women', *International Journal of Psychoanalysis* xiii (1932)

Irigaray, L. *Speculum de l'autre femme* (Minuit: Paris, 1974)
'When Our Lips Speak Together', *Signs* 6 (1980), 1

James, C.L.R. 'Wisdom: An Interview', in *Sturdy Black Bridges: Visions of Black Women in Literature*, ed. R.P. Bell *et al.* (Anchor Press: New York, 1979)

Jelinek, E.C. *Women's Autobiography* (Indiana University Press: Bloomington, 1980)

Johnston, J. *Lesbian Nation* (Simon & Schuster: New York 1973)

Kamuf, P. 'Writing Like a Woman', in *Women and Language in Literature and Society*, ed. S. McConnell-Ginet *et al.* (Praeger: New York, 1980)

Kaplan, C. 'Radical Feminism and Literature: Rethinking Millett's *Sexual Politics*', *Red Letters* 9 (1979)

Kristeva, J. *La Révolution du Langage Poétique* (Seuil: Paris, 1974)
Desire in Language: A Semiotic Approach to Literature and Art (Basil Blackwell: Oxford, 1980)
'Woman's Time', *Signs* 7 (1981), 11
'Psychoanalysis and the Polis', *Critical Inquiry* 9 (1982), 2

Lacelle, G. *La Femme, son corps, et la religion: approches pluridisciplinaires* (Editions Bellarmin: Montréal, 1983)

Leavis, Q.D. *Fiction and the Reading Public* (Penguin: Harmondsworth, 1979)

Lorde, A. *Sister Outsider* (The Crossing Press: New York 1984)

Lurie, N.O. (ed.) *Mountain Wolf Woman* (University of Michigan Press: Ann Arbor, 1961)

McRobbie, A. (ed.) *Feminism for Girls* (Routledge & Kegan Paul: London, 1981)

Mailer, N. *The Prisoner of Sex* (Little, Brown: Boston, 1971)

Marcus, J. 'Enchanted Organs, Magic Bells: Night amd Day as Comic Opera', in *Virginia Woolf*, ed. R. Freedman (University of California: Berkeley, 1980)

'Thinking Back Through Our Mothers', in *New Feminist Essays on Virginia Woolf,* ed. J. Marcus, (Macmillan: London, 1981)

(ed.) *The Young Rebecca* (Virago: London, 1982)

Marder, H. *Feminism and Art* (University of Chicago Press: Chicago, 1968)

Marxist-Feminist Literature Collective, 'Women's Writing: *Jane Eyre, Shirley, Villette, Aurora Leigh', Ideology and Consciousness* (1978), 3

Michaels, W. 'The Interpreter's Self' *Georgia Review* 31 (1977)

Millett, K. 'Prostitution: A Quartet for Female Voices', in *Woman in Sexist Society,* eds. V. Gornick and B.K. Moran (Basic Books: New York, 1971)

'On Angela Davis', *Ms,* August, 1972

Sexual Politics (Virago: London, 1977)

Mitchell, J. *Psychoanalysis and Feminism* (Penguin: Harmondsworth, 1974)

Women: The Longest Revolution (Virago: London, 1984)

Modleski, T. *Loving with a Vengeance* (Archon Books: Hamden, Conn., 1982)

Moore, G.E. *Philosophical Studies* (Routledge & Kegan Paul: London, 1948)

Mulhern, F. *The Moment of 'Scrutiny'* (New Left Books: London, 1979)

Neumann, E. *The Great Mother: An Analysis of the Archetype,* trans. R. Manheim (Princeton University Press, Bollingen Series: Princeton, 1955)

Paper, J. 'The Post Contact Origin of an American Indian High God: The Suppression of Feminine Spirituality', *American Indian Quarterly,* Winter, 1984

Pomeroy, S.B. *Goddesses, Whores, Wives and Slaves: Women in Classical Antiquity* (Schocken Books: New York, 1975)

Poovey, M. *The Proper Lady and the Woman Writer* (University Press: Chicago, 1984)

Pratt, A. 'Archetypal Approaches to the New Feminist Criticism', *Bucknell Review* 21 (1973) Spring

'The New Feminist Criticisms: Exploring the History of the New Space', in *Beyond Intellectual Sexism,* ed. J.I. Roberts, (David McKay: New York, 1976)

Archetypal Patterns in Women's Fiction (Harvester Press: Brighton, 1982)

Radway, J.A. 'Women Read the Romance', *Feminist Studies,* 9 (1983), 1

Ray, G.N. *H.G. Wells and Rebecca West* (Macmillan: London, 1974)

Rich, A. 'On Karl Shapiro's "The Bourgeois Poet"', in *The Contemporary Poet as Artist and Critic*, ed. A. Ostroff, (Little, Brown: Boston, 1964)

'Caryatid', *American Poetry Review*, II (1973), 3

'There is a Fly in This House', *Ms*, February, 1977a

Of Woman Born (Virago: London, 1977b)

On Lies, Secrets and Silence (Virago: London, 1980)

'Interview' *Spare Rib* (1981), 103

'Compulsory Heterosexuality and Lesbian Existence', in *Women, Gender and Scholarship*, ed. E. Abel and E.K. Abel, (University of Chicago Press: Chicago, 1983)

Roberts, J.R. *Black Lesbians: An Annotated Bibliography* (The Naiad Press: Tallahassee, Florida, 1981)

Robinson, L.S. *Sex, Class and Culture* (Indiana University Press: Bloomington, 1978)

Rosenthal, M. *Virginia Woolf* (Routledge & Kegan Paul: London, 1979)

Roszak, T. *The Making of a Counter Culture* (Faber: London, 1970)

Rowbotham, S. *Hidden from History* (Pluto Press: London, 1973)

Ruehl, S. *Sex and Love* (The Women's Press: London, 1983)

Rule, J. *Lesbian Images* (The Crossing Press: New York, 1975)

Russ, J. 'What Can A Heroine Do? or Why Women Can't Write', in *Images of Women in Fiction-Feminist Perspectives*, ed. Cornillon, S.K. (Bowling Green University Popular Press: Bowling Green, Ohio, 1973)

The Female Man (Bantam Books: New York, 1975

Ruthven, K.K. *Feminist Literary Studies* (Cambridge University Press: Cambridge, 1984

Schmalhausen, S.D. and Claverton, V.F. (eds.) *Woman's Coming of Age* (Horace Liveright: New York, 1931)

Schwarzer, A. *Simone de Beauvoir Today* (Chatto & Windus: London, 1984)

Sheldon, A.B. 'With Delicate Mad Hands', in *Out of the Everywhere* (Ballantine Books: New York, 1981)

Showalter, E. *Women's Liberation and Literature* (Harcourt Brace Jovanovich: New York, 1971)

Smith, B. *Toward a Black Feminist Criticism* (Out and Out Books: New York, 1977)

Home Girls (Kitchen Table Press: New York, 1983)

Smith-Rosenberg, C. 'The Female World of Love and Ritual: Relations Between Women in Nineteenth-Century America', *Signs* 1 (1975) Autumn

Snitow, A. *et al. Desire: The Politics of Sexuality* (Virago, London, 1984)

Spacks, P.M. *The Female Imagination* (Knopf: New York, 1977)

Spender, D. *There's Always Been a Women's Movement This Century* (Pandora Press: London, 1983)

Spivak, G. 'The Letter as Cutting Edge', *Yale French Studies* 55/56 (1977)

'Unmaking and Making in *To The Lighthouse*', in *Women and Language in Literature and Society*, ed. S. McConnell-Ginet *et al.* (Praeger: New York 1980)

'French Feminism in an International Frame' *Yale French Studies* 62 (1981)

Sprague, C. (ed.) *Virginia Woolf* (Prentice-Hall: Englewood Cliffs, NJ, 1967)

Stephen, L. *Hours in a Library* (Smith Elder & Co., London, 1874)

Strachey, L. *Eminent Victorians* (Chatto & Windus: London, 1928)

Walker, A. *In Search of Our Mothers' Gardens* (The Women's Press: London, 1984)

Walters, M. 'The Rights and Wrongs of Women: Mary Wollstonecraft, Harriet Martineau, Simone de Beauvoir', in *The Rights and Wrongs of Women*, ed. J. Mitchell and A. Oakley (Penguin: Harmondsworth, 1976)

Warner, M. 'Art of Fiction: Interview with Rebecca West', *Paris Review* 23 (1981)

Washbourn, P. *Seasons of Women: Song, Poetry, Ritual, Prayer, Myth, Story* (Harper & Row: New York, 1979)

Washington, M.H. 'These Self-Invented Women: A Theoretical Framework for a Literary History of Black Women', *Radical Teacher* 17 (1980)

Weigle, M. *Spiders and Spinsters: Women and Mythology* (University of New Mexico Press: Albuquerque, 1982)

West, R. *Henry James* (Nisbet & Co: London, 1916)

'Women as Artist and Thinker', in *Woman's Coming of Age*, ed. S.D. Schmalhausen and V.F. Calverton (Horace Liveright: New York, 1931)

'Miss West, Mr Eliot and Mr Parsons', in *The Spectator*, 15 October 1932

'The Event and Its Image', in *Essays by Diverse Hands*, ed. P. Green (Oxford University Press: London, 1962)

A Celebration, (Penguin: Harmondsworth, 1978)

Widdowson, P. *Re-Reading English* (Methuen: London, 1982)

Williamson, J. *Decoding Advertisements* (Marion Boyers: London, 1978)

Wittig, M. and Zeig, S. *Lesbian People's Material for a Dictionary* (Avon: New York, 1979)

Wolfe, P. *Rebecca West* (Southern Illinois University Press: Illinois, 1971)

Woolf, V. *The Second Common Reader* (Penguin: Harmondsworth, 1944)

A Room of One's Own (Penguin: Harmondsworth, 1945)

A Writer's Diary (The Hogarth Press: London, 1959)

Contemporary Writers (Harcourt Brace Jovanovich: New York, 1965a)

The Death of a Moth (Penguin: Harmondsworth 1965b)

Collected Essays (Harcourt Brace Jovanovich: New York, 1967)

'Introductory Letter', to *Life as We Have Known It*, ed. M. Llewelyn Davies (Virago: London, 1977)

The Captain's Death Bed (Harcourt Brace Jovanovich: New York, 1978)

Women and Writing (The Women's Press: London, 1979)

Three Guineas (Penguin: Harmondsworth, 1982)

Yates, G.G. *What Women Want* (Harvard University Press: Cambridge, Mass., 1955)

INDEX